WHAT THE BUDDHA NEVER TAUGHT

WHAT THE BUDDHA
NEVER TAUGHT

By

Tim Ward

CELESTIALARTS

Berkeley, California

Cover design by Andrew Smith
Author photograph by Peter Ward

First published in Canada by Somerville House Publishing

FIRST CELESTIAL ARTS PRINTING 1993

Library of Congress Cataloging-in-Publication Data

Ward. Tim, 1958–
    What the Buddha never taught / Tim Ward
        p. cm.
Originally published: Toronto Somerville House Publishing, 1990.
ISBN 0-89087-687-8 $14.95
1. Ward, Tim 1958–   2. Monastic and religious life (Buddhism)—
Thailand.   I. Title.
BQ995. R3A3 1993

294.3'657' 09593—dc20   92-39702

                                                              CIP

Printed on paper
containing over 50%
recycled paper including
10% post-consumer fibre.

2 3 4 5 6 7 8 9 10 / 97 96 95 94 93

Contents

Acknowledgements

Thanks . . .

First, my gratitude and respect to Ajahn Chah, who made it possible for people from all over the world to come and live much as the early Buddhists lived. Many thanks to the monks of Wat Pah Nanachat, the lay-community of Bung Wai which supports them, and my friend Jim Bulkley, who all share this story with me. I have done my best to portray our individual struggles with karma, death, boredom and mosquitoes as accurately as possible.

Many people helped bring this book out of the jungle and into print. Jim and Lee Gander let me use their vacant Bangkok apartment and portable typewriter, on which the first three drafts were constructed. Thanks to Ali, Shawna and Kara Birkenstock who befriended me like family as I sweated through those initial drafts.

When I returned to Canada eight months later I found that my sister Wendy had thoughtfully made up several reading copies. Bede Hubbard generously offered to edit my manuscript, gently suggesting I delete reams of philosophical musings of dubious luminosity (my readers owe him thanks for this too). During May of 1986, my good friends Stephen and Andree Cazabon-Hotz made me 'writer in residence' at their Ottawa apartment, permitting me full use of their word-processor and refrigerator to help write the final drafts. Frank Holober, my future father-in-law, let me loose on his PC for retouching the end product. He also did a 'maahvellous' job proof-reading and making copies of the finished manuscript.

Thanks to Ray Woollam for a well-placed kick, after which the last page rewrote itself. Ray also introduced me to Colin Limworth and Michelle Mills of Banyan Bookstore in Vancouver, who helped me locate my publisher. Many thanks to Element Books and, in Canada, Somerville House Publishing, for getting the book into print at breathtaking speed, and to my agent, Denise Bukowski, for swiftly concluding contracts despite the hassle of having an author half a world away.

Thanks to my wife Julie for her perfectionist's touch on the final proofs. And most of all thanks to my parents for their boundless love, support, prayers, photocopying, mailing of manuscripts, searching for photographs and forwarding of mail all the years I've been in Asia.

And my thanks to the Buddha, for everything he taught.

Tim Ward
Tokyo, January 1990

CHAPTER ONE

The Farang Wants to Go to a Wat

I told Nimalo, the Australian novice, that they ate deep-fried cockroaches on the bus. I expected him to laugh. 'Beetles, not cockroaches', he told me in all seriousness. Of course. Silly of me. Certainly beetles would be a much tastier snack.

I rode all day. It was dark when the bus neared the city of Ubon Rajathani, less than fifty kilometres from the Laos border. Then I started asking other passengers where to get off for Bung Wai village. The Thais blinked at me, smiled politely and let me babble as if it was for my own entertainment. Finally the driver got it into his head that I wanted off. He stopped the coach and let me out into the night. It was raining. I found a local bus stop nearby.

'This stop for Bung Wai bus?' I said to a young Thai soldier in uniform. He grinned at me.

'Bung Wai bus?' I said to a man wearing glasses and a wristwatch. He shrugged his shoulders, smiled shyly and looked away.

A farmer's wife controlling two whining children glanced at me nervously. I kept quiet. A bus came. Everybody climbed on board. I put one foot on the steps.

'Bung Wai bus?' I said to the driver. He looked at the ticket girl, a short young woman who wore the regulation blue skirt and fat legs. She gave a helpless little smile.

'Bung Wai bus to Bung Wai village', I explained.

1

She looked wordlessly at the driver. He revved the engine, and looked down the highway. I stood my ground, not getting on, not getting off.

'Bung Wai. Bung Wai!'

The driver gestured impatiently, beckoning me to board. I knew he hadn't understood. I gave in. Shaking the rain from my rucksack, I sat down next to the most-likely-to-be-educated person on the bus, a student wearing a white shirt with three ballpoint pens in his breast pocket.

'This bus go Bung Wai?' I tried again.

The student looked back at me, polite but puzzled.

I unzipped the outer pocket of my pack and pulled out a small white book. Finding the name I was looking for, I pronounced it several times in various tones, hoping I'd hit a combination understandable to his Thai ears.

'Pah Nanachat. Pah Nanachat. Me go Wat Pah Nanachat, Bung Wai bloody village.'

The young man's smile turned a bit wary at my insistence. I flipped through the pages, hoping for a picture of Ajahn Chah, but it was in the other book, four hundred kilometres away in Bangkok. I drew my legs up and folded them under me, then placed my hands together in my lap, straightened my spine and closed my eyes meaningfully for a few seconds. I opened them again and looked piercingly at the student. He scratched his head. But the soldier called over to him, and mimicked my posture. The student grinned openly and nodded his head. Everyone on the bus looked relieved. The *farang* wants to go to a *wat*.

The bus, however, had reached Ubon Rajathani by this time. My hazy sense of direction told me I would have to backtrack to reach Bung Wai. The student got down with me in the city. Apparently he knew what I wanted, but not where to find it. He seemed determined to help. He was tall for a Thai, almost my height, but skinny and younger than I first had thought: fifteen perhaps. My new guide stopped a group of soldiers on the street. One of them seemed to know the place for which a foreigner like me would be looking. He smiled and spoke in broken English.

'You go *farang wat*? Wat Pah Pong, Wat Pah Pong.'

'I go Wat Pah Nanachat, Wat Pah Nanachat. Ajahn Chah.'

'Ajahn Chah, Ajahn Chah. Wat Pah Pong, Wat Pah Pong', he corrected me.

'I see. Why not? Wat Pah Pong then.'

Everybody seemed happy about this decision. The soldiers hailed a *tuk-tuk* for the student and me. Wat Pah Pong was also mentioned in Ajahn Chah's books so I assumed somebody there would at least be able to speak English. In Bangkok, one can be lazy. English will get you by. Out here in the northeast you might as well speak Portuguese.

The *tuk-tuk* driver said he would take us to Pah Pong monastery for thirty *bhat*. The three wheeler drove us east through the rest of the city then out along a muddy dirt road into the jungle. In twenty minutes we arrived at a set of great iron gates. They were locked tight. The student found a small side door in the high concrete wall which was open. It was a black night and still raining. I pulled my flashlight from the bottom of my pack and went through the small entrance with the student clutching my arm. Beyond the wall we found a huge hole in the road about twenty metres wide. My light was reflected by puddles on the bottom. We could see that the sides were smooth, like an excavation pit.

'I guess Pah Pong isn't here right now', I said to my guide. He pulled me back through the gate. Outside, our driver was talking with the proprietor of a small noodle shop near the wall. His chairs were all piled up for the night on top of rickety wooden tables. A kerosene lamp flickered. He shook his head as we joined the driver. He pointed to the road leading west from the gates. 'Pah Nanachat.' I heard him say.

'Yes, Pah Nanachat!' I nodded furiously. Our driver took new directions and the three of us crawled back into his *tuk-tuk*. He stuck a dipstick into his petrol tank and muttered something quietly. Then he started the engine. We roared along the slippery new trail until it opened onto a different highway. There the driver hesitated. The student argued with him over which way to turn. Finally we turned right, back towards the city. But the student harangued the driver until he turned around and headed in the opposite direction.

3

When we neared the lights of a small roadside village, the driver stopped and left his seat to get help in a nearby house. He returned, giving us a confident thumbs up signal. Half an hour later we were completely lost. The engine began to sputter in the rain. The driver seemed ready to mutiny, let me off on the highway and go home. He and the student argued loudly. A wooden signpost loomed in our headlight. It was written in Thai and English: 'Wat Pah Nanachat. Bung Wai International Forest Monastery.' Together we made gleeful noises. The *tuk-tuk* followed the turn off. It was only a mud and gravel track. We were soon surrounded by jungle. A footpath appeared through the rain. The *tuk-tuk* slithered sideways in the open muddy space next to it. The driver left his engine running.

I gave him what he asked, one hundred *bhat* for the job, and thanked them both. I prayed they would have enough petrol to get back to town safely. My student waved at me as the machine swung around. After watching the little light disappear down the road, I clicked on my flashlight, shone it into the dense, wet trail and wondered what comes out at night when the rains flood the earth. Pack slung over one arm, I walked into the black jungle.

I expected a nerve-steeling walk of several kilometres before reaching the forest retreat. It irritated me when the grey outlines of buildings emerged after only five minutes. Ahead I saw lights. The path widened and the tree cover thinned as I reached a large barn-like building. A side doorway was open. It was a temple. At the front was an altar like a stage, dominated by two large brass Buddhas. Smaller brass figures knelt in worship on either side. Lesser images in front of the main idols glittered by the light of two candles. In front of the altar, five rows of red mats had been set out. In the back row sat a young man dressed in white. His head had been shaven. He sat in typical Thai meditation posture, legs crossed with the left foot resting on the right calf. His hands were folded in his lap, eyes closed, still as the Buddha images. He took no notice of me. He was Caucasian.

I bowed three times to the statues, as Tan Sumana Tissa had shown me, touching my forehead to the ground three

4

times from a kneeling position. I took a seat in the third row and folded up my legs, just to try the place out. To the left of the altar stood a glass case containing a complete human skeleton.

I repeated my bows, stood, and left the temple in search of an office. No one was expecting me. In the rain again, I noticed that light was coming from a window at the back of the temple. There was a door. I heard voices inside so I knocked. It opened. A white-skinned man wearing white robes blinked into the dark at me through steel-rimmed spectacles.

'Do you speak English?' I asked.

'I suppose so' he said humourlessly.

'I'm sorry I've come so late' I stammered. 'I took a day bus. The *tuk-tuk* got lost in the rain. I just arrived.'

'Yes' he said. He turned to an adolescent Thai boy wearing ochre robes seated next to a tape recorder on the floor of the room, and spoke to him in Thai.

'I will take you to the Ajahn' said the man, turning back to me.

I followed his white robes across the clearing, into the jungle again. They seemed luminous in the night. The rain had stopped but water dripped everywhere from the dense cover overhead. We came to a small wooden house raised high off the ground by stilts.

'*Swaddie krub*' said my new guide, as we walked up towards the dark building.

A dark figure appeared at the railing above. A voice spoke down to us in Thai. When the reason for the interruption so late at night was explained, the figure descended the wide wooden staircase. I shone my flashlight on him and was surprised to see he was another Westerner. The man was tall and thin, perhaps forty years old – but with no hair. He had a ski jump nose. His eyes seemed blue beneath his pink scalp.

'Thank you, Michael' the Ajahn said. The man in white raised his palms together in front of his face in a *wai*, the Thai gesture of respect. He turned, and walked back through the jungle like a ghost.

5

'We can sit down here' said the Ajahn. He wore the ochre robes typical of Theravada Buddhist monks, a muddy yellow-brown, but his accent was Australian. We sat on the marble surface of the foundation beneath his quarters, he on a low platform, me kneeling in front of him.

I explained briefly that a monk in Bangkok had given me two of Ajahn Chah's books on meditation and had recommended Wat Pah Nanachat as the best place in Thailand for foreigners to learn how to put the Buddha's teachings into practice. I said I wanted to stay for three months or so.

The head monk nodded. 'I've been expecting you. For now you can sleep in the guest room above the kitchen. Once you get to know your way around, you may shave your head. That's the sign you wish to stay for some time and practise. We will give you a *kuti* to live in once you have been shaven. You may think it is strange that we attach so much importance to shaving the hair, but people are attached to their hair. Here we teach how to overcome our attachments. This is the way to end suffering. You start with the hair. There's no hurry though. When you are ready. There's a lot to learn when you first get here. I won't say much now. It's late and you will forget.

'You will hear the bell at three in the morning. Everyone is expected to be in the *sala* – that's the main temple – by three thirty for morning chanting and group meditation. The meal is at eight. We eat only once a day. Some people find this difficult to adjust to at first. It's easy to be attached to old habits. Now, I'll get you some blankets and show you where you will sleep.'

'By the way' I said, 'my name is Tim. I'm a Canadian.'

'Fine. Before you get up you may as well learn it's customary to bow three times whenever you come into the presence of an Ajahn and whenever an interview is over.'

I did my bows.

'Tomorrow we'll talk about proper ways of bowing and sitting' he said.

The room above the kitchen was huge, with a high roof and many windows. I opened them all for the cool. The whole building was made of wood. The floorboards held a dark glow. Painted on one wall was a familiar – but out of place – Tibetan Wheel of Samsara. In the centre of the wheel, a pig, a rooster and a snake chased each other in a circle. They represented ignorance, desire and hatred, the three causes of suffering which bind all beings to the endless cycle of existence. All living beings are continually reborn in the six realms which were shown as radiating outward from the centre circle of the wheel. In each realm there was suffering. The hell beings suffered physical torment; the hungry ghosts of the spirit realm, with their thin throats and huge bellies, were incapable of gratifying their cravings of thirst and hunger. In the animal realm, beasts suffered from fear and ignorance. Amongst the various activities of the human realm, there was poverty, cruelty and pain. The Titan-like *asuras*, envying the gods, devoted themselves to perpetual war with heaven. But even the gods in the *deva*-realm of bliss, suffered. All beings will die and take rebirth according to Buddhist doctrine. When gods die, they fall again into the lower worlds. They suffer the fear of death. The entire wheel, the realms of god and hell being alike, was clasped in the yellow teeth and claws of a red-eyed demon. This was the first Buddhist truth: life is suffering. Yet Buddha was also depicted in each realm of the wheel, preaching his message of release.

A bell rang in the dark. The clear tone reverberated through the jungle. I sat up on the floor to listen, to clear the sleep from my head and remember what it was. Three o'clock.

The air outside was cool. I joined other dark figures coming out of the jungle, moving towards the *sala*. Inside I sat in the back row with four other men, all dressed in white clothing. The row ahead of us seated three people wearing white robes. One of them was Michael. Ahead of them sat the monks and novices wearing ochre, about twelve of them altogether. The community was smaller than I had imagined, which pleased me. We sat in silence for an hour. A few monks stood up and walked to the rear of the *sala* where they paced back and forth. I had never seen walking meditation practised before. I closed my eyes and searched for the point of concentration, for the light sensation of air moving through my nostrils, rushing against my upper lip. Here I would learn *vipassana* meditation, the meditation which begins with simple awareness of natural body sensation, the feel of feet on the ground, of inbreathing and outbreathing, returning the mind to that which sustains it, establishing it there, free of the illusions and fantasies which crowd our everyday lives.

Images whirled behind my closed eyes, though I tried to concentrate. Fresh yellow pineapple wedges eaten on the bus. Sugar cane juice sticking to my fingers. Hair like black raw silk falling down the back of the Tourism Information Officer. Her Thai smile. Phra Sumana Tissa in Bangkok, tickling me when I tried to bow to him. Rambutan, all red and hairy on the outside, sweet and white inside, a most exotic fruit. What could be more disgusting than fried cockroaches, served up in a sterile plastic bag?

A small gong sounded from the front of the *sala*. The walking figures returned to their seats. Everybody knelt in formal posture, buttocks resting on heels, back straight and palms pressed together at the chin in the *wai* position. The Ajahn crawled forward on his knees towards a photograph in front of the Buddha statues. He lit a candle on either side of it. In the dim light I could see it was a picture of an old Thai monk. A special mat had been set in front of the picture. Anyone who was seated on it would naturally be facing the monks, not the Buddhas. It was the teacher's seat for Ajahn Chah. Only his photograph faced us.

The gong rang again. The Ajahn's voice rose in a strong deep monotone chant, 'YO SO', vowels drawn out, vibrating through the quiet dark hall. The monks, novices and white ones joined their voices to his in praise of the Buddha. 'BHAGAVAN ARAHAT SAMASAMBUDDHO . . . ' They chanted in Pali, the language of Theravada Buddhist texts, reputed to contain the original words and teachings of Gautama Buddha. Pali was once the common language of northern India where Gautama Siddhartha Buddha lived. In Thailand, Pali is a mystical religious language, chanted by all devotees but understood only by a small minority of educated monks. It filled the *sala*, creating a rhythm out of long and short sounds. There was some intonation in the nasal hum of it, but it remained free of song, free of the swell of emotion. A severe, a solemn, a detached offering to the silent brass images before us.

Then it was dawn. Outside light leaked into the *sala*. We sat in silence until the bell rang again. Three times we bowed to the altar. Three times we bowed to the photograph of our absent teacher, Ajahn Chah. In silence the monks and others stood. They rolled the mats and returned them to a shelf at the rear of the hall. We all took small grass brooms from a large wicker basket and swept the floor clean, gathering dust and dead moths together with hundreds of tiny black ants caught while foraging for food. All was brushed into a pile then swept into a dustpan and shaken out of the door. Not a word was spoken, not a sign from anyone that a new face had joined them in the night.

The monks began readying themselves for alms round, cleaning their bowls and wrapping themselves in their outer robes. Although I knew this was an international *wat* and had expected *farang* monks, I was surprised to see that only three of them were Thai. I had not noticed this in the dark. In the light the white and pink heads, the tall, ungainly forms and the blue eyes were a shock to see, shrouded in the Thai traditional ochre robes.

I left the *sala* and went in search of a small open area in the jungle. Finding a suitable spot, I removed my sandals and began to pace, eyes cast down a metre in front of me, head bent, body moving slowly and deliberately, mind concentrating on every sensation of muscle movement. I had never tried walking meditation before. I felt as if I were going to fall over.

A black creature, about eight centimetres long, crawled slowly across my path. My eyes bulged. I knelt to watch. It had claws like a scorpion and the same black arthropod body. But instead of a scorpion's arced tail, a thin translucent needle like a hypodermic jutted out from the rear of its abdomen, horizontal to the ground. The needle glistened as the creature crawled off the path and back into the dry

leaves. It moved as if it too were practising walking meditation this morning. Straightening, I resumed my pace, more
fully aware of the ground in front of my feet.

In the morning light I could see that the *wat* was beautiful,
surrounded by jungle. Between the *sala* and the kitchen a
dozen paths crisscrossed through leaf-carpeted wild patches.
Trees almost canopied the sky. Jungle is different from forest
as we think of it in the West. Green creepers twined everything together, wrapped themselves up tree trunks, clung
from one branch to another. They connected and strangled
at the same time. Ferns and palms shot up between broad-
leaved deciduous trees. I could recognize only a few varieties. Mango. Teak. Nothing from home. Where the pathways
were swept the smooth sand was reddish brown.

The kitchen was alive with activity when I returned to the
guest room. Actually, my room was above two storage rooms
and a large concrete floor space which had water jugs and a
few charcoal stoves to serve as a kitchen. Several Thai villagers were busy cooking food, peeling vegetables, washing
great white serving basins, chattering and enjoying themselves. In addition to whatever the monks would bring home
from alms round, we were served food made for us by
whoever showed up in the morning to cook. Traditionally,
monks only eat what they collect by begging, but I supposed
the extra food was put to good use by foreign visitors. Better
than a monk having to carry two bowls. Our breakfast looked
as if it was going to be a feast. One must fill up, I thought,
with only one meal a day.

I wandered back into the empty *sala* and noticed a black-
board on the back wall. The daily schedule was written out
in English.

> 3:00 – Rise
> 3:30 – Morning chanting, daily reflection and meditation
> 5:00 – Clean sala
> Dawn – Alms round
> 8:00 – Meal
> 2:30 – Drink
> 3:00 – Chores

Lots of time, it appeared, to sit and watch the body breathe. Or walk back and forth among the scorpions.

A little before eight I went into the kitchen and helped the villagers carry white bowls full of food into the *sala*. The monks and novices were seated on a low platform against the wall along the far side of the temple. They formed a single line which was continued by the ones in white robes and those in plain white clothing. But the ones in white sat on the floor in front of the platform, not up with the monks and novices. The Ajahn beckoned me, and told me briefly to remain in the *sala* with the villagers until the monks had begun to eat. Then I could leave and eat in the kitchen with those who had brought the morning food offering. He told me once I had shaved my head and put on the white clothing, I would become a 'layman' and be permitted to eat on the floor of the *sala*.

I watched the monks pass the food along the line, ladling out the contents into their black enamel bowls. Everything they collected on alms round went to the kitchen in the white basins. At mealtime they were brought back out and passed around for everyone. There were about twenty dishes, mostly Thai-style curries and fresh tropical fruits. After the monks and others had filled their bowls, the Ajahn led them in a short chant of blessing. The Ajahn began to eat first, using a soup spoon and a knife. After him, the second monk began, and so on down the line, each one waiting until the one seated to his right had begun. Following the villagers' example, I carried the white serving bowls back to the kitchen. I was hungry after watching all the food go by. I had had no supper the night of my arrival and knew there would be no lunch or dinner. Not for a long time.

One of the village women crouched, setting a huge bowl full of food in front of me on the floor of the kitchen. I had been travelling in Asia for over a year, so the sight of so much food triggered an automatic response to shovel it all in before someone could take it away. I dug in with a little tin spoon.

'Hi, this must be the kitchen, right?' said an American voice above me. Instinctively, I grabbed my bowl, then looked up over my shoulder into a lean and grinning face that matched the voice. It belonged to a tall young male who sat down crosslegged next to me.

'I was told to get something to eat in the kitchen. My name's Jim; what's yours?'

'Tim, Jim.'

A Thai villager set a load of food in front of the newcomer and gave him a spoon. Jim dropped a little blue student's day pack from his back and attacked his food with a meditative enthusiasm equal to my own. It was irritating to have him here. I had lost my unique sheen. Not that anyone had noticed me. But now there were two new guests: a Tim and a Jim. That would make for trouble, I thought. We looked too much alike. Our accents were similar, our hairstyles, features and glasses the same. From the annoying way Jim's first few words grated on my ears, I concluded that our voices must also sound very much alike.

But the intrusion couldn't spoil the meal. The food was excellent. The variety of fruit amazed me. I had been given bananas, oranges, pineapple slices, grapes, a mango and a handful of ripe jackfruit segments. There were also small red-skinned rambutans, papaya, lichee fruits and mangosteens, with their purple rind and sweet white flesh. A large pale yellow thing stuck to the side of my bowl like a giant slug. It smelt of sweet creamy garbage. The infamous durian – delectable to all Thais, repulsive to anyone else. I left it alone.

Jim spoke to the villagers in Thai. They came over and sat with him, delighted that this new *farang* could speak their incomprehensible language. He explained to me he had been studying Thai history, culture and religion for the past year at Chiang Mai University in northwestern Thailand. This was his sophomore year abroad.

After breakfast I took Jim to the Ajahn's place. The Australian monk seated himself on a cushion on the marble patio beneath his elevated teak hut. In full daylight the ochre robes looked even more out of place on his gaunt and pink frame. He was well over six feet tall but years of living on a monk's diet had emaciated him. His bald head would have appeared skeletal if not for his nose which stuck out like a beak. He looked at Jim with pale blue eyes and spoke in a quiet, halting voice.

'You must be the American. I was a little confused. I thought you had arrived last night.'

'You got my letter then, sir?' said Jim.

The Ajahn nodded. 'I thought Tim was you at first.'

'Well, he's not, but I am. As I said in my letter, I'd like to stay for about three months and be ordained as a *pahkow*.'

'And you?' The monk turned his pale gaze on me.

'I don't really know much about the place. I said last night I wanted to stay about three months, but it could be two or five. I'm in no rush. What's a *pahkow*?'

'They wear robes like a monk, only white. You met Michael last night, didn't you? Actually, it's a fairly new development in Thai tradition to ordain men as *pahkows*. It used to be only women who became *pahkows* since in Thailand there is no longer an order of nuns. Usually Thai men go straight into the monkhood, unless they are very young, even if they are only staying for a few months. Of course because they have grown up with Buddhism it's quite easy for them to become proper monks. For Westerners who are not familiar with the tradition it's more suitable for them to be ordained as *pahkows*. It allows them to become accustomed to the discipline and practice without the pressures of monkhood. Then when they are ready they can become novices. Eventually they take the vows of a *bhikkhu* – that's the Pali term for a monk. Of course, you don't have to decide this right now.'

'What's the difference between a *pahkow* and a novice?' I asked.

'The only real difference is that a *pahkow* keeps The Eight Precepts and a novice keeps The Ten Precepts. A Westerner usually remains as a *pahkow* for several months before considering being ordained as a novice.'

'Why not just be ordained as a novice and take two more precepts?' I asked.

'It's a difference in how others will look at you' said the Ajahn. 'A novice is seen by the Thais and the *sangha* as someone in training for the monkhood. A *pahkow* is a lay person adopting basic, temporary vows.'

'Right. Then I want to be a *pahkow* too' I said.

'First you both will have to pass some days as guests in the monastery, just to learn the rules' said the monk. 'We are a community here and so we have to have certain rules set down telling us how to live with each other. If we didn't have rules, we wouldn't have harmony. The rules we follow are the same ones the Buddha laid down in the *Vinaya* over twenty five hundred years ago. It's not just a set of arbitrary rules; it's an ancient tradition you will be following. The monks follow two hundred and twenty seven training precepts. You should recognize that everything the monks do is laid down as a rule. As much as possible you should adopt the same behaviour. At the present time, I'll just go through the five precepts laymen and guests must follow and the additional three you will take if you become *pahkows*.

'The first precept is to refrain from killing. Most of us are pretty good at not killing other human beings and large animals but you should avoid killing even insects. You may find that hard, especially with the mosquitoes and ants around here. A monk isn't even supposed to cut plants or dig in the earth, according to the *Vinaya*. But this is something you, as non-monks, may be required to do.

'The second precept is to refrain from taking what is not given. This is more than just not stealing. If something is the communal property of the *wat*, you should still ask for it before you use it. Sometimes people take things without thinking or are careless with a limited resource. This can cause disharmony even if they don't realize they are doing it. So don't take what is not given.

'The third precept is to refrain from incorrect speech. Lying is only one of the four kinds of incorrect speech. You should also avoid slander, harsh words and frivolous chatter. As you watch the monks, you will notice how calm and silent they are as they go about their daily duties. At least that's how they're supposed to be. They do not bother each other with idle words.

'The fourth precept is to abstain from all erotic behaviour.

14

For this reason the women's section is kept at a distance from the rest of the *wat*. The real temptation many men face when they come here is masturbation. You are not supposed to do it. Once you have been ordained, if you break this precept you must come and confess it to the senior monk. It's worse if you are a *bhikkhu*. Then a meeting of the *sangha* is required and penance must be handed down. The guilty monk has to sit at the end of the food line. For seven days no one can do anything for him. It's really embarrassing. I remember one fairly senior monk had a serious problem with this. Whenever the villagers came in to bring us food in the morning, they would see him sitting at the bottom of the line and laugh. It's a tough penance, but shame is a good incentive to develop will power. Some men get worried about pressure building up if there is no release. But there is a natural release through wet dreams. Since you can't help having them, they are not an offence. However, if you wake up in the middle of one, you should not actively encourage it to continue. No rubbing or body movements. That's forbidden.

'The fifth precept is to refrain from taking alcohol or drugs that lead to heedlessness. This has seldom been a problem at Pah Nanachat, even though we include smoking in the list of forbidden drugs. I suppose if an addicted smoker came here I would permit him or her to smoke outside the monastery grounds. But alcohol is definitely not allowed. Actually, there is one small loophole I've been indulging in during the last two years, and that's chewing tobacco . . . '

'But Ajahn, I've seen monks all over Asia chew betel nut' I said.

'And in Thailand a lot of *bhikkhus* do smoke' Jim added.

'But the point is to stick to the rules as they are laid down, even if interpretations vary in different places. Chewing tobacco is not forbidden here. Smoking is.

'Now, the sixth precept is to refrain from taking food at improper times. That means any time after noon and before dawn. Here we take this to mean one meal a day, which we have in the morning. You may be surprised that we some-times take chocolates or candies with our afternoon drink.

The definition of food in the *Vinaya* is not what it is in the West. Sugar, honey and chocolate are actually hardened liquids, not solids. We are permitted these any time of day. Since we share all offerings though, we only eat these together at drink time. So we may have fudge with our cocoa, but we can't use milk in it, because milk is considered a food according to the rules.

'The seventh precept is to refrain from singing, dancing, listening to music, watching shows, wearing perfumes, garlands or beautifying cosmetics. This precept isn't much of a problem here. The previous Ajahn used to bring in video movies sometimes, saying they were about *dhamma*, and so were allowable. But some of them had a pretty shaky connection to *dhamma*, I think.

'The eighth precept is to refrain from sleeping on a high or luxurious bed. We have no beds here, other than the one in the Ajahn's quarters, so this isn't a problem. You've both got your sleeping mats? Good. Any questions?'

Jim and I looked at each other. Neither of us dared to ask about the bed.

'What are the other two precepts for a novice?' I asked.

'Actually, there's only one more precept. The seventh precept is divided in two parts to make ten. A novice must refrain from touching gold and silver. That means money. Sometimes you may be asked to go into town with a novice or a monk to carry money for them if they have any business to do.

'In addition to the eight precepts and the two hundred and twenty-seven precepts you will catch on to, you should also learn the Thai traditions and customs which we follow at Pah Nanachat. Most of us here are not Thai. As guests in the country we take it upon ourselves to blend in properly. The local people support us and we try not to offend them. A little courtesy goes a long way in Thailand. This is a much more formal culture than our own. It usually takes Westerners a while to adjust. I've been here twelve years. For me the adjustment is pretty well complete. The Thais appreciate this. It makes for a harmonious relationship with the lay community. For example, Tim, the way you are sitting now would be considered rude by Thai standards and an insult to me as a monk.'

'Sorry' I said quickly, uncrossing my legs, not knowing where to put them.

'And if you were wearing *pahkow* robes right now, you would have just exposed yourself. So you see you must learn to pay attention to all the details of life. This way you will develop mindfulness. That is the key.'

'Tell me, Ajahn, how should I sit?'

'Look at Jim. He is sitting perfectly, with both legs folded back to one side, away from me. You should never point your feet at anybody in Thailand, especially a monk. It is also incorrect to cross your legs when facing a senior monk. Jim, your letter said you have spent a year in Thailand.'

'Yes sir, at Chiang Mai University. I felt it wasn't enough to study Buddhism. I need to come and practise in a monastery too. I've done some meditation before but nothing formal with a teacher. I guess that's why I'm here.'

'And you, Tim?'

'Theravada Buddhism is new to me but I spent three months last summer in a Tibetan monastery in Ladakh, in northern India.'

'Mahayana Buddhism?'

'Yes. It's about as far from what I've seen of Thai Buddhism as the Catholic Church is from the Salvation Army. But I'm open to learn whatever Pah Nanachat has to teach me.'

'We don't give much by way of formal teaching. There are just two things to remember: follow the rules and be mindful. So much of the bad *kamma* we build up in this lifetime is due to ignorance of the precepts. Keep them and you will find your meditation will follow naturally. Be mindful of all things. Mindfulness makes your meditation practice a twenty-four-hour-a-day effort. Pay attention to what you are doing in the present. Don't think about the future or about the past, or about some resentment or longing that you feel. If you are walking, walk; if you are sitting, sit. Apply this to everything you do, from eating to defecating. The rules themselves are really just a tool for mindfulness. Some of the rules seem foolish in a modern context. They seem more trouble than they are worth. We want to throw them out. This just reveals a lack of patience, a lack of willingness to submit. So every rule has a teaching for us. I remember when I first came here twelve years ago, thinking I would just stay for six months, get enlightened and then move on. I couldn't stand all the rules. They seemed to slow everything down. Of course that was their purpose. I just couldn't accept it at that time. I was in too much of a rush. Only in the last year or so have I begun to see just how important the rules are. Follow the rules. You will be surprised how everything else fits into place.'

'But what about meditation?' said Jim.

'It has a place. But there isn't a lot one can say about it. I suppose at the beginning you need some guidance. Usually we start visitors off just with practising concentration on a word as they breathe. The word we use is "Bud-dho", breathing in on the "Bud" and out on the "dho". The word itself isn't important. You can use any word you like. It's just something to help the mind get established on the breathing. As soon as that is done, you can drop it.'

'What about walking meditation?' I asked. 'I tried it this morning and kept feeling as if I were going to fall over.'

'You shouldn't walk so slowly. We think walking meditation should be done at a normal pace. In this way no barrier is set up between the meditation and normal walking. Let everything be your meditation. Any more questions?'

'One more, sir' said Jim. 'What's the condition of Ajahn Chah? Is he still able to give any teaching?'

The Ajahn turned his gaze on Jim. 'He's in Bangkok right now. Doctors say his condition is stabilizing. The stroke left him completely paralysed three years ago. He has to be fed intravenously. They can't determine if any of the personality is left inside. They hope to bring him back to Wat Pah Pong eventually.' He sighed. His words were spoken heavily.

'You were one of his disciples, weren't you, sir?'

'Yes.'

'Do you think there's anything left of him?'

'I have no view. Now I'll get you some blankets.'

Jim and I bowed three times to the man who had just

become our spiritual teacher. I mimicked Jim's bows well enough not to draw further comments from the Ajahn and withdrew.

I wandered back to the *sala*. Inside I met a young Thai woman writing English in a notebook. She told me her name was Dukita, a nickname that meant 'Dolly'. She said she lived in the nearby town of Ampher Warin. During school vacations, she stayed at the *wat*. She had a round face and cheerful dark eyes and looked more like a thirteen-year-old than a high school senior. We chatted easily.

'Where did you learn such good English?' I asked her. 'I haven't met anyone in the Northeast half as fluent as you. Did the monks teach you?'

'Oh no' she laughed, 'I went to school for a year in America. I got a scholarship to go back and study there at university next year. You just arrived this morning, didn't you? You're from America, right?'

'No, you must be thinking of Jim. I'm Tim, from Canada.'

'Pleased to meet you, Tim. Have you seen my mother yet?' she asked with a beaming smile.

'No. Does she stay here too?'

'I'll show you.' She led me to the front of the *sala*, next to the altar. I thought perhaps we were going to look at one of the miniature figures on the glittering side tables in front of the Buddhas. Instead, Dukita crouched down near the glass case containing the skeleton. The bones hung from the top of the case by a metal wire so that the toes dangled just off the ground. In front of the skeleton's feet was a black and white portrait of a Thai woman. She had short hair and a sober expression on her lips. Her face was boyish but beautiful.

'This is my mother' said Dukita, a smile on her round young face. She turned to me and said in a cheerful voice, 'She shot herself' as if she were conveying a trivial but curious detail of her mother's life.

'What?'

'Through the head, see? Here's the bullet hole.' She pointed to a perfect black hole in the right temple of the skull.

'I'm sorry' I said feebly.

'It's okay. She had cancer. It was really bad so she shot herself.'

'How did she end up here?'

'In Thailand it's not permitted to burn suicides like we do for everybody else. They have to be buried. My daddy gave the monks permission to use her skeleton for the *sala*.'

'A reminder of mortality, right?'

'I guess so. Mother used to spend a lot of her time in the *wat*.'

'I'm pleased to meet her.'

Dukita looked at me a little strangely. She smiled.

'Will you be staying here for long, Jim?'

I winced. 'I'm Tim. Jim is the other one. I'll be here between two and five months.'

'That's good. What other one?'

'Jim.'

Dukita looked confused. 'Well, I hope you like it here. See you.'

'See you, Dukita' I called after her as she bounced out of the *sala*, leaving me alone with her mother.

> Mother of Dolly,
> suicide
> is not a ticket off the wheel of rebirth
> nor an end to suffering.
> What does your pretty face have to teach
>   me?

CHAPTER TWO

How Big
is a Stick?

'How big is a stick?' Ajahn Chah once asked his disciples. 'It depends on what you want to use it for, doesn't it? If you need a bigger one, then it's too small. If you need a smaller one, then it's too big. A stick isn't big or small at all. It becomes so as a product of your desires. In this way, suffering is brought into the world.'

On the first day at the *wat* I came down from my room above the kitchen and watched Pahkow Michael prepare coffee and cocoa for the afternoon drink. With him were two Westerners: a small, sullen teenager named Herbie, dressed in a white undershirt and trousers, and a grey looking Englishman wearing ochre robes who squinted at the kettles through little round-rimmed glasses. The young Thai novice I had seen the night before squatted on his haunches nearby, watching the three *farang* with a secret smile.

'The trick is to balance the sugar just right' said Michael, heaping big spoonfuls into the kettle with a soup ladle. He watched the young Thai out of the corner of his eye. 'Isn't that right, Meow?'

The Thai stood up. He crossed his arms, frowning for an instant as if he were an overseer.

'You don't want it too bitter' Michael went on hastily. 'That's not so bad for coffee, but cocoa just has to be sweet or you can't drink it. Maybe a wee spoonful more.' He dumped in another heaped ladle-full. Meow coughed politely.

On the pillar near the table where Michael was fussing, a sheet of paper enclosed in clear plastic was posted. It gave detailed beverage making instructions in English, complete with a breakdown of maximum and minimum quantities allowable per kettle of coffee, tea, ginger tea and cocoa, as well as corresponding rations of sugar and Coffeemate. Underneath the chart a notice read: 'Please stick to the given quantities. Do not follow your personal preferences. Drinks are for the whole community and supplies are limited. On normal days, minimum quantities are sufficient. Maximum quantities are for work days only.'

'Now I hear rumours that I'm a *pee bah*' said the Englishman in ochre to Michael in a plaintive voice.

'What's a *pee bah*?' asked little Herbie.

'It's because sometimes I have a way of staring at things' said the Englishman, as if in explanation. 'Some people find it odd. Now the villagers are saying I'm a *pee bah*, for goodness sake. On *bindabhat* I've noticed some of the old women seem frightened of me. They are afraid to put food into my bowl.' He sounded sad.

'What's a *pee bah*?'

'I don't know what to do about it, Michael. I try to stop but sometimes things are just so interesting to look at. I can't help it.'

'I understand, Eddie' said Michael. 'Those villagers, once they get an idea into their heads, it passes from mouth to mouth pretty quick. They don't have much else to talk about other than the *farang* monks anyway. So they think you're a *pee bah*? If they believe it, maybe that will keep them from poking through the jungle near our huts every morning looking for mushrooms.'

'What's a *pee bah*?' Herbie's patient question now sounded like a refrain.

Eddie removed his wire glasses and squinted at the teenager. 'A *pee bah* is a forest sprite. Sort of a ghost, for heaven's sake.'

Herbie gave a short laugh, a little exhalation of breath. A

smile crossed over his face in a flicker. Then he was sullen again.

'Perfect!' cried Michael. 'Meow, try this cocoa and see if it's sweet enough for you.'

The little Thai took the offered cup with a smile like a Cheshire cat.

Herbie and Eddie each picked up a kettle and carried them across the compound. Michael and Meow followed. I fell in line behind. I was hungry.

'Bring a cup from the kitchen' Michael said over his shoulder, not looking at me. I hadn't noticed that they each carried a cup as well. On a small table against the store room wall I found a rack with a dozen plastic mugs and a few glasses. They were uninspiring. I selected an off-white cup with a chewed up base, then hurried towards the coffee kettles disappearing out of the compound and into the jungle. Meow stopped to ring the bell. It was 2:30 pm.

Drink was held at the Ajahn's place on the marble foundation underneath his raised rooms. We removed our sandals. The marble was cool on our feet, but the air was hot and heavy. Jungle air. We sat with our legs folded to one side, away from the Ajahn. Monks sat near the front, novices, *pahkows* and laymen further back, according to their places in the hierarchy. Jim and I stayed in the rear. The community sipped the sweet cocoa and coffee with Coffee-mate in silence. All of us brushed at mosquitoes. Their humming filled the air. Dark sweat covered the ochre backs of the monks in front of us. I had waited all day for drink break. Now the time stretched endlessly. I shifted my posture. My ankles and knees throbbed on the hard marble. I had to rub my feet and neck constantly to keep away the insects. Jim seemed placid, absorbed in drinking his coffee. I envied his adaptation to Thai customs, his facility with the language and his ability to endure Thai sitting postures for long periods of time. I had arrived in Thailand only a week before, after a year on the Indian subcontinent. My market-place Hindi, Ladakhi, Nepali and Bengali languages were useless to me here. I was starting all over again. Even my sojourn in a Himalayan monastery seemed of little relevance in a steaming Thai jungle. Jim had laughed at my Tibetan bows. All I had was experience at starting from zero. I wanted to place myself within the ancient Theravada tradition in order to judge the fruits of Buddhist philosophy in a living community of monks. The Buddha told his disciples not to accept his words but to practise them and believe only what personal experience revealed. It was an experiment I could not resist. I was not here to seek enlightenment, I reminded myself, not even to demand the truth. I was here only to open myself to experiencing what the Buddha taught.

Finally the Ajahn spoke. 'No mail today. In three more days it will be time for head shaving. Any visitors wishing to shave should see Tan Casipo in the next day or two.'

No one looked at Jim and me. We had nothing to say. Silently the monks drained their cups. They bowed three times to the teacher. After they had finished, the back rows bowed. The monks rose to return to their huts and the community dissolved into the jungle.

It took a few days before the white and ochre robes lost their aloofness and I could begin to sense people underneath them. Jim and I still had our hair. We hadn't yet adopted the uniform and uniformity of the community, so we shared a feeling of isolation. This drew us together. Knowing that many tourists came to Pah Nanachat for only a few days, we could understand why the monks seemed remote and uninterested in new faces. We had received no instruction for training other than our first session with the Ajahn. He gave us a few books to study then left us alone in the guest room. The only people who spoke to us personally were other guests, a few of the laymen, and one New Zealand monk whose job it was to teach us the monastery routine. Through this monk, Tan Casipo, word gradually got around that we were not just passing through. The new boys were going to be ordained. That fact, plus our own growing familiarity with the place and its peculiarities, slowly made conversation with others possible.

Jim and I decided to join in the bi-monthly head shave, held at the washing area near the robe-dyeing shack at the far edge of the monastery grounds. I asked Pahkow Michael to scalp me. Jim went under the knife in the hands of an Australian novice named Nimalo, who seemed calm and even tempered, even by monk standards. The two of us soaped our heads as instructed, rinsed, and soaped again. Dripping suds, we sat side by side on a board bench set up near the wash pump.

'We can race' said my barber to Nimalo. 'That is, if you've got your confidence back after your last attempt. Phew! That was a lot of blood.'

Jim laughed a little nervously. I felt the scrape of a razor on the crown of my head.

'Do you want the ears on or off?' asked Michael.

I thought he was joking when he soaped my eyebrows but he removed them neatly as I sat with suds and hair dripping down my face.

'It's an old tradition in Thailand for the monks to shave their eyebrows' Michael told us. 'It used to be that the Burmese sent spies into the country disguised as monks. They were hard to catch. Nobody dared to arrest a genuine *bhikkhu* by mistake. So the king decreed that all Thai monks should shave their eyebrows.'

'Why didn't the Burmese just shave their eyebrows too?' I asked.

'They did. But then when they got back to Burma they were spotted by the Thai spies in the Burmese court and dealt with appropriately. Clever people, these Buddhists, yes? Go rinse.'

Michael won by half a head.

Strange, the scrape of a razor on my scalp. Strange, the feel of cool wind around my ears and the direct heat of the sun on my pate. I put my head under the pump spout. Cold water hit like a shock. Strangest yet, the sudden dryness when the water ran right off. Drip dry skull.

After the haircut we returned to the *sala*. Tan Casipo gave us white linen trousers to wear. Together with our own undershirts, these formed the official uniform of the laymen. Wearing them and shaving our heads signified our intention to stay in the monastery, even though we had not yet been ordained. The effect of the costume was what you would expect to find in the violent wing of a sanitorium. Next, Tan Casipo assigned each of us a private hut in the jungle, called a *kuti* in Thai. He loaded us each with a kerosene lantern, matches and a kettle. He showed us the locations of our new homes on a map at the rear of the temple, then sent us off into the trails. From the guest room we had brought with us our blankets, pillows, sleeping mats, books, mosquito nets and small rucksacks. Thus equipped, Jim and I were ready to begin the homeless life.

Our huts were a ten minute walk from the *sala* along a narrow trail. Tan Casipo had placed us next to each other, separated by only fifty metres of dense overgrowth. The placement was only natural. After all, hadn't Jim and I been childhood friends? As I feared, the community already considered us a single entity. Nobody believed we had not arrived together, nor that our identical intentions to stay and be ordained were as coincidental as our physical similarity. Now that we were both bald and wearing white clothing, the only way to tell us apart was that Jim was a little taller and I was a little broader. Even our glasses looked the same. When Tan Casipo spoke to us, he never referred to us individually by name. I knew he couldn't tell which was which. How could anyone be expected to differentiate? When the Ajahn suggested we be ordained together in a dual ceremony, we eventually accepted the fact: we were each possessed of a double.

Fortunately, in spite of all my fears, Jim and I liked each other. We soon became grateful for the company, especially in the beginning when the rest of the community seemed cold and impersonal. Their quiet lack of interest would have been isolating and frightening if either of us had arrived alone. Jim was twenty one, five years younger than I, a second year history student at Swarthmore College in Philadelphia. He said they called it 'Sweatmore' because its academic pressures were so intense. He planned to study law. Jim was articulate, a debater by nature, with a cynical bent. Since he had studied Thai Buddhism and culture for a year in Chiang Mai, he became my most reliable source of information. For him, I was a balance to his analytical and critical perspective. I had a degree from the University of British Columbia in western philosophy and had been on the road for a year, through the *ashrams*, temples and cheap hotels of India, learning something about the ways of the East. To Jim, I was a world traveller. He valued my experience and endured my reminiscences. We quickly discovered that we argued well together, as one would expect from an iconoclastic lawyer and a mystic philosopher trapped together in a Southeast Asian jungle. We intended to follow the rules at first, avoiding 'frivolous chatter' with each other as much as possible. But the community had already moulded us into a single entity, even twinned us in our huts. We shared our experiences and leaned on one another for support and insight as we tried to understand the meaning of Wat Pah Nanachat.

How big is a hut? Small, but big enough. Two and a half square metres. Two paces by two paces. It was raised four metres off the ground by wood and concrete stilts to keep out snakes, scorpions and other living beings that creep in the jungle. There was a porch at the top of the stairway where I could sit and stare at the trees and creepers which grew close around. A window in each wall allowed breezes to blow through no matter from which direction the wind came. The hut was built of rough wood, stained walnut brown, simple and bare, except for the lathe-turned slats on the porch railing. The roof was made of corrugated tin. Although the trees and the wind provided some coolness, the sun beating on the roof radiated an oven-like heat at midday. There was a single object inside the room. A small wooden statue of the Buddha sitting in meditation posture. The stub of a candle stood beside it on a shelf beneath one of the windows. Walking on the floor boards, I discovered dozens of black sticky pellets the size of rice grains. A noise in the rafters soon revealed the cause. I shared my *kuti* with a lizard. He was about thirty centimetres long, shy and quick. He had a reddish-grey complexion and was covered with ugly little bumps. That may have accounted for his retiring behaviour in the daylight. But at night, as I soon discovered, he often thumped and thrashed on the roof as if wrestling alligators in his dreams. Still, I appreciated the company. I named him Gonzo. Having to shake lizard turds off my mosquito net was an irritation to me, but I'm sure my stomping about at three in the morning made my hut-mate just as tense. After all, he was there first. A broom had been provided, so I swept the floor clean. Then I climbed down the stairs to clear the private track between the main trail and my hut. The last twenty metres was a smooth sandy stretch like a runway, designed for walking meditation. My new home had all the facilities a would-be *bhikkhu* could want.

Pahkow Michael asked me which *kuti* I had been given.

'Number ten' I said.

'Little Herbie's old *kuti*? That's a good one.'

'What do you mean? Did Herbie move out of ten to another hut?'

'Just a few days ago.'

'Why?'

'He said he didn't like the scorpions.'

'The scorpions?'

'And he didn't like the king cobra. It lives somewhere along the path between your hut and the wash pump. Haven't you seen it yet?'

'I've just moved in.'

'It's a good eight feet long. As thick as your leg.'

'And Tan Casipo gave this *kuti* to me?'

'Don't worry. They don't hurt you. They pick up your attitude. We've got a German monk, he's in Bangkok now, who went to the toilet here one night. He had just squatted down when he noticed a cobra coiled up behind the door. It reared right up at him, two feet from his face, eyeball to eyeball.'

'This is not comforting me, Michael. What happened?'

'He very calmly straightened up and walked out. Nothing happened. Man, that monk's got a lot of *metta*. Cobras, they know. They pick up the vibrations. Respect them and they respect you.'

'So I've just got to be mindful, right?'

'Right. And don't stomp on anybody.'

The moon was full that evening. It was Wai Phra, the Thai equivalent of Sunday, celebrated on the full, new and half moon nights, four times a month. Devout Thais came to their *wat* in the evening for chanting and prayers. Many arrived in the morning to prepare a special meal for the monks and then to stay at the monastery enjoying a day of rest, talking and relaxing around the *sala* and kitchen area. Those who came took the eight precepts for the day and wore white cotton clothes like the laymen. I was surprised that over a hundred Thais had gathered in the temple at nightfall. No one had told us anything about the order of the evening service. I found Tan Casipo filling his kettle with water from one of the large water tanks that collected rain from the *sala's* eaves.

'Tan Casipo, tell me, what's the programme for tonight?'

'It starts at seven with an hour of sitting meditation. At eight we'll start chanting. We do it both in Pali and Thai for the villagers. They keep chanting for hours, but at nine the monks and novices go to the Ajahn's *kuti* for a *dhamma* talk.'

'*Dhamma* talk? A talk on truth?'

'It's sort of like a sermon' said the New Zealand *bhikkhu*.

'At last, a teaching.'

'But it's only for monks, novices and *pahkows*. Laymen have to stay here in the *sala* with the villagers until we come back. That should be about nine thirty. Then the Ajahn gives a general *dasana* to the people.'

'What's a *dasana*?'

'It's just the Pali name for a *dhamma* talk.'

'Good. Does he give the same one twice? I suppose it doesn't matter since I'll only hear the one for the villagers anyway.'

Tan Casipo looked at me a little timidly. 'Of course, it will be spoken in Thai.'

'I see' I said.

'It will probably last a few hours' the monk added swiftly in a business-like manner. 'But before he starts there's drink. Usually we have strong coffee to get us through to the morning, and we eat some medicine. On Wai Phra we are supposed to sit up all night and meditate.'

'What's the medicine for?'

'Constipation. Many monks need it, especially after the morning meal before Wai Phra.'

'It was good food this morning' I said. Sitting in line with the other laymen that day I had counted twenty one dishes go by.

'The sticky rice tends to clog you up though' said the monk. 'So we get pickled olives tonight. Medicine is permitted in the *Vinaya*. It's not breaking the rules. Just be careful you don't eat too many. They are a powerful laxative.'

Although I regretted not hearing the *dhamma* talk, the chanting was pleasant to listen to. The villagers formed a segregated congregation, men on the right and women on the left side of the *sala*. They alternated lines of Pali and Thai verse. It was a strange combination of tongues. Pali is spoken in long and short monotone syllables, while Thai is a sing-song of five varying tones. The villagers actually put a lilt into the Pali, transforming the sober chants into forbidden music. I relished it. When the monks came back from the *dhamma* talk, we were served our coffee and medicine. Then the Ajahn climbed up into a high ceremonial seat on a cushion for the *dasana*. His audience listened attentively – those who understood Thai. Our teacher seemed much more at ease in this tonal language than he did when talking to us in Australian English. When at last the sermon ended, we sat together in silence. The big clock against the side wall chimed twelve times. At this signal many of the Thai villagers pulled themselves stiffly to their feet. They shuffled out into the compound, heading towards the kitchen area where they would spend the night. Several monks and others from the community slipped out quietly into the darkness.

On his way by, Tan Casipo stopped and whispered to me, 'If you like, you can go back to your *kuti* until morning meditation at 3:30. Just sit up and try to stay awake. If you fall asleep don't worry about it; it's not an offence.' The tone of his message was compassionate and lenient. But I knew what nightshift work was like. You can't stay awake sitting alone in a comfortable spot. My legs were stiff after five hours on the floor. My knees ached in every permissible posture. I stood with difficulty. Pacing back and forth along the rear of the darkened *sala*, circulation returned painfully and my feet ceased to tingle. They had gone numb during the *dasana*. I walked, but there was little meditation in it. My mindfulness consisted of remembering not to fall over. I knew if I stopped I would sleep. During nightshift on an oil rig, at least there was always something to do. Jim's gangling form leaned back against a pillar in meditative slumber, his white head lolling down at an angle. Only three monks and half a dozen villagers remained in the hall.

Suddenly, walking slips to watching the body move. Dream-like, it drives itself. The mind is in the back seat, just watching. It surprises me that the body knows what it is doing. I don't need to touch it. This agitates the mind. It tries to jump back into the driver's seat. I feel tired. Knees begin to wobble. The mind, now at the steering wheel, pleads for a rest, just ten minutes to sit down. It's too tired to drive. When I keep on walking, the body again takes control. It manages to pace and turn without stumbling. Why does the mind get so anxious? It wants control, even though it doesn't really want the task at hand, that of simple, endless walking. In the back seat it jumps around like a hyperactive child. In the front seat it only wants to sleep. Perhaps this is the value of the Wai Phra vigil. In the exhaustion of deep night, the mind loosens its grip. Then, if one can watch oneself, what is it one begins to see?

I yawned through morning chanting. By dawn I was past sleepiness. When the monks left for their morning alms round through the villages I had to resist the temptation to retreat to my *kuti* and doze until the meal. I didn't want to miss it. Outside, the cool air of early morning helped me to resume my pacing at the edge of the compound. But my mind wandered out of control into the realms of philosophy.

The Pali name for mindfulness is *sati*. When *sati* is concentrated on a single object so that the meditator is absorbed in it, this is called *samadhi*. When the object of concentration is the breath, this is called *anapana*. The mind becomes pure observer in this state, feeling the body breathe. The observer learns that in the breathing there is no self, no I, no ego. Turning *sati* upon any physical object or activity, such as walking, leads to the same conclusion. When *sati* then is turned on the objects of the mind, it finds no substantial, permanent entity, no self. It watches memories rise and fade. They are not self. It watches thoughts flicker and vanish. They are not self. It watches emotions rage and dissipate. They are not self. Where is the self? What is the self? I felt it in the restlessness of the previous night's walking, the struggle for control. What is it that struggles? Who is there? *Sati* looks to itself and disappears.

Through the practice of *sati*, *vipassana* will emerge. Insight meditation, it is called. It is more than the realization gained in *samadhi* that 'I am not this, I am not that.' *Vipassana* is the knowledge of what is when the curtain of illusion has been drawn aside. It reveals itself in silence. It is a knowledge that cannot be taught in words, for words themselves are the fabric of the curtain.

After breakfast I met a monk who had arrived that morning just in time for the meal. I had never seen him before, but I knew he was a resident *farang* at Pah Nanachat by the way Michael had greeted him when he first came through the *sala* door. He was about fifty years old, with a round belly and sagging jowls. His eyes were bright blue and lively despite the bags under them.

'Get much sleep last night?' he said to me playfully when our paths crossed in front of the *sala*. He had a distinct Mid-Western accent.

'Not a wink, Mr Chicago' I replied. I held up my hands, and pressed my palms together at the nose in the respectful *wai* one is supposed to make when meeting a monk. The monk scowled at the name. Michael had called him that. It was true to the accent.

'You should call me Tan Sumeno, kiddo' he told me with a reproving grin. 'You're Jim, right?'

'No, I'm the other one. Tim. I'm from Vancouver.'

'Washington State. Nice place. I used to fly to Seattle every couple of weeks to check on my business interests. That was before, of course.'

'The other Vancouver. The one in Canada.'

'Same difference. So you plan to get yourself ordained and leave all that craziness behind?'

'As a *pahkow*, yes. I'll let go of the craziness for a few months anyway.'

'Why not stay and ordain as a novice? You could be a monk in a couple of years.'

'I've thought about it, Tan Sumeno. But at this point in my life, I'm not ready for it. I'm still travelling. It's not in my plans.'

'That's just the point, kiddo. It's those plans which keep you in with the crazies. This is the place of letting go and getting in touch with reality. Out there, I tell you, it's a mad house. Believe me, I know. I ran enough of it in my time.'

'I don't know, Mr Chicago. If the world is crazy, maybe it needs a few sane people in the middle of it. Why do monks lock themselves up in monasteries? What's the good of solving your personal suffering if the solution keeps you isolated from everyone else's suffering?'

'What a lot of questions you got! You've got to leave those arguments and rationalizations behind you, boy. You think it's so easy to help a crazy man? You don't know what *samsara* is. It's pure lust, hate and delusion out there. Believe me, I know. How are you going to help the crazies? Will you pay their bills? They'll just become dependent on you. Will you let them cry on your shoulder? They'll soon be sitting on it. Will you make them laugh? They'll expect you to keep them entertained, then blame you if anything goes sour. Believe me, I know.' Mr Chicago paused for breath. He looked up at the eves of the *sala* and through the trees to the blue sky beyond, considering his words. 'Not that I think people are bad. They're just trapped. I like people, sure. But you can only change yourself. You start worrying about others and they'll just drag you down into the mess. The world is full of suffering.'

33

'And you say let it be?'

'I say you can't change that. If you think you can, go ahead. You'll end up even crazier because you can't end it. You can't change *samsara*. It's like Mother Teresa in Calcutta. She's been there for years and I bet there are more beggars on the streets now than there were when she started. You try to cure Calcutta and it will drive you crazy.'

'Have you been to Calcutta, Tan Sumeno?'

'Nope. No desire to go there, either.'

'I have. You're right about the city. It's packed full of beggars in grey rags. They live on the street corners, under canvas or bits of cardboard. They build fires out of coconut shells and pick through mountains of rotting garbage for food. If they are lucky they can pull a rickshaw or push a cart. They work like animals for enough rice to eat. Old withered women used to touch my feet, asking for a rupee. I'd give them ten paise. It doesn't do any good. But you're wrong about Mother Teresa. You know she's not crazy. I went to the home she runs for the aged and infirm. It's in one of the worst slums in the city, right next to a hog tannery. The stench made me gag. Rivers of bile and slime choked the open gutters on either side of the streets. People lived in little tin and canvas hovels alongside the bridge over the railway line, thousands of them packed in with their own filth and garbage, a big stinking human maze. I got lost. I found a dead dog on the railway track. Its head had been cut off by a train. It must have been some kids' idea of fun. Even though the sun was beating down, it felt dark in there. Eventually I came to a high stone wall, painted dull yellow. There were palm trees growing on the other side. It was the home. Inside, the sisters showed me around. I saw hundreds of old and mentally retarded people dressed in striped cotton clothes. Red for the women, blue for the men. The nuns brought in people they found on the streets who couldn't care for themselves. They were given food to eat and a bed of their own. Perhaps for the first time in their lives somebody cared for them. The wall was not to keep them in, but to keep what was killing them out. I watched a group of ten old women laughing at a fat lady. She was screaming at a young retarded woman who was teasing her. The fat one kept trying to catch hold of her, but she was too slow. It was funny. Even the fat lady couldn't help grinning occasionally as she swatted at the girl. When the young one saw my white face, she ran at me, holding out her hand like a beggar. She called out in a garbled voice. Her eyes were crossed and her movements jerky. I felt embarrassed. I tried to move away. She seemed to think she was still out on the streets chasing a tourist for rupees. I ignored her. The rest of the women looked on and laughed. Finally, the girl grabbed my hand. I couldn't pull it back. She held on tightly. Then she gave it a shake, like a formal handshake. "Hello" she said in careful but distorted English. Her brown face gave me a big smile. She let go and ran back to the fat lady, who was waiting for her with her hands on her hips. I was ashamed, Tan Sumeno. I thought she was begging so I flinched. She just wanted to say hello to a guest. That's Mother Teresa's work. Sure there's still suffering, still thousands just like her out begging and being raped on the streets. But now there's a smile that wasn't there before. There's suffering in this slum. Mother Teresa doesn't end it. She brings love into it. And love is more real than suffering.

'I was lucky to catch a glimpse of Mother Teresa herself before she left for Ethiopia. She was leaving her convent, Mother House, on her way to the airport. She looked old, more bent over than I had imagined. There was a car in the lane waiting for her. Three ragged beggars pushed their way in through the side gate. They threw themselves down in her path and raised their empty hands to her. They pleaded for her to give them something. I don't think it mattered what. One of them, a man with a matted beard and torn grey undershirt, was in tears. Mother Teresa patted him gently on the arm. She met his eyes and shook her head. Then she calmly walked around them into the waiting car. She left me stunned. She wasn't sucked in at all by the beggars. Even if they really did need money, she knew they had just come for a handout. She didn't try to be responsible for them. She wasn't distracted from her task at hand. If they had a need, there was probably some way her organization could help. But she was not affected by emotional pleading. The lady gives her life to the poor. If she turned them down, it wasn't because she was too busy. She knows what is and isn't her work. Still, she didn't treat them like dirt, like everybody else does. I can't describe how gentle was her touch on the man's arm. She saw them as people, not beggars. To me that's how a saint lives in a crazy world. Do the task at hand without delusions that you can cure all suffering. It's enough, isn't it, to give a retarded beggar-girl a love which lets her shake hands with a smile and say hello?'

'That's good' said Tan Sumeno. He surprised me. 'Thanks for that story. I appreciate you sharing it with me.' He had listened to my monologue attentively. My words may have won our argument, but his response won the conversation. I liked this middle-aged monk. Not only was he interested enough in a newcomer to initiate discussion, he was a good listener as well. A teaching at last.

CHAPTER THREE

Samadhi Suicide: Our Example

M ichael told me that he and Herbie were going to the nearby town of Ampher Warin to do some shopping. He asked me if I wanted anything. I asked him to buy a cup I could use for drink time. I wanted something personal.

'Any particular colour?' asked Michael.

'Red. Real red. The redder the better. I don't have any red, only white. I need a little red in my life' I said.

Next morning at meal time I found at my sitting place a fine plastic mug which could have been an accessory on a fire engine.

'Turn it upside down and it doubles as a police flasher' said Michael, who was pleased with himself. 'I thought we'd never find a cup like that in Warin. But there it was, right in the centre of the display, as if it were meant for us.'

'Perhaps it felt a calling to come to the *wat*. It's a perfect red. Thanks.' I said.

'There was a *bhat* change so I got something extra for you' said the *pahkow* in a low voice. I peered into the bottom of my cup and saw the secret: two wrapped toffees.

Jim and I prepared for our ordination. The ceremony, which must be performed in Pali, involved taking our vows from the Ajahn. We were required to recite by heart the eight precepts and the triple refuge. The triple refuge is a Theravada Buddhist's profession of faith:

I go to the Buddha for refuge.
I go to the Dhamma for refuge.
I go to the Sangha for refuge.

Buddha, *Dhamma* and *Sangha* are three sources of spiritual
nourishment and shelter for a Thai Buddhist. They are a
trinity called the 'Triple Gem.' The Buddha was the historic
founder of the faith, but in this fuller context the meaning
expands to include 'The One Who Knows' within each of
us. It is the wisdom which comes forth through the practice
of meditation. *Dhamma* is the name given to the teachings of
the Buddha which were recorded in the Pali scriptures. Yet
it also means truth itself, even if that truth is not found
within the Pali canon. *Sangha* is the community of monks.
But the human forms which wear the robes do not complete
the meaning of the *Sangha*. The *Sangha* are those who tread
the spiritual path together, supporting and being supported
by one another as they practise diligently the *Dhamma* of the
Buddha.

Jim had memorized the ordination ritual before he came to
Pah Nanachat. He explained to me that his original intention
while in Chiang Mai was to be ordained as a monk. He had
been rehearsing for this much longer ceremony for over a
month.

'I knew a Thai man and his wife who wanted to sponsor
me. It's a big deal for a *farang* to be ordained as a monk.
They would get a lot of spiritual merit for their role in it.
The Thais believe that a son who ordains as a monk, even
if only for a week, brings great spiritual credit to his parents
in their next incarnation. My sponsors didn't have any children, so my ordination was very exciting for them. They
organized a feast, robes and gifts for the monks at the *wat*
in the city where I was to be ordained. They even arranged
a head shaving ceremony. I'd heard about Pah Nanachat
and planned to come here. But I wanted to spend ten days
in Chiang Mai first to help me get comfortable in the robes.
I figured that way I could come to the jungle fully prepared
to meditate.

'My sponsors took me to meet the abbot of the *wat* I was

going to live in. He was the most disgustingly fat monk I have ever seen. He reminded me of Jabba the Hutt from *Star Wars*. All the time we talked he chain-smoked. He had beady red eyes. For the first time I stopped and asked myself just what I was doing. I'm an outsider in Thailand. I'm not even a Buddhist. I like the meditation part of the philosophy, but some things are really repulsive to me, like that abbot. I realized I didn't have the right to take on the role of a religious actor. I wouldn't be true to the expectations placed on me by the culture. I had to ask myself what my reasons were for wanting to be a monk. They seemed pretty shallow. It was all a big ego trip. I had written my friends back in America, telling them I was becoming a Buddhist monk. I was going to wear robes, shave my head and beg for my food. If I backed out they would think I had lost my nerve. I had been telling myself my motivation was for the sake of meditation. But it was just a kick to be different.'

'I looked around at the fuss everyone was making over me. My sponsors and other Thai friends had spent about five thousand *bhat* on the ceremony. That's over two hundred American dollars, a lot of money here, and these people aren't rich. I'm an atheist, but I hate it when religion becomes a business. Stores selling religious articles make a lot of profit from Thais who want to buy merit. It made me sick to be in the middle of it. My only reason left for not cancelling everything was that I didn't know how to explain why I had changed my mind. They wouldn't understand. And they had spent the money. Can you believe it? I was going to be a monk so I wouldn't waste two hundred dollars worth of merit.

'At that time I met a Thai monk who had spent several years in Pah Nanachat. I told him my problem. He suggested I become a *pahkow*. I didn't know men could be *pahkows*. I knew right away it would be a better role for me. Maybe a Thai can justify jumping straight into ochre robes. He grows up with the religion all around him. I guess it's in their blood. For me, I knew it wouldn't work. It was hard to swallow all my pride and tell my sponsors I was backing out. I tried to explain why I had decided to be a *pahkow* instead, but they didn't listen. They said they were sorry I had lost interest in their religion. I think they took it well. It must have been a loss of face for them, but they had no bad feelings.'

'Did anybody understand?' I asked.

'Maybe one of my professors. Everyone else just wrote me off. That's probably a good thing. Now I'm here without anybody else's expectations of me. I'm glad. Can you imagine me waltzing in here pretending I'm a monk just because of the robes? Could I sit further up the line in the hierarchy than Nimalo who's been a novice for three years? The right place to start was at the bottom, as a guest. From layman to *pahkow* is as high as I ever want to go.'

'I agree' I said. 'I thought about monkhood, but it isn't right for me either. I don't know if in your position I would have had the guts to cancel the show.'

'You didn't come face to face with a Thai version of Jabba the Hutt.'

Tan Casipo gave me a small tape recorder and a cassette of the ordination ceremony. He was a helpful monk, shy and slender. I think he was in his mid-twenties. Age means nothing here, I was told. It was not a question to ask. His eyes were tranquil. In his smile there was a subtle sense of the ridiculous. He had dropped out of his final year of a degree in applied physics.

The tape was only fifteen minutes long. Almost everything the initiate says is simple repetition of the Ajahn's words. The Pali pronunciation was difficult for me to master. Short and long vowel sounds had to be spoken with absolute precision. I practised for hours in my *kuti*. Jim came over occasionally to help. We sat either on my porch or under the shelter of my mosquito net and rehearsed. He knew it backwards, giving a Thai inflection to his syllables. We were also able to support each other through the preparation. We both had doubts about what we were doing, but we were determined not to back out. Vowing to follow the eight precepts was not a problem. Although the precepts are similar to the Ten Commandments in content, they are not imperatives handed down from heaven. The Buddha taught his followers to practise *sila*, moral purity, as an essential preliminary to meditation. He said wrongful actions produce guilt and fear. When the mind is agitated it is incapable of tranquillity. Right actions produce a natural calm. This calm is necessary if meditation is to arise. The precepts are simply a means to meditation. Jim and I could make these vows sincerely. However we were both uneasy about taking refuge in the Triple Gem. Neither of us were Buddhists. I was a Christian. Jim was an atheist. From these opposite extremes, we were reluctant to declare Buddha, *Dhamma*, and *Sangha* as our sole refuge. Our Ajahn told us not to worry about the meaning of taking refuge. Just go through the ritual, he advised. Understanding will come gradually. Faith takes time to grow. We weren't sure just what kind of faith would grow in either of us. Perhaps we could accept it under the more esoteric interpretation of Buddha as the 'One Who Knows' and *Dhamma* as truth in general but neither of us felt ready to submit to the community of monks as if they were divine. The Buddha had challenged people to test his words against their experience. For us the test now involved submission to the monks. This called for a faith neither one of us possessed. But for the sake of the test we decided to follow through with the ritual together and join the ordained hierarchy of Wat Pah Nanachat.

The rehearsals filled all my mornings, all my quietness, all my stillness. They soaked up my calm. Meditation fled. Apparently I couldn't meditate and do anything else in the same day. If this was true, then what was the value of meditation, unless I was going to spend my whole life in a *wat*? If I came here to meditate, then what was the point of this irritating chanting which clogged my brain like an advertising jingle?

The mind is like a monkey, say the Buddhists. It hops from place to place, restless and wild. We have no control over it. Our sensations, perceptions, memories, wills and thoughts chatter erratically in our heads. There is no peace. The aim of meditation is to learn first how to control the monkey mind; then to be free of it. This is not how the West views the mind. The scientific and artistic traditions of the human race are not erratic chatter to us. We exalt our minds. We raise our consciousness. Our sense of self is our most important possession. We cannot comprehend what the Buddha taught.

But the goal of meditation can also be considered in terms of science, according to right brain/left brain psychology. The two hemispheres of the cerebrum control different activities. The left hemisphere generates linear thought. It is conceptual, abstract, verbal. It gives us our words and ideas. The right hemisphere generates non-linear thought. It is intuitive, creative, imaginative. The left hemisphere is the dominant partner in most human activities; it seldom relinquishes its control. It thrives on complex tasks and if not fully taxed, will wander distractedly. The right brain is easily absorbed with just the sort of simple activities the left side finds tedious. For example, if required to concentrate on the mundane simplicity of breathing, the left brain will rebel. It will want to think of something more interesting. But if attention is continually returned to breathing, the left may eventually give control to the right brain. When this happens, a distinct mental shift will be experienced. Restlessness will cease as the right brain takes over. A person in this condition will relax into peaceful contemplation. Viewed in this way, meditation is a therapy for lessening left brain dominance. As the passive right brain learns how to be in control, enabling us to lead more creative and intuitive lives, this restores a balance in our own human nature.

I sit on my porch and concentrate on the trembling sensation of breath in my nostrils. The ease of absorption begins to come at last. 'Hey, now I'm getting somewhere! This is meditation!' Concepts spring into awareness, shattering the calm. One word, one thought leads to the next. The chattering left brain takes over like a bully. 'Yes, I'm finally meditating. Well, almost there for a second. Sure is hot now. When's coffee break? Remember coffee break back on the rigs? Fudge brownies. Damn mosquitoes.'

One tool for restraining the monkey mind when it breaks unbidden into meditation is the use of a *mantra*, such as the 'Bud-dho' suggested by our Ajahn. The right brain may be too weak at first to sustain control of so subtle an object as the breath. The left can easily intrude when it has not been tamed to be silent. Repeating a *mantra* forces the flow of thought back to a single sequence. The left brain can tolerate this for a short while, because a *mantra* is at least verbal. But it is boring. Repeating 'Buddho, Buddho, Buddho' a hundred thousand times is not its idea of fun. It will struggle to break the sequence. But like links of a chain, the words are firmly connected to one another. Many Buddhists repeat their *mantras* while counting the repetitions on a rosary. The rhythm of the words and the beads in the hands help to still the left brain and activate the right.

'Bud-dho, Bud-dho, Bud-dho, Bud . . . what time is it now? I must have been sitting near to an hour. Where's the coffee bell? The Ajahn – I'm not meditating. Bud-dho, Bud-dho. Cof-fee. Thoughts keep creeping back in. I have to concentrate hard, keep repeating Bud-dho, Bud-dho, and perhaps there will be cocoa. Does Coffeemate violate the *Vinaya*? Argh, Argh, Bud-dho. Why not Buddha? Bud-dha Bud-dha, Bud-dho, Bud-dha. Perhaps – Stop it, stop it! Out damned thought.'

The effort to silence a thought is itself a thought. Yell 'Stop!' and it only shatters your calm. As soon as one says 'Oh dear, I'm thinking now' the left brain is back in control. An act of judgement is a left brain function. A meditator must refuse to judge even the quality of his meditation. Ajahn Chah told his disciples not to be absorbed by thoughts that arise in meditation. Note their arising, but do not become attached to them, he said. Observe a thought which intrudes, but don't question it, don't deny, evaluate or dwell on it. It's just there, the same as breathing is there. No one judges breathing. Accept all states of mind as they arise. This diffuses the left brain activity of labelling everything good or bad. To accept what is, is a right brain activity. It has a way of comprehending in a flash of insight that comes before the words. In meditation that insight can be turned to the intruding thoughts and they will wither to their roots.

Bud-dho. These thoughts and concepts whirl through my mind as I pace on the runway in front of my *kuti*, perspiring in the afternoon heat. I conceptualize my failure to meditate, and devise theories to overcome my theorizing. Words to tear a curtain of words.

Tan Casipo led Jim and I to a large wooden cupboard at the rear of the *sala*. We were to be fitted for our new role in the hierarchy.

'We have some used *pahkow* robes in here' said the helpful monk, 'but I don't think there will be enough *sabongs* for both of you. You need three sets each. There's lots of linen. We'll just have to make up some more. I sent Meow to get Yenaviro. He's the Malaysian monk in charge of supplies.'

Tan Yenaviro arrived. I had noticed him before. His Chinese-Malay features marked him out from the other monks. He sat next to the novices in the morning meal line, which indicated he was the junior *bhikkhu*. He was the only non-Thai Asian in the international *wat*. He took a set of keys from the front of his ochre sash and opened the cupboard. He pulled down a pile of white linen which looked like bed sheets.

A *sabong* is a simple wide strip of cloth. Wrapped once around the waist, it covers one to the ankles. It's the common dress of rural people throughout Southeast Asia and India. Usually it's made from bright patterned cottons. As a religious uniform, it is ochre for monks and novices, white for *pahkows*. There is a special way those who have taken vows must secure them. Tan Casipo and Tan Yenaviro showed us how. The wearer wraps the cloth around his backside, holding the ends together at arms' length in front of him. He rolls the two ends together until the *sabong* is tight around his waist, with the rolled cloth against his stomach. A thick cotton belt is then worn so that the string ends are tied over the top end of the linen roll. Fastened like this, it won't slip or unwrap. The result is a midi-skirt with a spring roller like a furled sail in front. It allows for maximum modesty and mobility. The only dangerous position is a full squat. Spreading the knees and bending can unroll the bottom of the sabong's roller enough to permit full view of all that a *pahkow* wears underneath; in the tropical heat, that's not much. To tie the belt on properly, the roll must protrude about four inches above the waist, forming a large knob which comes up to the navel. It looks like a great white phallus. While Yenaviro searched for a belt, I was left gripping this knob in my hand, holding the roll in place. Jim and Casipo suddenly started to giggle. Yenaviro turned around from the cupboard, puzzled, then he too started to laugh. Perhaps the outfit was meant to be a constant reminder of the third precept.

Above the waist, ordained members of the community wear a cotton or linen sash draped over the left shoulder, fastened beneath the right armpit. It falls across the chest, discreetly covering both nipples and the protruding white reminder. Pahkow Michael, however, wore his sash in a roll, just looping it over his shoulder to stay cool. I told Yenaviro I liked the style.

'It's not appropriate in the *sala*. You must cover your chest' said the Malaysian.

I pointed to the gleaming idols at the front of the temple. 'But the Buddha shows a nipple' I said.

'We don't make the rules. We just follow them' he told me.

Pahkows do not share the burden of an outer robe, which the *bhikkhus* and novices must wear at rites and on alms round. Especially during the humid Thai summer before monsoons clear the air, the robes are hot and constricting. But monks must follow the rules. The only disadvantage of a *pahkow's* outfit is the colour. When I grumbled about the large size of my new wardrobe – three *sabongs*, three sashes, two bathing clothes, two sitting clothes and a white carry bag – Yenaviro told me I'd need them all unless I wanted to wash my clothes every day.

'Those whites don't stay white too long after a few mornings out walking through rice paddies on alms round' he said. 'You'll spend a lot of time doing laundry meditation as it is.'

The monks are lucky. The ochre robes they wear are a good match for the reddish brown soil. Some *bhikkhus* even use mud to dye their bathing clothes the prescribed colour.

A tall *farang* monk in his late twenties entered the *sala* and joined the fitting session. He was the German monk who had calmly backed away from the sleeping cobra in the toilet. Recently he had returned from Bangkok, where both his knees had been operated on. Too much sitting meditation had damaged them. At the meal he sat on a cushion, easing the pressure off his joints. The day he returned he showed the others the tensor bandages wrapped around his legs for support. Despite his injury, his face was always a smile. Ajahn Chah had given him a Thai nickname which he preferred to the Pali name assigned him when he was ordained. He was called Ruk, a nickname meaning laughter.

Michael said Ruk was built like a tank. He was famous for having eaten fifteen mangos at a single meal. He was tall and had broad shoulders. Yet like most Westerners who spend years in a monastery, he seemed below a normal weight. His frame was big, but he was a lean looking tank. Still, he worked like a bulldozer. He was always active. The day he returned to Pah Nanachat with bandaged knees he began collecting deadwood in the jungle. I watched him cut and stack it under the roof of the robe dyeing shed for the rains retreat. He sweated like a horse. His robes were always wet. Perspiration often ran down from his bald head, over his bald eyebrows and onto his gold-rimmed spectacles. He went about his self-motivated tasks cheerfully. If his vows did not prohibit singing, the air around him would have been filled with music.

When he wasn't dragging dead branches out of the jungle, Ruk was invariably in a small side room of the *sala*, sweating over the sewing machine. Meow had told Ruk the two new laymen were going to need new *pahkow sabongs*, so he had come to volunteer his talents.

'I love to sew' he told us. The German accent was still noticeable in his voice. 'In fact, I have to be careful, because sewing can easily become an attachment for me. I used to spend a full week every month in the sewing room. I'd make robes for anybody who asked me. Of course the others would sooner give them to me than let me teach them.' He laughed. 'Even when I tried to explain, if they couldn't do it right I would just take the job over anyway.'

Ruk led us to the front of the *sala*, near the sewing room. He got a measuring tape and began to measure us for new *sabongs*. We stood beside the skeleton of Dukita's mother. While Ruk worked, I asked him about the woman and how her bones ended up on display in our temple.

'It's common in Thailand to have a skeleton next to an altar. It reminds us of what we are. She used to come to the monastery often. She liked to be here. When she died, since she could not be burned, she was buried in the jungle nearby. Her husband gave permission for her body to be exhumed a year later when it was suggested the bones could be used in the *sala*. One of the monks was a good friend of hers. Her death made him very sad. He took it upon himself to prepare the skeleton for display. When the body was dug up, they left it out for a while, to completely dry. Then the monk spent a few hours every day cleaning the remaining flesh from the bones. He did it as his meditation on death. He worked alone in the jungle. He was devoted to his task and he used only one tool: his food knife. At the end of every day, he would clean it, then use it for the morning meal.'

Jim and I examined the skeleton while Ruk wound up the measuring tape. It was exquisite, a giant dangling sculpture in perfect balance. From the slender spinal column delicate ribs curved out into space. From the pelvis and clavicle arms and legs hung motionless, yet free to move. Her fingers and toes were all precisely tooled. Covered with living flesh, these bones were the miracle in each of us. We stood in awe of her beauty.

'What about the other reminders of mortality, Ruk?' I asked, walking over to the altar. I touched a clear plastic box about half a metre high, filled to the top with formaldehyde. Inside it sat a small pink figure with its eyes closed. The skin had a rubbery tone, but it was real. A dead human baby, less than a year old.

'Did the parents donate this?' I said. Ruk shook his head.

'What about this?' I pointed to a photograph, framed in black wood, which was sitting on top of the baby's case. It was a black and white picture of a naked meditator sitting crosslegged in the lotus position, grinning. It seemed at first glance that he must have been sitting that way for a long time. The ascetic was emaciated. I looked more closely and noticed that the skin had come away between his ribs. The pelvic cavity was just a gaping black hole. Each toe bone could be seen clearly. So could the joints where his elbows joined his forearms. The head was a skull wrapped in leather. The blissful but insane smile on his face was there because his lips had pulled back and withered away.

'They think he was a monk' said Ruk. 'They found his body alone in a cave a few hundred kilometres north of here. He died in *samadhi*. His posture was so perfect, his body did not fall.'

'Sure looks like he died happy' I said.

'It's hard not to smile when you don't have any lips' said Jim.

'Ruk' I said, 'what I want to know is why is his photo here in front of the *sala*? Is he supposed to be a warning to us, or a good example?'

'A good example, of course' said Ruk, a little surprised at the question.

'He's not my example' Jim muttered as the two of us left the *sala*.

Did the monk die a natural death, I wondered, or did his meditation kill him? Ajahn Chah warned his disciples of the danger of addiction to *samadhi*:

> That which can be most harmful to the meditator is absorption samadhi, the samadhi with deep sustained calm. This samadhi brings great peace. Where there is peace, there is happiness. When there is happiness, attachment and clinging to that happiness arise. The meditator doesn't want to contemplate anything else, he just wants to indulge in that pleasant feeling. When we have been practising for a long time we may become

48

adept at entering this samadhi very quickly. As soon as we start to note our meditation object, the mind enters calm, and we don't want to come out to investigate anything. We just get stuck on that happiness. This is a danger to one who is practising meditation.[1]

Perhaps this cave monk became addicted to absorption *samadhi* and never came back. I imagined him in perfect bliss, perfect contemplation, while his body stiffened in the lotus position and began to dehydrate. As an aware meditator he would have noted these events as they arose but they would not have disturbed him. There would have come an instant when he knew his limbs were about to lock in place, that there would be no more help for him, lone hermit, if he did not move at once. He would have watched that instant come and pass without abandoning his calm. As the days passed he may have noted the gradual deadening of sensation as the life dried from his extremities. Circulation would begin to clog. Toxins would slowly poison his body. Some masters of meditation can greatly reduce their rate of metabolism. Perhaps the hermit lived like this for many months, well past the time of natural death. He may not have been emaciated when he first took his seat and entered this fatal *samadhi*, observing the whole process of death and decay from the beginning. Was he still aware as his skin began to crack and rot, as his bowels hardened and the veins closed in his folded legs? His body continued to sit erect and balanced while his spine fused to a petrified rod. He watched his breath, inbreathing, outbreathing, until there was no more moisture left to wet his lips or tongue and the passing of air turned to a dry rasping over dead flesh. After his lungs collapsed, after his heart sagged in his chest, ceased pulsing and finally fell loosely from its place into the decaying mess below, perhaps even then there were a few flashing electrical impulses inside his skull observing pure bliss until the day some rude photographer took his picture and his bones were

[1] Ajahn Chah, *Taste of Freedom*, Wat Pat Pong, 1980, Ubon Rajathani, Thailand. (pp. 18–19).

carried out to the cremation grounds and burned. It could have been the monk's intention, when he first took his seat, to meditate on death by living through the event. This knowledge he would carry into his next rebirth. Surely there would be few lives left before his final release from the wheel of *samsara*.

I wanted to ask Jim what he thought of this cave monk on the way back to our *kuties*. It had begun to rain, cooling the air. The red mud of the trails was sticky on our rubber sandals. In the shelter of the jungle, little rain penetrated at first. We walked carefully and slowly, aware of the pattering on the treetops. My twin walked ahead of me.

'Jim, what do you think of suicide?'

He stopped, turned and looked at me strangely.

'I don't mean like Dukita's mother, out of pain or despair. I mean like that monk in the photo. I think he committed *samadhi* suicide.' I stopped beside him on the path.

'I don't think you can separate a suicide out of despair from a philosophical suicide' said Jim. He spoke slowly, carefully articulating each word, staring through me rather than at me. 'Despair is only an excuse. I think we all have curiosity about death. It can be very attractive sometimes. When living becomes difficult, there is less you think you will be leaving behind.' We started to walk again. The rain began coming through in large drops. We heard thunder.

'Sounds like you've thought a lot about it' I said.

'You're the philosopher. Have you ever read Camus' essay, *The Myth of Sisyphus*? He said suicide is the most important philosophical question. Why not do it?'

'But Camus did come up with an answer. My memory of it is hazy. Maybe the answer was too. He said life is absurd, but that you should accept that absurdity, even rejoice in it. Like Sisyphus you roll the rock up the mountain again and again even though you know it will roll back down. You accept futility.'

'That's not it, Tim. You don't rejoice despite absurdity, but because of it. Life is absurd so nothing compels you at all. There is no logic and no necessity. You do what you do out of freedom. You are always free to choose. Life's absurdity means you are never compelled to commit suicide.'

'What about Kirlov, Dostoyevsky's character in the novel *The Possessed*?' I said. 'He tells everyone he must commit suicide in order to prove there is no God. If God existed, according to Kirlov, it would be against His law to kill yourself. But Kirlov knows God does not exist, so there is no law. As a free, sane man, he can perfectly well choose to kill himself. There is nothing stopping him. He chooses to do it deliberately as a necessary proof of his freedom.'

'So freedom compelled him to commit suicide? I understand that. Nice philosophy.'

'But Jim, how much of your interest is strictly philosophical?'

'I'm trying to tell you, it can't be strictly philosophical. It never is for anyone. What could be more personal than your own death?'

'Personal counts more than philosophy, I admit. For me that's a confession.' I looked at him silently, waiting. We had arrived at the fork in the trail leading to Jim's *kuti*. Huge raindrops slid down from the drenched leaves onto our naked heads.

'I know what you're asking.' Jim looked into the jungle. 'Twice. First time the gun misfired, of all the cartridges in America. Second time, the train was late. That was a year ago. It seems to come around in cycles.'

'So when are you due next?'

Jim grinned at me and laughed. 'Any time in the next six months. It's getting faster.'

'If you ever need somebody to talk to, out here in the jungle, I'm just a hoot away in the next *kuti*. I don't have much to say, advice or anything . . . '

'God! Advice is the last thing anybody needs then. Just someone to be there and be human. I'll tell you about a dream of mine sometime. We're getting soaked.'

'All right. See you at coffee.'

'Thanks' said Jim. He turned and began sliding along the path to his hut.

'Careful not to slip too deep in *samadhi*' I warned.

CHAPTER FOUR

Refugees in the
Triple Gem

I sat on the porch of my *kuti*, struggling for the calm of that dangerous and elusive *samadhi*. But meditation was thwarted by my constant violation of the first precept. I murdered mosquitoes. The Ajahn said don't kill them. Just brush them away. They whined around my ears searching for new sites to drill, as persistent and distracting as my thoughts. I gave my head a good clout, and flailed as if I was swatting bats. I contemplated the meaning of that vicious swipe. It felt like self defence. But if a mosquito has already begun to bite, the poison is already under the skin. Killing won't reduce the itch that follows. In fact since the bug slurps up much of the juice it has injected, it's actually less painful to let her finish once she has begun. And the sting often hurts less than the self-inflicted slap. It makes far more sense to let her bite and be done.

A mosquito landed on my thumb. Instinctively my hand raised for the kill, but I checked the blow and watched the hungry insect probe my skin, searching for a soft place to penetrate. Poor bug, I thought. Perhaps you are driven by blind forces and accumulated *kamma* from past lives to search for blood. I give you permission to take a drop from me. I felt the familiar sting, and fought my reflex to squash. Panic arose as I watched her fill her belly. Everybody knows mosquitoes are cunning, malicious darts of the devil, devised for human torture. Let one bite you and it will breed a million more. Ecology and theology cry out against giving permission for one to bite you. Yet permitting destroyed my perception of evil in its intent. It defused my anger. I had not realized I was angry – at an insect. I had always believed mosquitoes bite in order to irritate. That is why they always land on hard-to-reach spots between the shoulder blades or cunningly bite feet and fingers in the dark. They know when a human has both hands full and is unable to retaliate. I believed all this. My upraised arm against the pests was an instrument of just vengeance upon them. The one on my thumb finished feeding, pulled out its proboscis and, heavy with red blood in its belly, flew away. It left a little white swelling on my skin. Ruk said if you love mosquitoes, they won't bite you. You can learn from them.

Mid-morning, the most difficult time of day to meditate, I would return to my *kuti* after the daily meal and sit on my porch. A light breeze soon brought the mosquitoes. Gradually I learned to tolerate being bitten one at a time. But the greedy insects preferred to descend in droves, driving me indoors and under the shelter of my mosquito net. The net protected us from each other. Then the sun heated up the tin roof like an oven. Sitting made my head broil. The only bearable posture was lying down. The heaviness of sticky rice and mangos would overcome me and I would doze until the afternoon bell rang for coffee break. The only solution was walking meditation. Although my runway was exposed to the searing sun, which often forced me to cover my bald head, at least the air outside was cooler. Mosquitoes swarmed around me, but if I kept my pace brisk, few of them could land. Often my legs would falter as my stomach struggled to digest the heavy meal. I would slow and stumble. Only the mosquitoes spurred me forward. My mind wandered once it grew accustomed to the pacing routine. It began to rebel against meditation. It led me into a world of fantasies about my future. I dwelt on my desires to teach and to write, and designed whole courses of Buddhist philosophy in my head as I dragged myself back and forth beside my hut in the jungle. Preoccupation slowed my stride. The only thing which drew me back to the present were the sudden stings on my feet or neck. My hand would jerk in

response, seldom able to stop itself for the sake of my vows.
I had no gratitude.

Once, while staggering through my morning walking, a
mosquito landed on my forehead and I was able to hold my
arms to my sides while she ate. I gave her permission.
Another suddenly bored into my ankle. It irritated me that
she couldn't at least wait until her sister had finished. Two
at a time was hard to tolerate. Then I noticed that while
concentrating on the ankle biter, the sensation of the head
biter's sting disappeared. The moment I thought of this, I
could feel the itching on my scalp, but the ankle bite faded.
I could only be aware of one sensation at a time.

It seems awareness functions like a radio. There are millions
of stations we can tune in to, but only one channel can be
played at a time. The Buddha taught that the dial of this
radio is in the grip of the monkey mind, which cranks it
around and around, twiddling from frequency to frequency.
The radio plays a jumble of disconnected noises, part of a
word, then static, a note of a song. This is the normal state
of human awareness. The listening consciousness screens
out most of this jumble, selecting fragments here and there
across the band. From these it fashions human thought, like
an archaeologist reconstructing an ancient civilization from
a few fragments of bone and pottery. This is how we build
our reality. All that we perceive is real, but we never stay
tuned to a single frequency long enough to listen to it. With
a few blips and random notes we create songs in our mind,
filling in gaps on the basis of our memories of previous
tunes. Our past experience constructs our present. It imposes
overwhelming interpretations on the random signals we
receive through our awareness. Like the nuclear model of
the atom, our reality is composed almost entirely out of
empty space.

The Buddha called the mental structures we make from
our past *sankharas*, the formations of *kamma* which we take
with us from life to life. They are the objects of our thoughts,
our conceptual building blocks, our words. They range from
physical things like chairs and tables to abstract things like

mathematics and our desires. Conscious activity is the arrangement of these building blocks into various patterns. They are the flow of words in our heads. But *kammic* formations arise within us as a product of the past, not of the present. When we are aware of our thoughts we are aware of something which is different from the reality of the present. Meditation directs awareness away from *kammic* formations towards more subtle frequencies. It stills the monkey's hand to focus on what was previously only a blip on the turning dial. When this happens, thoughts disappear. One can only be aware of one thing at a time. Focusing awareness on the sensation of breathing excludes thought. Deeper into meditation, even awareness of breathing disappears; the sensation becomes too subtle to be defined as an event. One sits in empty silence as awareness holds steady on that single frequency. Then, so the Buddhist sages say, without thoughts arising, the awareness vibrates with a music unlike anything created by our *kamma*. It is fresh with the present. If meditation has a goal, it is to gain this direct contact with reality.

After the drink, the Ajahn tells us today is sweeping day. Monks, novices, *pahkows*, laymen and guests, all of us take bamboo brooms with stiff straw bundles tied to the ends and sweep the sandy compound area. We sweep down the trail behind the *sala* to the robe dyeing shed and through the winding paths in the jungle that lead to each solitary hut. Even the Ajahn sweeps alongside us – sweeping leaves, big broad jungle leaves, little red and black berries fallen from the trees, small twigs and lengths of creepers brought down by yesterday's storm. Fifteen men, sweeping leaves, sweeping leaves in silence, sweeping leaves with mindfulness, the task a tool for meditation, as we sweep to clear our mind of thoughts, as we sweep to clear the path of leaves. Sweeping leaves, sweeping leaves. 'What are you sweeping?' said the silent voice.
'Leaves.'
'What are leaves?'
'Leaves, I know them now' I answered. 'They are the

55

product of my *kammic* formations, moulded from a few grasped snatches of the past while my monkey mind twitches the dial. Born into thought, their true nature is unknown to me. That which they are is covered by the shape of leaves.'

'And where are all the leaves you have swept?'

'In the forest.'

'No. They arose as your *kammic* formations, they dwell in your mind as *kammic* formations. For this reason when you put your broom away, you will still be sweeping leaves. Tonight when you sleep you will dream these leaves again. The song you have written will play on. These are your memories which you sweep. You have called them to life, so they will return again. You called them up from a fragment of awareness, a brief fluxion perceived in an instant, covered now by a carpet of that which you label leaves. A pure and vibrating fluxion lies beneath the illusion you have created. Some instant passed when you grasped that fluxion, when it fluttered in your awareness . . . .'

'And if I can learn to attend fully to that flutter, to that which sparked the first thought "leaf"?'

'Then no *kammic* formations will arise. Then there will be no memory.'

'Then, how will I remember it? What will I learn? How can there be learning without memory?'

'Perhaps there is not.'

'What will there be?'

'Only the un-sweeping of un-leaves called leaves.'

'And when I finish un-sweeping sweeping, will the un-leaves called leaves return to haunt my dreams?'

'No. They will stay in the forest.'

People come, people go. Our community in Wat Pah Nanachat is in constant flux. Only the robes remain the same. Mr Chicago left for Bangkok. Pahkow Michael will soon travel to Malaysia for a visa renewal and a holiday. The British novice Edgar disappeared some time ago. The other laymen have all left to continue their travels except little Herbie, who looks glum because Michael is going. But new laymen have arrived and Pahkow Mark has become ordained as a novice. He dyed his white robes ochre. All our monks went over to Wat Pah Pong for the ordination ceremony. It required twenty monks and a *bhote* – a special ordination temple – for the ritual. Pah Nanachat didn't have enough *bhikkus*, and our new *bhote* was still under construction. Those of us further down the hierarchy were not invited to attend. We simply watched Mark leave in his white robes. He returned later in the evening wearing dusty yellow. He was wrapped so tightly it looked as if he was wearing a shroud with only his skinny, skeletal head poking out of the top.

'So do you feel any closer to *nibbana*?' I asked him.

'Don't feel any different at all' Mark said.

'Then why did you do it?'

'Just the right time for it, I guess. What I really get out of this place is the feeling of community. I've always been a lone wolf. I've never lived at close quarters with other people if I could avoid it. It's good for me here. There's respect for each other in this community, not like back home in New Zealand. I suppose I was ordained because I wanted to participate in it more fully.' Mark sat in Edgar's old place at mealtime.

A new Englishman arrived, a middle-aged man named Percy who seemed as eccentric as the novice who had vanished. Percy had close-set eyes and hair which was greying without distinction. He combed it forward, less to hide the thinning on top than to create a bit of the 'mod' look which went out of fashion fifteen years ago. He wore new blue jeans low on his hips so that his belly was not constricted. There was a slightly self-conscious limp in his walk which he habitually tried to turn into a saunter without ever achieving the desired effect. Percy spoke with the kind of British accent that makes me feel the speaker is pulling a tremendously funny joke, seeing how far he can carry it. It was the kind of earnest voice which describes the battle of harvesting last season's radish crop in minute detail. I always waited for the punch line. It never came. Percy told me he was perfectly keen on Buddhism. I could not believe that he was not in a London suburb, raking fertilizer into a shabby lawn which would never grow anything but weeds. He seemed a born fusser, a putterer always at odds with the garden shears, someone for whom the world would never co-operate. I wanted to ask him what he was doing here, so far away from his dying begonias. The question came out a little more civilly.

'Why did you decide to come to Pah Nanachat, Percy?'

'I thought it would be a good place to learn Buddhism. I'm frightfully keen on doing meditation, you see.'

'Have you practised *vipassana* before?'

'*Vipassana*? Is that how you say it? It's the one with the breathing, isn't it?'

I nodded.

'I haven't actually done it yet, not *vipassana*.'

'Have you done other kinds of meditation?'

'Not much. Not really. No. Perhaps you can tell me a bit about it, then?'

'I just got here a week ago myself. You should talk with the Ajahn if you want instruction.'

'But you've done it before, haven't you? Meditated?'

'I was in a Tibetan monastery for three months last summer, in Ladakh.'

'Ah yes, Ladakh, Ladakh. And where is Ladakh?'

'India. Near the mountains in the north.'

'That would be the Himalayas then, wouldn't it?'

I nodded.

'It sounds frightfully interesting. Did you go to Bombay too?'

'Bombay?'

'It's a city in India.'

'I know.'

'Then you've been there?'

'No.'

'Oh.'

'Have you been there, Percy?'

'No.'

'Oh.'

'But I've met people who have. They are all frightfully keen on it.'

Do not speak unless you can improve on silence, said a Buddhist sage.

I watched Percy sit during group meditation next morning. His legs were bad. I could tell he was in pain. They stuck out in front of him, barely crossed, in a posture a Thai would think definitely rude. His kneeling was even worse. He couldn't seem to bend his knees past ninety degrees. Instead of resting his weight back on his feet, he teetered crookedly upward from the waist, hunching over a little to the side, looking like a broken jack-in-the-box. It must have been excruciating. His bow was little more than a flop on his face. I looked graceful by comparison.

When meditation was finished and the monks had left for their morning alms round, I went to the back of the kitchen to find a sturdy broom. After the first sweeping day, the Ajahn had made it known that it was the responsibility of guests and laymen to sweep the compound area every morning. He said it keeps us out of trouble while the monks are away on *bindabhat* and helps keep the place looking orderly. I resented this at first. Early morning was my favourite time for walking meditation. To thoroughly sweep the compound often took longer than alms round. Every activity should be a meditation, they said. Renunciation is the road to liberation, they said. Scorpions live under the leaves, they said. I started sweeping.

I watched Percy grapple with his broom. He had chosen the scrawniest, spindliest one for the job. His sweeping was little more than ineffectual scratching in the sand. He made pathetic little jabs at the leaves, as if trying to nudge each one individually off the path. The ground he swept remained strewn with leaves, twigs and berries. I watched as he swept right over the top of them.

'I suppose that should do for today' he said as I approached him. He put his broom up and mopped his barely wet brow.

'We should do the road too, Percy, at least some of it. There's a lot of leaves' I said, not breaking my own sweeping rhythm. For some reason Percy felt I was in charge. Nobody else paid much attention to him. I remembered my own isolation when I had arrived so few days ago. To Percy, I must have appeared to be a permanent part of the community. I knew the rules.

'Yes, I see. So it's the road then, is it? Mustn't forget the road, I suppose. Yes, all right. Well, I'll go over there and start, since it must be done.' He headed down the gravel pathway gloomily.

'Remember, Percy, the Ajahn wants the leaves swept up into piles in the centre, then carried to the side and dumped. Don't sweep from the middle out.'

'Of course not. Piles in the centre, then carry to the side. Can you tell me, why is that?'

'Otherwise, all the gravel will end up in the jungle.' I quoted the Ajahn.

'Well, we certainly wouldn't want that, would we?'

I looked at him sharply, searching for just a hint of sarcasm in his expression. But I found only grim determination as he nibbled at his stiff upper lip. His gaze was riveted to the leaf-strewn path ahead.

'How much of the road must we do? Perhaps we should save some of it for tomorrow.'

'That's a good idea. We'll just work at it until we've had enough.'

He inverted his broom with a deep sigh and began scratching his way down the centre of the road. I found myself beginning to like his good-natured courage in the face of helplessness. He would be easy to abuse, even despise, I thought. A little praise, however, seemed to go a long way. Any encouragement produced renewed determination to combat untidiness. His language, so carefully propped up with clichés, was a shield behind which he seemed engaged in genuine struggle.

After breakfast, Jim and I rushed back to our *kuties* to change into our new white robes. It was time for our ordination ceremony. I felt giddy wearing the robes through the jungle for the first time, feeling my legs swishing without the restriction of cotton pants. The linen of my best robe, the one Ruk had made, was stiff. It felt like a wedding gown.

'You look dazzling' said Jim, who was waiting for me at the fork to his *kuti*.

'Thanks, *bhikkhu*. You're stunning yourself.'

'You look like the Man from Glad in drag' he chuckled as I straightened my front roller. 'Better cover that other nipple.'

'And you look as if you're wearing a main sail. I think you'd look better in ochre. You sure you don't want to be a monk?'

Jim laughed, and led us at a quick march through the jungle to the temple. Tan Casipo waited for us there.

'Where's the Ajahn?' Jim asked.

'Waiting for you in his *kuti*. You need to take an offering to him. I'll help you get it ready' said the New Zealander.

Beside the altar, just behind the glittering little side tables, there was a stack of incense sticks and candles. Tan Casipo placed six candles and a handful of the scented sticks on a round tin serving tray. From one of the flower vases he removed two fresh lotus blossoms, completing the offering. The tray had on it a picture of a familiar gentleman in a top hat striding briskly across the centre. Across the top it read 'Johnnie Walker Black Label.'

'You want us to take the Ajahn an offering on a whisky tray?'

'It's the thought that counts' said the monk.

'I like the thought' said Jim. 'It's too bad we didn't bring a little chewing tobacco to offer as well.'

'*Swaddie krup*' Jim called up to the top floor of the Ajahn's *kuti*. The teacher answered the greeting in Thai. He came stiffly down the stairs and motioned wordlessly for the two of us to take our places on the marble patio beneath his rooms. He seemed pale and detached as he settled himself into the elevated ceremonial seat. He gazed at us with his sombre, pale blue eyes. We bowed to him three times.

'Which one of you will go first? You, Tim, since you were the first to arrive. Just for the sake of convenience, you will also be considered the senior *pahkow*. Jim, you will be the junior. Although there is no difference at all between people, this designation will prevent confusion in the order of seating at meals and such things. Now, Tim, you can begin by offering me the offering.'

I crawled up close to him on my knees as Tan Casipo had instructed and carefully presented him with our ceremonial goodies on the whisky platter. I shuffled backwards to my place beside Jim and knelt in my best Thai posture, resting my buttocks on my heels, hands raised to my nose in a polite *wai*. I had been practising the ritual for five days now. I felt more than ready.

'Before my ordination as a monk' the teacher began, 'I felt extremely confident. 'But when I said my first word, Ajahn Chah raised his hand to stop me. Then he stood up and walked out of the *bhote*. I didn't know what I had done that could possibly be so bad to cause him to walk out. I was shattered. He came back a minute later with a tape recorder. He sat down in his seat, raised his hand high, then pressed the record button. He looked at me and gestured me to start again. He had a way of keeping any of us from getting too sure of ourselves. Now are you ready to begin?'

I nodded.

'Just remember, hold your *wai* steady. I noticed in our rehearsal you tended to bob your hands like a metronome.'

Hands rigid, serenity shattered, I began to chant.

'AHAM BUNTE, TI SARANENA SAHA ATTA SILANI YAJAMI.' Venerable monk, give to me the eight precepts.

The ritual went smoothly. The deep nasal monotone required had by now become familiar, almost comforting to repeat. Even the dreaded seventh precept did not trip me up, though it had remained a tongue twister until the final day.

'NAGAGITA VADITA VISUKADASANA MALAGAN-DHA VILEPANA DHARANA MANDANA VIBUSANA-THANA VERAMANI SIKHAPADAM SAMADHIYAMI.'

With those words I formally surrendered singing, dancing, music, shows, perfumes, jewellery, garlands and beautifying cosmetics for the period of my ordination. Jim followed my performance without flaw, using his Thai tonal pronunciations for the Pali. We took our refuge in Buddha, *Dhamma* and *Sangha*. A strange pair of refugees, the Christian and the atheist before the Australian abbot. The Triple Gem still had not become for us a shelter from suffering. It was more like a new cave we had been challenged to explore.

When Jim had finished, our teacher told us to sit at ease. We could now properly call him our teacher, for in taking the eight precepts from him we had entered into a formal religious arrangement. He was our guru; we were his disciples, bound by our vows to obey him in all things.

'Now that you have been ordained, you should be instructed about the behaviour and duties that will be expected of you as *pahkows*. While you were laymen all that was expected of you was that you follow the five precepts and conform to the daily routine. As *pahkows* you have taken on a position and a role within the hierarchy which involves new responsibilities both to those above you and below you. To the guests and laymen you must be examples of proper behaviour and respect. They will be watching you when they are unsure what to do themselves. You should look to them and help them to learn the rules. Visiting Thai people will also watch you just as they watch the monks. You must be careful not to offend them by behaviour they would consider sloppy or rude for an ordained person. Tim, I notice in the *sala* you still sometimes sit with your feet pointing straight out in front of you or clasping your knees in your hands. Please correct this. It could offend people. Be careful, especially now that you are wearing robes. You must always be mindful of them, or else you may heedlessly expose your testicles. This is embarrassing, not only for you but for the whole community, especially the Ajahn who is responsible for you. You also have new duties to those above you in the hierarchy. You must learn how to serve the monks. You must learn their vows. At times you will be required to perform tasks forbidden to them, such as handling money and certain kinds of work. The rules forbid a monk from digging earth or cutting plants. You should be willing to do this work should the need arise. A monk can't even ask you directly to do such work. Learn to listen for hints and do what you think needs to be done.

'There are many complex rules you should learn about

food as well, not only for your own eating. Monks have a special relationship with their alms food. A monk can only eat food which has been offered to him. If another person touches a monk's bowl or a piece of offered food, then the *bhikkhu* can't touch it unless it is offered to him again. Be willing to offer a monk's bowl to him properly, bending low so you don't tower over him. Then come in close so he does not have to reach. A monk should never reach for anything. He must live without desiring. Only what is placed directly into his hands is fit for him to receive. *Pahkows* at this *wat* are also permitted to go on alms round every morning with the monks. *Bindabhat* has many rules. Remember you represent the *wat*. The villagers will be watching you closely. Don't swing your arms. Don't talk. Don't look directly at the people who give you food. Just do exactly what the monks in front of you do. As *pahkows* you can further help the senior monks by offering to carry their bowls back to the monastery. Since you have brought your own bowls with you, I will show you how to care for them.'

The Ajahn spoke to us about our bowls and the regulations surrounding this important possession for half an hour. Tan Casipo had given us our bowls that morning. He instructed us to take them with us to the ceremony. They were about the size of large bowling balls, made of metal and coated with black enamel. Each came with an orange woollen cover with a strap attached so it might be carried around the neck while walking through the villages. The rules governing the use and care of bowls were extensive and sometimes strange. Still, one could easily imagine the human foibles which led to the creation of these rules.

A monk must not look inside another monk's bowl.

A monk must not cover up the curry in his bowl with rice to make it appear he hasn't been given any curry.

A monk must not scrape the inside of his bowl with his fingernails.

A monk should not leave his bowl near a ledge or on the edge of a table.

A monk should not leave his bowl where it may be kicked.

A monk should not hold his bowl by the bottom, but grip it securely by the rim.

A monk should not stand while cleaning his bowl, but set it on the ground, and dry it in his lap.

The majority of these rules reflected a time when bowls were made of clay, not metal. A single moment of carelessness could produce unpleasant changes in such transitory and unstable objects. The Ajahn explained, however, that although the modern bowls could not be broken, the rules have been maintained so monks can develop mindfulness.

'There are still many rules for you to learn' our teacher concluded. 'Don't worry if you can't remember them all at first. Follow the monks' example and you will catch on. If you do as well with the rules as you did with the ordination ceremony, you will make out well here.'

Jim and I bowed to the seated ochre figure, tall and stick-like in his immobile posture.

'And Jim' he said, reaching for the whisky tray with our offering still on it, 'you can take these back to the *sala*.'

'So how does it feel to be legal in the robes, Jim? Any closer to *nibbana*?'

'Holy *pahkow*, Tim, I feel more like I have just joined the army rather than a monastery.'

'But now we have got our sitting papers. We're licensed to meditate.'

'Do you realize that we talked with the man who is supposed to be our teacher for over an hour, took refuge from him, took the precepts, listened to all the rules all over again and a whole bunch of new ones, and the one subject that never came up once was meditation?'

'He did say to be mindful about cleaning our bowls.'

'Did I have to come all the way to the border of Laos to learn how to wash my dishes?'

'I know what you mean. Everybody talks about the *Vinaya*, not about *vipassana*. All we got was that one little book of Ajahn Chah's to read when we arrived. Did you read the notice at the back of the *sala* saying reading should be kept to a minimum? How are we supposed to learn anything here? You and I, at least we've had enough contact with Buddhism not to be totally lost. But people like Percy, for example, who know nothing about meditation, what good does it do them just to follow the rules? Maybe they can teach Percy how to bow properly. But does he need to bow before he can practise?'

Jim wiped the beads of sweat off his skull. 'Do you sometimes feel that though we bow to Buddha, *Dhamma*, *Sangha*, it's only *Sangha*, *Sangha*, *Sangha* that we ever hear?'

Percy raised his hand at the back, then cleared his throat. 'Will there be a teaching or something sometime soon?' he asked, over the sweltering hush of afternoon coffee break.

'We don't teach meditation here' said the Ajahn in a flat, emotionless voice. 'All we do is lay down the precepts and the rules of practice. Follow this and your meditation will bear fruit naturally.'

Percy bit his lip. The Ajahn looked around at the crowd of laymen and guests in white. The faces had all shone with sudden interest. Even the two new *pahkows* were staring at him. The Ajahn seemed compelled to say more.

'There's not much I can say about meditation. Look to yourself. Where do you resist? Where are you heedless? The rules will reveal your defilements to you. Perhaps you don't like bowing to the monks or even to the Ajahn. Remember it is not the person you are bowing to, it is the robe. Bowing is a great tool to break the pride of ego. Perhaps you don't like coffee served with so much sugar, or maybe you would like it with more. Living in a monastic community you have the opportunity to surrender your personal preferences. These are only delusion and ignorance giving rise to desire. If resentment arises, recognize it as aversion. The defilements reveal themselves to you when you begin to follow the rules. Persevere with the discipline and the defilements will gradually drop away, leaving your mind clear and peaceful. Establish the rules in your heart, follow them with mindfulness and you will stop your craving and thirsting, even for meditation. Here we teach renunciation. Here you can learn to give up cherished ideas of self. Once they are given up to the *Vinaya*, you will see they were only burdens after all.'

The teacher gazed around at us intently. 'However, I have noticed a certain slackness and lack of enthusiasm in recent days. I was surprised when I first came back here not long ago that evening chanting had been discontinued. I think that is a bad sign. As of tonight we will again assemble at seven pm. I've been thinking about this for some time. Now is as good a day as any.' Many of the monks shifted uncomfortably as the Ajahn looked from face to face. 'This afternoon will be a work day' he concluded.

CHAPTER FIVE

Sore Feet on the Noble Path

E very day after drink time we did our daily chores and hauled water. The first three men to the well had the privileges of pulling the can up, emptying it into the pails and holding the mesh net through which the water was strained. The water was for washing, not drinking. The pails were slung on either end of bamboo poles, then carried by two men to the various washing areas in the compound. Water sloshed back and forth out of the buckets unless the haulers walked smoothly in step with each other. The work took less than twenty minutes when everybody helped. There were only eight of the giant ceramic cisterns to fill each day – three in the kitchen, one for each of the two toilets, two near the *sala* for bowl washing and one for the Ajahn's *kuti*. We worked vigorously. I enjoyed the opportunity to stretch some muscle.

One day while water hauling to the monks' toilet, Yenaviro said 'I suppose you could dump that wash jar over if you wanted to.'

'Why should I want to?' I said, amazed. 'It's three quarters full. Two buckets should fill it.'

'Maybe you want to' he said.

'For the sake of mindfulness? If you want to do it, go ahead. Seems like needless work to me.'

'I can't' said the Malayan monk, suddenly embarrassed.

'Why not?'

'Because it might contain mosquito larvae.'

'Oh, so you can't kill them. Why do you want me to dump it then?'

Yenaviro turned red. 'Because it might contain mosquito larvae' he blurted out. 'If it does, someone has to pour it out because monks can't use it.'

'But if you think it might, you can't dump it yourself or it's an offence, right? So you want me to dump it?'

'I can't tell you that' said the monk.

'But if there are mosquito larvae inside, then I break my precepts by spilling the jar.'

'You wouldn't actually be killing them' said Yenaviro, who was getting increasingly agitated. 'Monks are specifically forbidden to pour out water which may contain living beings.'

I was being rude, I knew it, and becoming self-righteous as well. Less than a day into my robes and already I was preaching to a monk. I gripped the thick rim of the water jar, and pushed it. It rolled to the side. I steadied it, pouring its living contents into the sand.

'You better not watch' I said to the monk.

'You don't have to pick on me' he said.

After water hauling, Ruk asked me if I would help him collect wood for the day's work project. I was grateful for his smiling offer and readily agreed. We pulled one of the rusty pushcarts down a trail and into the jungle. Machetes in our hands, we climbed through the brush a little way to a fallen tree Ruk said he had found the day before.

'I couldn't do this one alone' said the industrious *bhikkhu*. 'I needed help from someone who's not a monk.'

'Why? I know you can't cut any living plants but this tree is already dead.'

'But look how the creepers are.' He pointed to the green cables which were wrapped around the tree. Vines had continued to survive even when their support had fallen.

'Can you *koppy* these for me?' he asked, tapping his blade on one of the creepers.

'You mean cut them?'

'I can't ask you to do that. It's against the rules. Just make it allowable.'

'What?'

69

'It says in the rules a monk can't cut a plant or ask anybody else to do it. But if you give me permission to cut one, then I can do it.'

'That's in the rules?'

Ruk nodded. His large frame was already beginning to perspire in the afternoon heat.

'That seems like a mighty tight little loophole.'

'What's important is the mindfulness.'

'Does mindfulness make a difference to the plant? I thought monks weren't supposed to kill things because that clogged up their *kamma*. The bad deeds would come back to them. And because it brought suffering to other beings. So how can I make it allowable for you?'

'It's the intention that counts, that's all.'

'But Ruk, if your intention in bringing me all the way here was to cut plants, then aren't you going against your vows? It's just a convenient way of getting around an inconvenient rule.'

'But what's wrong with that?'

'The Ajahn was just saying today that when the rules conflict with personal desires and preferences, that reveals defilements. Then we should submit to the rules.'

'That's right.'

'But you're just finding ways around the rules when they conflict with what you want to do, right?'

The big monk laughed good-naturedly. 'Am I not following the rules?' he asked, swinging his machete in the air.

'Really, Ruk, I don't care. I don't want to have to argue that cutting plants is evil. Maybe it is. I *koppy* you, over and out. Can I cut some too, on my own initiative?'

'You can. Just don't ask me about it.'

We hacked away merrily at the clinging creepers, ripping them away from the trunk where they snaked out from the ground. I was still nervous in the jungle. Although I knew there were no large animals near the *wat*, deadwood and leaves are good homes for snakes and scorpions. Ruk seemed perfectly at ease. He watched with a smile when a viper slipped out from under a branch in front of him. I saw it wriggle into the brush and wanted to run. It was difficult for me to concentrate on the cutting, especially in my rubber thongs. Every leaf which brushed my heels felt like a scorpion. Ruk laughed when I told him so. He said he once lived in a *kuti* for eight months which was infested with them.

'I used to catch about thirty or forty every month. I was only bitten once. That was by a baby.'

'So it didn't know any better?'

He laughed again. 'The last monastery I lived in before coming home to Pah Nanachat was in the northwest of Thailand. There were still tigers in the area. Sometimes if I went out walking I would find fresh tracks. I always wanted to see one face to face but they were too shy. If you love living beings, they will know, and will not harm you.'

Ruk's compassion towards living beings was genuine. It extended even towards scorpions and the red army ants which marched through our jungle like Vietnamese troops, ready to attack anything in their way. In a second they could cover your leg, biting with a venomous sting. By the rules we were not supposed to kill them. Once while sweeping the compound I stepped into a nest. I had no time for compassion. I had to swat and stomp and beat my legs in panic.

'Last year one monk stayed out here all through the dry season' said Ruk. 'He felt it was cooler than his hut and more peaceful.' Ruk pointed to a small clearing near the fallen tree. A faded plastic clothesline hung between two trees.

'In the open? On the ground? This monk –, tell me Ruk, how long have you been here?'

'Five years now. I first came to Pah Nanachat at Christmas four years ago. When I came I thought I would only stay for a few weeks. I never left, except to *tudong* to other monasteries.'

'Have you ever gone back home?'

'To Germany? No.'

'What about your parents? Do they miss you? What do they think?'

'They know I'm doing well here. I wasn't very happy when I left Europe. I write to them.'

71

'I'm glad. I think it's important not to drop parents like some cults want you to do.'

'I think parents are a very important *kammic* connection.'

'What were you doing before you left Germany that made you so unhappy?'

'I was a student. I got hepatitis in my last year of mechanical engineering and had to drop out. I decided to go to India. I travelled there for a year before coming to Thailand.'

'Do you plan on ever going back home for a visit?'

'I'd like to go back and live in Germany again but I can't do that until my five *pansa* are past. I have three more to complete.'

'What's a *pansa*?'

'It's the rains retreat. Every monsoon season the monks all have to stay together in their monastery for three months. A junior monk must complete five *pansa* before he can travel anywhere on his own. Right now if I want to go somewhere I need to have a senior monk with me. In a few more years I can go where I please. That's what Ajahn Chah did. He spent many years alone in the deep jungle, meditating.'

'But what would you do in Germany? Start up a monastery?'

He laughed at this, sweat dripping down his smiling face. We had cleared the last of the creepers from the tree and together hefted it onto our shoulders. We started to carry it towards the pushcart when I felt a sharp prickle along my neck.

'Ants! The tree is full of ants!' I hollered, flinging my end of the tree as far away as possible. Red monsters were swarming all over our shoulders and arms. I danced and cursed, violating my first precept again and again. They bit hard, stung like wasps. Ruk kept on laughing, astonishing me as he shook the tiny creatures from his sash. He brushed them gently but rapidly from his arms.

On our way back to the woodpile at the end of the afternoon, Ruk told me about a Japanese monk who had lived with him in the northwest.

'One day we were out walking through a field. He was ahead of me. We were laughing and joking. Suddenly, a

walk over gravel roads and paddy dykes. Each morning they travel in groups of three or four to the clusters of nearby villages. I decide to follow the Australian novice, Nimalo, who habitually goes with Sun Tin, a Thai farmer turned monk. Sun Tin has a blue lion tattooed on his left forearm and a crazy crooked smile. He leads us off into a dawn drizzle at a quick march, bowls slung over our left shoulders, umbrellas up for cover. A thoughtful devotee donated twenty or so umbrellas to the *wat*. For monks in Thailand, an umbrella is almost as essential as an alms bowl. The gravel on the road to the gates cuts into my soft and tender feet. I didn't count on this kind of suffering. I hobble slowly over the rocks. My two companions leave me behind. It takes ten minutes to reach the monastery gates which are flanked by two large plaster tigers, garishly painted with bright red lips and vivid stripes, perhaps to keep out *pee bahs*. This is the first time I walk through the front gates of Pah Nanachat. The direct sunlight makes me blink. Since I arrived at the *wat* I have been submersed in jungle. Now I see that beyond the jungle the *wat* is surrounded by rice paddies. There is a gas station half a kilometre away. A truck rolls down the highway. It surprises me to see a truck. My journey to the temple was an ordeal in darkness. Our jungle *wat* seems remote enough from the inside, but it is not as isolated from the rest of the world as I had thought.

Walking into open space is exhilarating. Pink smear of dawn in the eastern sky, the world quiet and empty. My eyes hungrily absorb the vibrant green of new rice, the clumps of forest off in the distance, the pools in paddy fields reflecting the clouded sunrise. Sun Tin and Nimalo wait for me by the gates. As I emerge they form a single file. Nimalo instructs me to walk behind him, no closer than two paces. Sun Tin charges off across the gravel, then veers off the road. He strikes out along the tops of the slippery mud dykes between the paddies. I slither in Nimalo's tracks, balancing my bowl and umbrella. Like a boot camp sergeant, Sun Tin plunges up to his knees in brackish water without slowing his stride. He wades across the last paddy before the highway, Nimalo on his heels, an experienced trooper. The new recruit is far behind. I clutch the lid of my bowl and struggle to keep my slipping feet from splashing red mud all over my white *sabong*. I hold it up like a skirt. There is no solid bottom in this paddy, just oozing, bubbling muck. By the time I reach the road, the others are well ahead of me. My feet are red and disgraceful. Mud flicks up from my toes, spattering the hem of my robe. The highway is made of rough asphalt, sharp and jagged. At the sides, small pebbles and gritty sand make walking more bearable. I force my feet to march. They will resemble raw meat when the ordeal is over. The noble path teaches a monk to overcome suffering, I tell myself. And I can't even walk barefoot down a highway.

Leather-footed Sun Tin and Nimalo wait for me again at the entrance to our first village. Following their example, I slip the bowl strap from my left shoulder and neck onto my right. Nimalo reminds me to keep my left hand on the lid, supporting the rim of the bowl with my right, arms still as I walk, head reverently bent. Throughout the walk we are to say nothing and never look into the eyes of the villagers. I remember the Ajahn's warning never to speak to the givers of food. Once in the past a *farang* novice actually thanked a woman for a handful of rice. She was so offended she came to the monastery and told the senior monk she and her family would never give alms to the *wat* again. Devotees give to the robe, not to the wearer. They believe it is a ritual for the making of merit, for a better rebirth. If a monk thanks the giver, then by treating it as a personal favour, merit is not gained. Along the muddy village path, old women, little children, school girls, grey-grizzled and bandy-legged old men come down from their wooden stilt houses and kneel. Each member of a family holds a little basket full of steamed sticky rice or a bowl of fruit to offer. As we approach the first cluster of devotees, Sun Tin veers close, bends a little towards them and removes his lid. He offers the empty bowl to an old woman with grey matted hair, her teeth rotting and stained black from chewing betel nut. She pulls a small handful of rice from her basket and drops it into the alms bowl without touching him or it. A woman must never touch a monk, not even his robes. She repeats her action twice more for Nimalo and me, then touches the little basket to her head and mumbles a few words in prayer. Her generosity to our robes will bring its reward.

The ritual is a humbling one, repeated fifty or sixty times that morning until my bowl is heavy with rice, mangos, bananas, dried meat, fishes, and sticky sweets wrapped in leaves. Do these villagers know where we have come from, our lands of swimming pool suburbs, aeroplanes and revolving restaurants, to walk through their rice paddies and pathways strewn with scraps of lumber, cardboard and buffalo dung? Their houses are spacious but rough, made out of unplaned wood. They wear patterned cotton *sabongs* or shorts. The younger ones have bright polyester shirts and blouses. Some of the older women wear only secure brassieres above their *sabong* wraps. A brassiere is a status symbol in rural Thailand. It's suitable morning dress during the hot season. Do they think about the world we have left behind? Few of them have even seen Bangkok, I suppose. Do they wonder why we left our Western heaven to come begging barefoot at their doors, or do they only feed the robe?

It hurts. It hurts like needles shooting up into my feet as I pick my way along the gravel road back to the monastery. The others leave me far behind. I reach the *sala* doors and gratefully rinse my feet in the little square footbath by the side entrance. After cleaning off the mud I sit to examine my soles. They throb painfully. There is no blood. They are not even blistered. Jim hobbles in behind the Ajahn's squad. He carries the senior monk's bowl as well as his own, his eyes fixed on the ground in front of him. He bares his teeth in a grim smile as he approaches the footbath. The Ajahn enters first. Nimalo comes out from the *sala* and crouches down next to the teacher. With his hands he washes the dirt off the senior monk's feet. Meow stands nearby, waiting with a towel. The Ajahn receives the cleansing and drying without a word. The three of them enter the *sala* leaving Jim and I alone.

'This must be what the Ajahn means when he talks about helping the monks and learning the practice of humility' my twin said to me as he stood alone in the footbath.

'That's a pretty cynical remark for a *pahkow* who's just carried the senior monk's bowl all the way back through the rice fields' I said.

'Maybe that's why I'm so cynical. He told me to do it.'

'Lucky you to be singled out by the master for a special teaching. I couldn't even catch up with the lead monk in my line. You did well.'

'Nobody seemed envious.'

'You'd think the monks would all be vying for the opportunity to wash our feet. It would be much more humbling to wash a *pahkow's* toes, don't you think?'

'That's Christian humility you're talking about, Tim. That's not how it works in Thailand. That would go counter to the laws of status. A superior would never wash the feet of an inferior. It would be gross.'

'You're a good Thai *bhikkhu*, Jim.'

'I can hardly wait until my next rebirth. It was funny on alms round though. The villagers don't think we understand Thai. Several times I heard them talking about me. They thought I was so tall. "And did you ever see such a big bowl!" they said, "but look how nicely he bends for us." I really wanted to say something back to them, but of course I couldn't.'

'So do they think the *farang* monks are something special?'

'Of course. We're converts from a heathen culture – a high status heathen culture. Of course they're interested in us. But it's funny to be talked about on *bindabhat*.'

'I guess it comes with the robe.'

Putting on the robes changed quite a few things for Jim and I. The monks paid more attention to us. They frequently reminded me not to expose my testicles when sitting sloppily in the *sala* and not to dry my bowl while standing or squatting. Unfortunately, sitting outside without my sitting cloth dirtied my *sabong* so I preferred to stand. When I did this, sooner or later some *bhikkhu* would tut-tut me. The rules said I should sit. I insisted on squatting on my haunches in a position I had adopted while touring the toilets of India. This only won further frowns from the men in brown. I often wondered if something was flapping heedlessly in the breeze. Despite occasional paranoia of judgment, I felt a tone of acceptance by the community where before there had been complete indifference. Our vows as *pahkows* gave us the right to feel we belonged here, however temporarily. We moved up in the meal line, ahead of all the laymen, including Herbie who had been at the *wat* for several months when we arrived. We sat one row closer to the front during group chanting and were no longer obliged to help with early morning sweeping. By watching the monks we learned many of the rules quickly. The routine of the monastery fast became second nature. This knowledge was power since it was part of our job to instruct the guests and laymen in their duties and their places in the hierarchy. It was all too easy to treat newcomers with the same dispassionate indifference which we had received at first.

I found I had less and less interest in those far below me in the pecking order. When I had first arrived, there had been three *pahkows*. With Michael gone and Mark ordained as a novice, the senior *pahkow* sat just next to me in the food line. He was a Thai who spoke no English and communicated nothing. One day he disappeared. Herbie told me the *pahkow* had only come for a holiday. Once he left, I became head *pahkow*.

'But you don't have to wash my feet' I explained to Jim.

'Should I bow to you?'

'Just make sure I keep my testicles under cover.'

It was hard to tell how Herbie felt about these adjustments in the middle rungs of the hierarchy. I felt he had become touchy since our ordination. It had jumped us over his head. I thought he might resent us for taking the robes so quickly. Of course it could have been partly because Michael left. Herbie felt he wasn't coming back and they had been friends. Or perhaps I was just learning more about his naturally sullen and difficult nature. It was hard to understand why he had stayed for so long without being ordained. Sometimes he seemed hostile towards the world in general. His face was often clouded with dark intensity. Then suddenly he would laugh, quickly looking to see who was watching. If I caught his eye he would grin in a flash as if we shared a practical joke. Whenever I carried water with him during chores, I watched the knots of tension across his scrawny back. He would almost run with the pole, tripping me up in my skirt. Finally I concluded that he was not resentful of Jim and me. We were just closest to him in the hierarchy so we knew him better. Jim's theory was that Herbie was a runaway. He was only eighteen and avoided personal questions like an ex-convict. Jim thought he was troubled, not just silent. At meals he ate only sticky rice and mangos with a few mouthfuls of curry. He said he had been constipated for two months. Sticky rice had plugged him up like glue. Now that Michael was gone, Jim and I agreed to keep an eye on him.

When Wai Phra came again, Herbie ate all my left-over olive medicine. The vigil was a rough one. Although I had slept for a few hours in the afternoon, it took all my energy to stay awake at night. My mind slithered and wandered along the past morning's *bindabhat* trail and fell again and again into memories of my past life. Meditation was impossible. My knees ached from sitting in one spot for so long. I tried walking but staggered and almost fell in the darkness. The night was cool. I had worn a white undershirt beneath my sash but goosebumps covered my arms. A heavy rain lulled those of us who remained in the *sala*. It drummed on the roof and beat upon the metal water tanks. Huddled in a flannel blanket, I sat leaning back against a pillar, waiting for the three-thirty bell for morning chanting. Jim said his knee had begun to swell where he had an old skiing injury, and he had returned to his *kuti*.

'What is the point of this?' I asked myself, 'sitting through the night in the cold, in the dark, for the sheer sake of staying awake when concentration is beyond my grasp?'

'Diligence' said the silent voice. 'Diligence will lead to mindfulness. Better to stay awake and suffer than to crawl back to your hut and sleep. If you suffer through drowsiness, meditation will come. If you yield, how will you gain strength?'

'You too, monks' taught the Buddha, 'struggle on without shrinking back, saying to yourselves: "Gladly would I be reduced to skin and sinew and bones and let my body's flesh and blood dry up if there came to be a vortex of energy so that that which is not yet won might be won by human strength, by human energy, by human striving."'[2]

When morning chanting was over we were all given a cup of Ovaltine before *bindabhat*, to give us a little extra strength and to clear dreams of *nibbana* from our groggy minds. The hot drink was smooth and chocolatey. Dukita had baked a coffee cake to go with it.

'Did you have a good night?' Ruk asked me as I sat staring into my cake crumbs.

'Too tired' I mumbled. 'I couldn't concentrate or think or sit or walk or watch my breath. I practised futility meditation all night. You?'

'I had really good *samadhi* for a few hours. That was enough. Then I went to sleep.' The gentle monk smiled. 'Would you like to come *bindabhat* with me?'

I had dreaded the morning walk over the gravel road and the slippery paddy dykes, but Ruk's offer kindled a smile on my own lips. I nodded.

The third member of our group that morning was a Texan novice who had arrived at the *wat* the evening before. His name was Richard. He and a Thai monk had travelled from a place near Chiang Rai, inside the Golden Triangle, where they lived in a small cave monastery. Richard looked pale and haggard from the trip. His robes twisted loose once or twice as we began our walk down the gravel road. It looked as though he was not accustomed to his outer garment. Ruk led us out of the jungle through a side path which avoided the worst section of the gravel. When we broke free of the trees we saw a double rainbow arcing across the dawn-blue sky. Misty clouds hung above us, translucent. From them fell a drizzle, the remainder of last night's thundershowers. The three of us gazed at the multicoloured bow as we stood

[2] Ananda K. Coomaraswamy and I.B. Horner, Gotama the Buddha, Cassell and Company, Ltd, London, 1948 (p.60).

barefoot in the brown mud. Its delicate hues hung in front
of us as we walked through the paddies. Ruk's route began
with a shortcut through the flooded fields. Soon we were
knee deep in brown water. The rainbow's end played on a
tree less than a hundred metres from us.

'Should we go and fill our bowls with gold?' I said to
Richard who was ahead of me in the line.

'From the pot? You can, but I'm not allowed to. I can't
touch gold, right?'

'Better to leave it' Ruk called back to us lightheartedly.
'What you see is better than gold.'

We crawled up on a slope-sided dyke which Ruk followed
to a dry dirt track. He jumped a drainage ditch to gain the
road. Richard followed. I landed ankle deep in the watery
mud. Red splattered up the side of my *sabong*. It looked as
if I had slaughtered a goat. The rain began again. Richard
fell back beside me as we walked and began to tell the story
of his life.

'I've been travelling through India and Sri Lanka for six
months since I left Austin. I stayed at a monastery in Lanka
and ordained as a *pahkow* for a while. It wasn't like this
though. Where I was it was really slack. The monks didn't
even go out on *bindabhat* most of the time. I think it's good
we do it here. There we hardly ever did any chanting. A lot
of monks just sat around and got lazy. That's why I decided
to leave. Thailand is different. The monks here are really
concerned about meditation, although maybe not most of
them.'

'So do you think for a foreigner it's better to be a monk in
Thailand?'

'Definitely. Sure. But still it's got problems.'

'What problems?'

'I've only been in the country a couple of weeks. I was
only just ordained as a novice in Lanka before I came here.
Already I've had trouble with a Thai monk who is after me.'

'After you?'

'You know. He's gay. Maybe I can't say for sure that he's
gay. But I know what I feel when a guy comes on to me. It
used to happen a lot. I've got a boy's face. It gives me

trouble. Don't get me wrong. I hate it. I'm not gay. But this monk has made a few passes at me. That's the reason I left the monastery up north to come here. In fact, I was living in his cave. I had to get away from him. I didn't feel I could report him. He was doing things like masturbating in front of me. It was disgusting. He knew I wasn't asleep. I just pretended that I was. Afterwards, when I could get out, I told him I'd seen him. He could be thrown out of the monastery for that. But you need two witnesses. He just denied it. He told me he was meditating. Finally I went to the abbot. I told him I wanted to come to Pah Nanachat. I said I'd heard there were plenty of Westerners and I thought it would be the best place for me. So the abbot let me come.'

'You must feel a lot better out of there' I said.

'Not really. A novice isn't supposed to travel alone. You saw the Thai I came here with? That's the gay monk! I had to sit beside him all the way to Ubon Rajathani. I couldn't even fall asleep on the train because I thought maybe he'd try and stroke my hand. Thank God he's only going to be here a few more days before he leaves for Bangkok. If I weren't a novice I could at least give him a good smack. But it's against the *Vinaya*.'

We had fallen far behind Ruk who was waiting for us at the gates of the village. We fell silently into line, heads bent, bowls slung over our right shoulders. Humbly we walked into the village. This area seemed much poorer than Sun Tin's route. Most of the devotees gave only a handful of rice. There were no sweets, no dried meat, only a few bananas. Although the path we followed was slippery and muddy, it felt cool and gentle on the feet. Jim said he expected we'd contract ringworm and other exotic diseases walking through village gutters in this way. One can't avoid all the buffalo dung. Our group soon caught up with a string of six Thai monks on *bindabhat* from the local village *wat*. They seemed ridiculously short compared to Ruk. The German monk halted at one point, giving them extra space to keep ahead of us.

At the far side of the village we watched them turn left into their monastery. Richard and I were staggered by the

82

gaudy splendour of the *wat bhote*. The village *wat's* ordination hall rose up like a cathedral, narrow and high. It was painted burgundy, white and gold with a multi-tiered roof. Stylized dragons flew off the corners. The villagers lived so simply – in poverty by Western standards – while their monastery glittered like a castle of the gods.

CHAPTER SIX

The Fan Man's Rapture

A beautiful black cobra lay on the path as I hurried along with an armful of laundry. It was two and a half metres long. I startled it and it gave a sudden surge when I was three steps away, pulling its head back and flattening its hood. I froze and clutched my muddy clothing. No point in running. The creature tested the air with its tongue. The hood relaxed. It surged again. I saw the power in its coils. Silently it slid like a stream back into the jungle. I watched entranced until the black ribbon of tail disappeared.

I spent two hours at the wash pump trying to bleach and scrub the red mud stains out of my robes. Richard arrived with his washing and we soon fell to comparing notes about Indian cults. Richard was a talker, which seemed unusual for a novice. He spoke with a lazy Texas drawl. His comments and questions often came at random, as if he was more concerned with filling the airwaves than following a conversation. This had already begun to irritate some of the monks. I noticed their disapproving looks when they heard the two of us talking. Richard seemed oblivious of them. He had a talent for shattering serenity wherever he went. That morning after bowl cleaning, I heard him yell across the compound to get Tan Casipo's attention. Nobody yelled in Wat Pah Nanachat. That was the unspoken rule. One was supposed to come up to a person if one wished to speak. Richard preferred to shout. He had big, innocent eyes, thin red lips and a boyish face which made him look five years younger than his twenty-four years. Head shaven, he reminded me of the vampire Nosferatu, especially in the half light of dawn when his robes fluttered in disarray. His skull had a pointy ridge running along the top. His white, sculpted ears were pulled flat in against his head. It was easy to believe he was familiar with exotic Hindu cults.

'In Varanasi I got amoebic dysentery' Richard told me as we scrubbed side by side. 'It was so bad that for weeks I just lay in bed. The only time I got up was to go to the toilet. I did that a lot. It exhausted me. It was the hot season too, over a hundred degrees most of the time. My bed was always drenched in sweat and smelled terrible. The hotel was right on a main street. There was always some festival going on and people carrying dead bodies to the river to burn. I was too tired to move to another place. I was even afraid they were going to kick me out. I didn't know anybody and I thought if I died, no one would find me. When I finally started to get better I met some people from the Ananda Margi cult. You must have seen them when you were in India. They wear red clothes and red turbans.'

'I've seen them in Delhi. I thought they were some kind of Sikh.'

'The founder is a Sikh. So are many of his senior disciples, but you don't have to be a Sikh to join. It's a mystical, spiritual group open to all religions. They invited me to come to one of their meetings in the evening. I was feeling very lonely and weak and they were very friendly to me. At the meeting everybody started dancing a wild, crazy dance. They were singing this chant. Their faces were blissful and peaceful but excited at the same time. The music was terrific, drums and little bells, everybody clapping and dancing with their hands in the air, whirling around and around in a circle as if they were in another world. There was real energy there. I could feel it. When they asked me if I'd like to join in I thought sure, why not? As soon as I stood up and they put their arms around me, this sudden incredible and overwhelming emotion swept over me. Suddenly the feeling I had sensed in the room was inside me. I felt this intense love and joy and peace. I danced around and around with them, clapping my hands and crying sometimes. I knew everybody in the room felt the same feelings I did. There were no drugs at all. We danced for hours. I didn't ever want to stop. I didn't want to let go. Even when we did stop, the feeling stayed inside me, a warm, happy glow. I don't know if I can explain it to you. It was like an unseen presence in the room had danced with us.'

'What was it?'

'I don't know. Some higher being.'

'Did they tell you who it was?'

'There was no need to name it. They are Shivites. I think maybe it was Shiva.'

'Shiva? Be careful with him. Of course, the ecstatic dance of Shiva. You know when he begins this dance, it's the dance of destruction bringing to an end the present age of existence?'

'Something like that. They didn't talk too much about it.'

'If you've been dancing with Shiva, don't ever get on the wrong side of him. He's dangerous to cross. How did you ever end up wearing ochre and not red, shaving your hair and not wearing a turban?'

Richard shrugged. 'I don't know. Maybe it was too much for me and I couldn't handle it. When I got fully better I just wanted to get out of Varanasi. I couldn't stay, even for them. They said I could go back any time I wanted to. There were no problems. They even gave me some addresses of other Ananda Margi centres all over the world. They have a relief centre in New Zealand. I still think I might go there. One of the things I like about them is that they aren't just buzzed on the dancing. Social action is integral to their belief. Really they are revolutionaries. Their teaching is that the whole international, political and economic order must change. They run health clinics and international aid centres. They send supplies to Africa from India. They work hard, but they are political realists. Ananda Margi says the time will come when they have to use guns because the old order won't just give up its power to make way for the new.'

'Sounds like Shiva's boys to me, combining ecstacy, charity and guns.'

Several members of the community had arrived at the wash pump by this time. Tan Casipo and Meow had begun to bathe in silence, scooping cupfuls of cool water from the cisterns and dumping them over their bodies. Percy was shaving his face in front of the small mirror nailed to the robe dyeing shed next to the pump.

'But what do you think, Tim, are they a good group?'

'None of it sounds new to me, Richard. I don't like the guns. I doubt if any religion should be that pragmatic.'

'They do meditation too. You concentrate on these different spiritual centres in your body.'

'You mean *chakras?*'

'That was the word. Spiritual power centres in the body.'

'Sounds like they might be tantric. You didn't do any human sacrifices, did you? No? It's pretty well out of fashion these days, even among Shivites. I guess Shiva must be changing his tastes.'

'Rajneesh is the one who's big on sex, isn't he?' said Percy, bursting in on the conversation with zeal.

'What?' I said.

'He's a Hindu. He has an Ashram in Poona, only now he's not there, you know.'

This bit of information hung in the air like a bad smell. Richard and I stared at the Englishman who had totally derailed our conversation. I was unable to speak.

'I have a friend in Brighton who is frightfully keen on Rajneesh.'

'That's nice' said my voice. I winced at the escaping sarcasm.

'Could you shave me now?' Percy asked me, oblivious of it all.

'What?'

'My head. I'm ready to be shaved today.'

'You want me to do it?'

'You seem to know how.'

'I've never done it before. You'd better ask Tan Casipo.'

The helpful monk agreed without a smile. We all gathered around to watch as Percy lost his locks. The finished product was not too bad. The monk completed the task without a nick. Percy rinsed and went to the mirror. He gasped at the gleaming white dome where his hair used to be. I thought he had a good head for baldness, round and smooth, no bumps or ridges.

'It makes you look ten years younger' I told him with a smile. 'Welcome to our cult.'

I walked with Percy back along the trail where I had met the cobra. He had become a layman. He had joined us. For me he was suddenly a responsibility.

'So how does it feel up top?' I asked.

'All right. A bit cool, a bit cool. Bit of a shock in the mirror, you know.'

'But it's good to have you looking normal. You've got a nice skull.'

'Do you think it will help?'

'Help what?'

'Meditation.'

'It sure won't help you get girls. How is shaving your head supposed to help meditation?'

'Hair is an attachment, isn't that what the Ajahn says? When you shave it, you will feel less attached.'

'I suppose you're right. Do you feel less attached?'

He wrinkled his brow. 'Not yet.' He looked around behind us in the jungle, then said to me in a low confidential voice, 'You know, the Ajahn hasn't given me any teaching yet.'

'Didn't he speak to you when you first got here? Didn't he give you a book? What more teaching do you want? I don't think any of us get any teaching.'

'I know we're supposed to be mindful about the rules and all that, but then there's the breathing. I'm not sure if I'm doing it properly. It's like this. I'm awfully glad you mentioned *chakras* at the wash pump. Perhaps you're the one to talk to. You see, one of my *chakras* is blocked. That's why I'm having trouble with my breathing meditation.'

'Blocked? Which *chakra* is it?'

'The forehead *chakra*, here.' He touched a spot just above his nose. 'I think I need a special meditation to unblock it.'

'Do you think maybe an antihistamine would do the job?'

88

'It's not that sort of thing at all. It's not a sinus problem. It's a *chakra* problem. Spiritual, you know. I've done the test.'

'What test?'

'The test to see if the *chakras* are blocked. You see, if the *chakras* are blocked, it will affect your *karma*. A blocked *chakra* will bring you bad luck. Perhaps you might not win the lottery when really it's your turn, or you'll lose your girl. It can make you lose your job or break your leg. It's frightening.'

'How long has your *chakra* been blocked this way?'

'I don't know. It seems to be getting worse. I'm frightfully keen to fix it.'

'Who gave you the test?'

'The Maha Devi people in India. I stayed at their *ashram* for ten days. Luckily I was there during the full moon. It's best to test during the full moon.'

'How do they do the test?'

'I thought you knew. You have to wait until dark, then you light a candle and make an offering to the Divine Mother. Then you step into a bucket of salt water and hold your fingers out in front of you and say the *mantra*. It's very powerful you see, because all four primal elements are present at once. Fire in the candle, water in the pail, air in the lungs while you say the *mantra* . . . '

'And solid in the wax?'

'No. Solid in the salt that's in the bucket. That's why you put it there.'

'If you used solid from the wax, could you stand in fresh-water instead?'

'Perhaps' he nodded, pondering the point. 'Then you close your eyes, and concentrate vital energy on your fingers until they start to tingle. There's a *chakra* in line with every finger. So when all four primal elements are present under a full moon and you say the *mantra* and concentrate, the fingers will tingle according to the *chakra* that matches them.'

'That makes perfect sense.'

'This one finger wouldn't tingle. I stood in the water until my toes got wrinkled. The *chakra* was blocked. They told me it was obvious.'

'Maybe you didn't use enough salt?'

'There's no doubt about the tests' said Percy ruefully, as if terminal cancer had been diagnosed.

'The problem then is how to unblock it, right? Couldn't the Maha Devi people help you? There's not much point in a diagnosis without a cure.'

'It's not as simple as that, you know. Before they can cure you, you have to want to be cured. I thought I wanted to be cured. They told me I didn't. Not deep down really.'

'Do you deep down really want to be cured?'

'I don't want the bad luck.' We had reached the fork in the path which split off to my *kuti*. Percy stopped and ran a hand over his smooth scalp where his hair should have been. 'You know what causes a blocked *chakra*? Sinfulness.'

'Sinfulness?'

'Sinfulness.'

'So sinfulness blocked your *chakra*? That makes sense. It can certainly damage your *kamma*. So they told you to unblock your *chakra* you had to repent of your sinfulness?'

'I'll tell you what did it, what sealed it off completely.' He spoke relentlessly now, as if the whole sordid truth needed to be exposed. His eyes were fixed on a twig on the path. 'Confession is good. I know it is. I feel better just knowing I'll tell you. It was one of those hotels in Bangkok, the kind where they provide you with a girl for the night. Then in the morning the maid came in to clean the room. She startled me and I jumped out of bed, still in my underpants. I had a half erection under them. I think she could see it. There, I've told you everything.' He breathed a deep sigh, and rubbed his hand over the skin on the back of his neck. 'It's sinfulness that's blocked it. Just confessing makes it better. Were you a Catholic before you became a Buddhist?'

'No.'

'I hope this *vipassana* breathing will clear everything out all right. I just wish someone could help me be certain about the technique.'

'Remember to relax, that's all. Breath naturally and concentrate on the in-and-out sensation in your nose. Say "Buddho" to keep your mind from wandering. Follow the precepts and you won't sin. Forget about the *chakras* and they will unblock by themselves.'

'Thanks awfully for the advice' the Englishman beamed at me. 'I'll be off to the kitchen now to give it a go.' He gave a brave smile and limp-sauntered down the trail.

At bowl cleaning time, Jim and I were bent over side by side rinsing out the spittoons. Each member of the community has a spittoon beside him during meal, into which he throws peels, bones, leaf wrappers and mango pits. Part of our job was to empty and clean the pots after the morning meal. Then we had our own bowls to wash.

'Something attacked my *kuti* last night' Jim told me.

'A *pee bah*?'

'I'm serious. It jumped on the roof. I swear it was a big animal. I heard claws scraping.'

'Are you sure it wasn't a little lizard?'

'I know a lizard sound from a creature sound. This thing was big.'

'Maybe it was a tiger' said Richard, who was washing his bowl within earshot of us.

'No tigers in here' said Jim. 'This is a park, not a jungle.' He straightened up and I followed him to where Richard was squatting. We picked up our bowls, rinsed them with water from one of the big cisterns, added a little powdered soap and then crouched down on either side of the Texan novice. As we washed curry stains from our bowls, Percy came out of the *sala* and around the corner to collect the clean spittoons. He was now wearing the white uniform of a layman.

'How's it going, Percy?' Richard called in a loud voice. Several of the monks scowled as they sat against the outside wall of the temple, drying their bowls with their ochre bowl-towels.

'Not too bad, thanks. I practised mindfulness this morning while sweeping around the *sala*.'

Everybody looked at the sand. It was still littered with berries and leaves.

'How was it?' Richard continued good-naturedly.

'I think I developed some concentration. Yes, there was a definite sense of that.'

'Concentration is good' I said to him as he gathered the pots. 'But did the leaves get swept?'

A sudden burst of laughter came from the monks and novices. A private joke, I thought, surprised at something so spontaneous and unmonk-like. Percy carried the spittoons back into the *sala*.

'I don't like the way they laugh at him' Richard whispered to me.

'Who?'

'The monks just then. They were laughing at Percy, at what you said to him, because of the leaves. They talk about him. I'm a novice. I hear it.'

After Percy had had his head shaven, he became familiarly chatty towards the other members of the community, especially those just a little above him in the hierarchy. He would invariably interject the most trivial and banal details possible into any conversation, often related to the topic only by a misunderstood word. He reported to me regularly on his progress in meditation, although there was no change in his sweeping. Obviously the monks had noticed his inability to clear a path. His awkward posture during morning and evening chanting went against community aesthetics. Yet Percy acted with the bravado of one who belongs, oblivious to the laughter. He especially enjoyed disrupting my conversations with Richard about India.

'The Hari Krishna people, you know how they get new converts?' he said, thrusting the question into a discussion of Krishnamurti's philosophy.

'No, Percy, that's not the subject' I said, clinging to our train of thought.

'It's the food' he continued. 'They serve great vegetarian feasts at least once a week. You come for the meal and then you don't want to leave. After a week they want you to cut your hair like they do and wear their pink clothes. If you try and leave they get all upset and make you feel guilty because you've been eating for free.'

'But they have a lot of spiritual singing in the Krishna

movement, don't they?' said Richard, already riding down Percy's new track. It didn't seem to matter to him what the topic was as long as there was a mystical angle to it. Confusion didn't matter. As long as there were drugs, dreams, *devas* or demons, it was fascinating to the Texan.

'Percy, this is all very interesting, but we were comparing Krishnamurti's philosophy with Theravada meditation.'

'But, that's just the point, you know. That's why I like this Buddhism so much better than all the others.'

'Why is that?'

'Here, if you want to leave, they don't get mad at you. They even let you come back.'

'Do not seek the Truth' said Sankara the monk. 'Only cease to cherish opinions.' The Buddha taught that all views are held in ignorance. I preferred my views to Percy's. To the monks it was all frivolous chatter, a broken precept, conversation for the sake of intellectual arousal, inflaming the ego, that source of all suffering. It was talk to build a wall of self, shoring up the illusion that self is a solid entity while life slips by unnoticed. 'Happy indeed those perfected ones!' taught the Buddha. 'The thought "I am" is eradicated.'

An adder before breakfast. Herbie nearly stepped on it, jumping back just before the fatal moment. I borrowed Percy's spindly broom and nudged it gently back into the leaves. It moved with small spring-like leaps, coiling itself and then jumping. I was sorry to irritate it but the path was not a happy place to rest. That afternoon a scorpion was found beneath one of the metal water tanks at the edge of the *sala* where we collect our rain water. It was a full fifteen centimetres long. It glistened like oil, entrancing and deadly. By the water pump red ants had built at least two nests in the mango trees. Pulling leaves together and gluing them into hollow balls, they performed amazing feats of engineering and strength. I put up a finger near the site. Work ceased. A hundred feelers tested the air. Richard tried to touch a worker on the tree. Without hesitation it bit him. Richard shook his hand vigorously. They have no fear. Ruk says it is the coming monsoon season which makes life so active.

Eggs will be hatching in the damp. Flooding brings many creatures out from their holes in the earth. One morning after a storm we found three snakes during our alms round. Ruk nearly stepped on one of them, which was a surprise. Normally he is aware of everything that moves. 'Only a water snake' he said, recovering his poise. The serpent had startled him. It slipped out from under his footstep into the flooded paddy, a foot long ribbon of greyish blue.

The ground on our *bindabhat* route softened with the rain. Red mud squished through our toes. Baby freshwater crabs scuttled sideways across our path to plop into puddles for protection. They were a local delicacy. The villagers began turning the earth, preparing the paddies for the next planting. The vibrant green shoots of new rice already growing would be replanted over larger areas and seeded with more rice. Water buffaloes wheezed and snorted plaintively by the sides of the road and in the fields. Their large brown eyes always bulged in fear whenever we passed by. Poor gentle creatures, they seemed terrified of the ochre robes. Other villagers they ignored but they sometimes bolted out of control and plunged through the paddy when even the smallest of monks came near.

I went with Ruk every morning on alms round. Richard walked between us, often engaging me in conversation. I loved the silence of the world in those morning journeys outside the closeness and dampness of the jungle. But Richard felt compelled to talk. We shared a common tendency to explain more than we knew. This had a dissipating effect on me. Talking had become a vice I could not resist. Some days I tried to walk fast and keep up with Ruk, who left us behind with his long strides. Because he was a novice, Richard always walked in front of me. It was my place to keep two steps behind him. He would fall back and wait for me to pass. Then he would try to snag me with a tantalising question.

'Do you believe in hell?'

He always hooked me.

'Yes, but not the inferno of fire and brimstone. I think that's just a metaphor for the very real state of intense suffering people are capable of experiencing even in this life. The agony of hell is probably the endless self-infliction of the suffering we already have during life on earth. The one thing about hell that amazes me is that it's universal. Every major religion believes in it.'

'I believe in hell' said Richard. 'I once had a mushroom trip back in Texas where I went into a hell state.' His angle on the mystical and metaphysical was always intensely personal. 'It was a thousand times worse than any physical pain. There was no sense of time at all. It seemed it would never end. I thought there was no way back for me, that I was trapped there. A friend, Cheri, was there at the party with me. She noticed my face and asked if I was okay. I can't imagine what I looked like. I told her I was fine just so that she would go away. Then I ran outside and hid behind some bushes.'

'You didn't think she could help you?'

'Help? There's no help for you in hell. Do you know what hell is, why it's such incredible suffering? Because hell is separation. You are totally isolated from everything and everybody, alone forever. I knew I was at a party. I could even talk to Cheri. But it was all outside as if I was watching through bullet-proof glass. I was locked in. Nobody could touch me. When it started to fade, I was just so happy to be alive. I ran back inside the house. The party was still going on. These people were my friends, I realized. I really loved them, even though I knew almost nobody there. I started giving away all my money and some records I had brought with me. I wanted to give away my clothes but Cheri wouldn't let me. I guess she thought I was crazy. "I'm not in hell, I'm not in hell" I told her, which didn't help much. I started laughing and dancing. It just felt so good not to be in hell. The feeling lasted over a week. I gave away almost everything I owned. I know hell, alright. Hell is separation. There's no suffering worse than that.'

'You know Richard, some theologians define hell as separation from God. I'm glad you came out of it. It must have kept you off mushrooms for a long time.'

'It did. For a week at least.'

A Theravada monk from Bangladesh once told me a riddle
on the problem of merit, the credit one gets in future lives
for good deeds done in the present. Once there was a poor
peasant couple who both had to work all day in their miserable field in order to scratch together enough food to survive.
When the woman became pregnant, she could no longer
work as hard, and yet needed more to eat. They began to
starve. She told her husband that without rich food she and
their child would soon die. Then she explained to him her
plan to get food from the king's table.

'Shave your head and dye one of our bed sheets ochre.
Wear it like a robe. Then take our cooking pot and go and
stand at the palace gates in the disguise. The king will see
you and give you alms. You are thin enough to look like a
monk. Bring the food back to me and I will live.'

The husband was horrified at the deception and sacrilege
of his wife's plan, but to save her life, he did as she told him
and went to the palace gates. The king was just sitting down
to his lunch feast. When he looked out of his window he
saw the false monk.

'Surely this is a holy *arahant* at my gate. My good fortune!
I will gain much merit from a generous deed today.'

He called two of his servants and told them to take away
the feast and to fill the monk's bowl with the food. He
watched through the window with pleasure as his orders
were carried out. The monk left his gates with his bowl full
to the rim. Then a doubt crossed the king's mind. 'How do
I know this is really an *arahant*, and not some imposter?' he
thought. He sent for the servants again, ordering them to
follow the monk and report what they observed back to him.
The servants followed the husband to the hut at the edge of
the miserable field. They crept up to the window and heard
the man explain how his wife's deception had succeeded
and they would all live. The servants were horrified.

'If we tell the king he gave his feast to a starving peasant,
he will have them both killed' said one. 'And we will be
beaten for our trouble' said the other.

When they returned to the palace, the king asked them
what they had seen.

'My lord' they said, 'we followed the monk to the edge of the city. Then he disappeared into thin air, right before our eyes.'

The king was excited. 'Then he must be possessed of supernatural powers. He must be a holy monk indeed, perhaps an *arahant*. How great will be the merit I receive for this generous deed. Surely I will gain a *deva*-realm in my next rebirth.'

Did the king gain the merit gained for giving food to an *arahant*, an enlightened monk, or did he gain the merit gained for giving food to a peasant?

A few faces began to stand out from amongst the villagers who came to the *wat* every morning to prepare our food. One middle-aged man regularly brought a huge bowlful of mangos around to us in the *sala*, offering them to us with a wide grin. Another man, shrivelled and grey with age, always sat himself to the right of me. It was his job to pass the food bowls from Richard's place at the end of the line on the platform down to me, the first member of the lower line seated on the *sala* floor. He seemed well past sixty. His whole body trembled as if muscle control had begun to deteriorate. His head wobbled on a scrawny neck. His eyes seemed dull and watery, but his lips were always on the verge of a smile. Passing the bowls made him grunt. He spoke no English, communicating whatever was necessary with a shaky gesture.

One morning the two of us watched him as he discovered for the first time how the electric fans mounted on the pillars inside the *sala* worked. The fans were set about two and a half metres off the ground with a string leading down from each one. Curious, the old man grabbed one of the strings. He tugged and seemed surprised when the fan gave a click. It rotated from side to side, spreading a cooling breeze in its arc. The breeze touched his face. He was transformed by sheer bliss. For a minute he stood motionless. He held up his hand and felt the passing of the cool air. He clicked the string again. The breeze increased. He clicked it through all three speeds, then clicked it off again, completely absorbed in his discovery. He clicked through the full cycle twice more before shutting the fan off. Finally he turned his head back down to earth and took his seat beside me for the passing of the food. His eyes had cleared. They glowed with rapture. Next day the miracle of the fan was repeated, and again on the third day. It became a regular part of the morning ritual. Some days the Fan Man would systematically turn on all the fans on our side of the *sala*; other days he simply clicked the same fan through its cycle four or five times. Afterwards he would return to his place of duty next to me like a man blessed by a vision. It was the most mystical encounter I witnessed in all my time at Wat Pah Nanachat.

CHAPTER SEVEN

Bhikkhu Bob and Boomer Bunte Gird their Loins

I t was breeding season for the nits. Before mating, the three-centimetre-long insects we called nits grew slender, flappy wings. They flew from their nests in a swarm at dusk when the nights were warm and dry. The long wings barely kept them aloft. Before they could mate, their papery new wings broke loose, allowing them to pursue each other on the ground. There was a saying in the region, 'He is as clever as a nit. He can grow wings, but they soon fall off.'

At evening meditation a light is left glowing dimly in the *sala*, allowing *pahkows* and laymen to follow the monks' chanting in our Pali texts. Thousands of nits flutter to the light. Their bodies cover the floor beneath it. They fly in our faces. They batter themselves against the glowing white of our clothes. They flap crazily, desperately trying to knock off their fragile wings. They struggle and twist all around us, freeing themselves from the papery filaments which have given them flight. Once their wings are discarded, the nits chase each other, crawling everywhere through the *sala*. They wriggle down our necks, inside our *sabongs*, over the prickly fuzz of our skulls. Long wings whirl downwards in the dark air. They pursue each other in a frenzy between the rows of our mats, around and through the solemn figures of the monks. They climb on top of one another, struggling to mate. They fall like a living shower, crawling over our closed eyelids and indulging in an orgy of procreation while our chanting rings in the temple. It is as if the temple is suddenly bombarded by the flux of the universe, spinning between our still forms like a storm of unformed particles. The hum of wings blends with the rhythm of our chanting. The words of our Pali litany do not deny this flux. They affirm it:

> Birth is suffering
> Decay is suffering
> Disease is suffering
> Death is suffering
> Separation from the liked is suffering
> Association with the disliked is suffering
> And longing for what we would like is
>   suffering

> I am of the nature of decay
> I have not gone beyond decay
> I am of the nature to sicken
> I have not gone beyond sickness
> I am of the nature to die
> I have not gone beyond death
> All that is mine, beloved and pleasing,
> Will become otherwise, will be separated
>   from me.

The Buddha did not offer us comfortable words. His teaching began with the problem of suffering. Extinguish desires and suffering will cease, he taught. The goal is to escape the wheel of *samsara*, to be free from the cycle of rebirth. Eternal death.

The Buddha meditated for six years before penetrating the illusions of existence. Although his solution to suffering seems pessimistic, it did not lead him to a *samadhi*-suicide. He lived and taught for forty-five years after his enlightenment as an affirmation of living, despite the human conditions of decay, disease and death. Suffering is caused by our refusal to accept these realities, he taught. Once a young mother brought her dead infant son to the Buddha, weeping and grieving. She pleaded with him to bring the child back to life. The Buddha told her he would raise the child, but first she must bring as an offering a sack of rice flour from a household which had not known death. The woman ran through her town from house to house but everywhere the answer was the same. A mother, father, uncle, aunt or child had died in every home. The woman returned to the master, declaring death was known to every family, so she could not bring the offering. 'And so I will not raise your son' the Buddha said. When one accepts death, there is nothing left to fear. Those who follow Buddha's path describe it as a state of lightness and harmony with the universe. It manifests itself in the liberated person as compassion towards all beings.

'Do you know the best reason for a Westerner to be ordained in Thailand?' Richard asked me on alms round. 'It makes it easy to get visa extensions from the government.'

It was a bad day for Richard. He said he had been constipated since his arrival in Pah Nanachat. This was no surprise. It was a common affliction. Eating only one meal a day seemed to justify cramming one's guts full. Afterwards, sticky rice swells when one drinks water, corking up the bowels. Richard looked pale and wretched. He had asked Ruk if he could skip out on the morning rounds that day.

'Of course you can' said the monk. 'The rule is that if you don't go on *bindabhat*, you don't eat. You are always free to fast.'

Richard had then hastily struggled into his outer robe as we departed. He still didn't have the knack of wearing it properly. It takes practice. He caught up with us half way to the village, his robe loose and flapping about his knees. On a deserted stretch between houses, Richard's bowl lid slipped and clattered onto the muddy ground. When he bent to retrieve it, his robe fell fully open. Ruk told him curtly to fix himself. Fortunately nobody was watching.

'It's not as if I'm doing it on purpose' Richard said. 'I need

101

something to fasten the lid in place, that's all. It just pops off every time I try to keep the robe from slipping.'

Minutes later, on the outskirts of the next hamlet, Ruk's back stiffened as he heard the tinny clatter behind him again. I bent to pick up Richard's muddy lid. The novice's robes were slipping from his shoulders.

'We stop here and you put your robe on properly' said Ruk. 'It looks bad for all of us to have you so sloppy in the villages. Why don't you practise?'

I had never seen my gentle monk so exasperated. Ruk had a cold. His eyes were bloodshot and he snuffled all through the walk. Despite the freshness of the dawn and the green shoots newly planted in the surrounding paddies, it was a miserable morning.

'It's this stupid lid' Richard said sullenly.

'Then perhaps we get a new bowl for you tomorrow' said Ruk.

'Maybe I'll go back to Sri Lanka after all' Richard mumbled to me as we walked back to the monastery. 'I need a break.'

A judgment had somehow been passed on Richard. He had good intentions and a good heart, but it was plain that his was not the spirit of a devotee. Those above him in the hierarchy considered him sloppy and ill-mannered. It was a surprise to see this come out in Ruk. Perhaps Richard's problem was because he had come here wearing robes, but did not appear committed to a *bhikkhu's* life. If he had started here as a layman, as Jim and I had done, he probably would have been better accepted by the *sangha*. The root of his troubles was that he behaved with complete disregard for the finer points of the rules. There was nothing of a monk in him. To Jim and I it was refreshing. Sometimes his nonchalance made the others appear to be hiding inside their costumes. Richard suffered for it. He was being ostracized from the pecking order. It made Jim angry.

'I looked around at meal this morning and saw all those faces staring into their food, everyone totally absorbed in feeding their faces. Is that supposed to be mindful concentration? They look like pigs at the trough. I don't see much awareness' he said to me at bowl washing one morning.

I soaped my bowl beside him and listened, eyeing the monks leaning back in the sun against the side of the *sala* as they watched their pots dry.

'Richard acts a little differently,' Jim continued, 'talks a little loudly, forgets a few rules and they get down on him. It doesn't seem very compassionate. They are exasperated because he won't be a good little novice and quietly wash the Ajahn's feet. Nobody cares about him at all. A few days ago Tan Casipo said to me, "Some people come here with so much dust in their eyes it's unbearable to talk to them." What does that say about the monkhood? He can't tolerate people with "dust in their eyes." All that these monks have developed here is a safe little self-centred world which they call holy because the villagers bow down to them. Living in a forest and wearing a robe doesn't make you better than anybody else.'

'Come on over to my *kuti* and let's talk about it. I think we both need a little frivolous chatter' I said. 'Bring your cup and I'll break open my best kettle of water. Sorry the fridge is empty and I can't offer you more.'

Jim arrived with his tin cup and a spool of dental floss. We sat on my mat under the protection of the mosquito net and cleaned our gums. My twin resumed where he had left off.

'I met an American *bhikkhu* in Chiang Mai once who told me he thought following the two hundred and twenty-seven precepts was the mark of a noble being. Conceit! I could hardly stand it. Living here, it's hard not to be noble. How can we break a precept when there's nothing exciting to tempt us? There's no stress, no push. It's an easy life. We don't kill, lie or steal, but it doesn't do anybody else a bit of good. What's the point of it? Look at Nimalo. I go with him on *bindabhat*. I think he's probably the best human being in the *wat*. He's been a novice for three years. Do you know he only eats what's put into his bowl on alms round? He never takes food from the bowls we pass at meal time. He's patient, helpful, quiet. I sense in him a deep reserve of well-being. But I think he'd be pretty much the same outside a monastery anyway. Out in the world he would be able to do a heck of a lot more good than he does in here, washing the Ajahn's feet. It's been building up inside me for over a week now, Tim. This place reeks with the one thing I can't stand. Complacency.'

'Remember Ajahn Chah said don't look to other monks or you'll only suffer doubt and confusion. Look to your own practice. What do we know about the private meditation of the others?'

'Do you see monks on the path to liberation?'

'A Christian monk once told me a monastery isn't a place for holy men, but for sinners. Monks feel they would be weak alone, so they live together for the support of the brotherhood. That's a legitimate reason to be here.'

'Then why do we bow to them? Why do they set themselves up as holy, as models of virtue for the society? You'll never see the Ajahn washing Richard's feet. The monks believe in their holiness. Besides, if this place is a rest home for the morally infirm, what are you and I doing here?'

'Weak people following the precepts can be an example to strong ones trapped in *samsara*. We wouldn't be here if we thought there was nothing valuable in it. I admit, there's some complacency. Life is easy. But because there is no stress, we can really focus on meditation.'

'What good is that when stress is the condition of the rest of the world?'

'Here it's like a training camp. That stress you talk about makes it impossible to begin a meditation practice in the outside world. Here where there's calm we can develop something to take back into the world that can combat the stress we will be returning to. If some people decide to stay and train all the way to *nibbana*, good for them. They should become monks.'

'Is that what you see?'

'It doesn't matter if the monks we see are complacent. We can still train.'

'I disagree. I can't keep bowing down to people I don't respect. These *farang bhikkhus* have a great scam going. I don't have anything against Thai Buddhism. If the villagers want to support their own sons in extravagant temples, it doesn't bother me. But when I put on these robes, I make-believe along with the others that we are very holy beings and that by giving to us, the Thais go to *deva*-realms in their future lives. Staying here I am participating in a lie.' He balled up his dental floss, reached under the net and threw the strand out of the window.

'But Jim, the villagers aren't supposed to be feeding relatives. They feed the robe. In many ways the monks here are more worthy to be fed than in other monasteries. In most other places the monks are really slack. You told me so yourself. There are lots of worse places to stay than Pah Nanachat. You are getting something out of all the sitting and walking, aren't you?'

'Perhaps' Jim admitted. 'But what am I taking at the same time?'

After breakfast the Ajahn declared it a work day.

'All the leaves between the pathways in the compound should be raked together and dumped into the jungle away from the main buildings. Those leaves are the perfect place for mosquito breeding, especially with monsoon season coming on. It's best to clean the area now. Already the bugs are getting bad around my *kuti*.'

It was a major task. Luckily five or six new faces had appeared at the *wat* in the past few days. Of the seven guests, four of them planned on shaving their heads and becoming laymen. There was Julian from Australia, a friend of Nimalo's in his past life. Lorenzo came from Italy, Hal from America and Herman from Holland. I wondered if the Ajahn had noticed the additional mouths to feed and decided to take advantage of the large work force suddenly at his disposal.

A senior monk named Tan Bodhipalo had also returned to the *wat*. He looked about forty years old and was the most dour-looking monk I had ever seen. Tan Casipo told me Bodhipalo had been living in a cave monastery in the far northeast for over two years. The community there practised severe self-discipline. They even followed the ancient ascetic practice of refraining from washing more than once a month.

105

He didn't want to come back to Pah Nanachat, according to the helpful monk. They had to send for him three times before they could pry him out of his cave. Tan Bodhipalo sat next to the Ajahn in the meal line, taking Tan Casipo's place as the number two monk in residence. That morning, after our bowls were washed, he took Jim aside and asked the tall *pahkow* to help him clean the drains of the eaves troughs around the *sala*.

The rest of us raked until noon with great mindfulness. Our work disturbed many of the residents of the damp, matted leaves we were removing. We irritated millions of red and black ants, annoyed vipers, scorpions, giant centipedes and a few tarantulas.

'Tan Casipo!' I bellowed. 'A huge, hairy spider!'

'Don't worry. It's just a tarantula' he said with a smile. 'They can't kill you. Just watch out for the black centipedes with the red legs.'

'They're deadly?' I put down a handful of leaves.

'The bigger ones the size of snakes could kill you. We've never had anybody actually die of a centipede bite though.'

'So people have been bitten?'

Tan Casipo gave me a small smirk. 'We had one French monk here a while ago who used to search for centipedes and make them bite him. He said it was a meditation to observe pain. He didn't last long as a *bhikkhu*. We disrobed him pretty quickly.'

The sun sparkled through the cover of the trees and giant ferns. By midday we were all glistening with dirt and perspiration. Mosquitoes ate their lunch. The Ajahn laid down his broom and told us to stop work. We obeyed gladly. I headed eagerly back towards my *kuti*. Jim was setting up a large aluminium ladder to reach the eaves at the corner of the *sala*.

'Do you want me to steady it for you?' I offered.

'Sure' said my twin. 'I'll be up only a minute. Tan Bodhipalo told me to unplug this one eaves trough here where it drains into the main water tank.'

'This is disgusting' he said when he reached the top. 'It's jammed solid with black leaves and muck. It stinks – and it's full of ants. This goes right into our drinking water!'

A tin pipe ran from the corner where Jim worked to the top of the main water tank. The tank was a large concrete cylinder about seven metres high and three metres in diameter. Jim began pulling out handfuls of muck. The debris scattered below him. Most of it fell on me.

'It's plugged all the way through the pipe I think. We'll have to clean the bottom end from the top of the tank and then rinse the whole pipe clean.'

'We?'

'Do you have other appointments in the next twenty minutes, Bhikkhu Bob?'

'Bhikkhu Bob? Where did that come from?'

'It just seemed a good name for a Canadian monk. Nice ring to it. You don't mind if I call you Bob?'

'Nobody's ever called me Bob. Okay. You can call me Bob. But if this cleaning project gets too enthusiastic, I'll start calling you Boomer. I have a meeting with *samadhi* scheduled in twenty minutes in my hut.'

I filled three plastic buckets with water while Jim used the ladder to climb the side of the water tank. While pulling filth from the mouth of the drainpipe he suddenly stood up and started shaking and dancing fitfully.

'Ants! Thousands of them!' he yelped. 'And this crud is like fertilizer. We should all have typhoid by now, drinking water filtered through this.' He climbed back to the ground and wiped his hands on the side of the tank. Looking up I could see hundreds of little black spots moving frantically around the rim of the tank.

'Black ants?' I asked.

'The tiny ones. Lucky they aren't the red monsters. I wouldn't even consider cleaning the tank if we had to face those.'

'Cleaning the tank? You are a Boomer, aren't you Bunte? What about my meeting with meditation?'

Jim offered me his black fingers in reply. 'You like to drink this, Bob?'

The two of us stripped off our robes and girded our loins with the bathing clothes we normally wore as slips beneath our *sabongs*.

WHAT THE BUDDHA NEVER TAUGHT

'I've always wanted to work with my loins girded' I said, passing buckets of water up the ladder. We had moved the lower end of the pipe away from the hole in the tank, then returned the ladder to the eaves of the *sala*. Jim started flushing the pipe clean.

'What work? I'm the one up the ladder with the ants, Bob.'

'You're the Boomer, Bunte.'

When the water came through the pipe it ran down the side of the tank, black and full of sludge. Jim poured six buckets in the trough before the water turned clear at the lower end.

Sun Tin, the Thai monk with the lion tattoo and crooked smile saw us. He stopped to watch us work. He spoke no English but understood Jim's Thai quite well. He showed us how to drain the tank and led me to the tool house where I found two long-handled scrubbing brushes, a wire hand brush and a thick rope. Jim was sweeping ants off the top of the tank when I returned. He had removed the filter screen from the hatch.

'Ants all over the inside' he told me. 'The upper walls are black with them.'

We tied the rope to a nearby tree. Jim lowered himself down through the hatchway into the knee-deep water that remained at the bottom. I followed him into the murk. Sun Tin climbed the outside of the tank after us. He peered down through the little square of light, laughing. Inside, the walls were slippery with grey slime. The floor was slick beneath our bare feet. But the resonance in the tank was perfect for chanting.

'YO SO . . . ' Jim intoned in a booming voice which reverberated through the cylinder.

'BHAGAVAN ARAHANT SAMASAMBUDDHASA . . . ' we chanted in unison.

Above us, Sun Tin pulled up the rope, threatening to shut the lid and seal us in darkness. He grinned like a maniac. We shouted at him.

'That would be quite a spiritual discipline, three years in a water tank' said Jim.

'It would make an *arahant* out of you, Boomer.'

'Not if I were locked in with you, Bob.'

'Boomer, have you ever met an *arahant*? Or a *bodhisattva*? A saint even? I was thinking of our conversation about the monks. You're too cynical about religion. There are good examples.'

'You mean like Ajahn Chah?'

'I don't necessarily mean a monk. Do you know anybody personally? I know one man, he's not an *arahant*, but I think he may be a *bodhisattva*, even though he's not a Buddhist. He runs a meat exporting business from Canada to Thailand and the Phillipines. He spends about half the year in Asia. First he makes sure his customers are happy with their orders, then he goes into rural areas. He helps village communities set up fishing co-ops, dig wells and set up local industries. He has a talent for bringing people together, getting them talking and working out solutions to their problems. He supplies the capital needed to put the solutions into action and fades out of the picture. He was a Baptist minister when I first knew him. But I think he's found a more direct way of serving God through the meat exporting business.'

'If that's what you mean, I guess I have a *bodhisattva* in my life after all. If I'm cynical about religions, this guy keeps me from getting absolutely hostile. He's largely responsible for me being where I am. He's my religious studies professor at Swarthmore. The man has definitely found something more than most people are looking for. He's married with two kids in the suburbs, has a typical overloaded university schedule, gets frustrated in traffic jams. Yet even when he's angry, I can sense this deep lake of calm inside him. He's sort of a guru on campus, but aware of the dangers that leads to. My parents met him once. We're a devoutly non-religious family. My folks aren't the type to recognize spirituality. Even they were really impressed with him. He goes to a Presbyterian church, but his speciality is Thai Buddhism. He taught my course in Asian religions. I guess that's how I ended up here.'

'What made you take a course in Asian religions? It's hardly a typical requirement for law school candidates.'

'It was my sister's advice. She's good at telling me to do all the things she regrets she never did. Before my first year she told me to make sure to take something wild and exotic at university that I'd never thought of studying before. Now here I am, chanting in the bottom of a water tank. I should ordain as a janitor.'

We scrubbed and talked for two hours. It was cool in the tank so we were able to work vigorously. Eventually I crawled back up the rope which Sun Tin had been persuaded to lower again. I threw buckets of water at the upper inside rim, washing down the ants. The poor creatures were too confused to bite. They ran in circles, carrying little white eggs in their mouths. Jim and I violated our first precept a thousand times over. Sun Tin filled buckets for me from the tap at the bottom of the tank which connected to another water storage tank in the jungle.

'Okeee' the Thai called up to me with devilish enthusiasm. I hauled the pails up to the top by rope. When finally the ants had all fled or been washed away, I lowered myself back into the tank and rejoined Jim for a final scrub of the floor.

'Careful! Don't step on the toad' he said as I touched bottom.

'A toad? How could there be a toad in here? How could it get through the screen in the top of the tank?'

'How could it even get up to the top of the tank, Bob?'

'Maybe it was born here. Maybe this is his home.'

'We'll have to evict him anyway' said Jim. He called up to Sun Tin to lower a bucket. We began groping for the creature.

'More violence to beings. I don't like it, Boomer. Maybe the toad was meditating? On its way to becoming an *arahant*?'

'He'll be happier in the real world.'

We located the toad, a black lump in the murk. Jim scooped him into the bucket. He floated passively.

'Sun Tin, toad coming up on rope' Jim sang out.

'And what about the ants?' I said as we emptied the last of the tank and began our own climb up towards daylight. 'Where will they go?'

110

The tank was free of slime, free of toads, free of ants, sterile and lifeless. Sun Tin turned on the taps at the bottom and began to refill it with water from the storage tank.

'The water in the other one is probably as foul as it was in this one' said Jim grimly. 'At least now the tank's clean.'

'We've been drinking the water all along without any problems.'

'That doesn't mean it's safe.'

That evening, perhaps as a reward for the day's work, evening chanting was cancelled. We were all told to go to the Ajahn's *kuti* instead for a taped *dasana* by the famed American monk, the first Ajahn of Wat Pah Nanachat, Ajahn Sumedo. He was one of the first Western disciples of Ajahn Chah. The teaching we were to hear had been given at his new *wat* in Chithurst, England. Sumedo's name was revered. His picture hung on the *sala* wall. In his English *wat* the monks kept not only the *Vinaya*, but all the Thai traditions as well. *Bindabhat* was a problem at first, according to Tan Casipo. Often the British *bhikkhus* would walk through the Chithurst countryside at dawn and not receive a thing. Fortunately, a father of one of the monks bought a house near the monastery. He was happy to give alms food to the *bhikkhus* every morning. Tradition was thus preserved without anyone actually starving.

Even the laymen were invited to the *dasana*. It was exciting to receive a teaching at last from a famous monk, even on tape. We sat in the dark on the Ajahn's balcony. Sumedo's voice sounded lethargic but contemplative, habitually stretching one syllable words as if he was yawning through them – 'yeees'. It was tempting to follow his example. The *dhamma* talk was a disconnected ramble on the five hindrances to meditation: desire, aversion, restlessness, inertia and doubt. The theme was that the hindrances are not our enemies. By patiently enduring we can learn from them. Most of the talk dwelt on the problem of lustful desires arising during meditation. The most widely recommended antidote for desires of the flesh is for a monk to concentrate on the aversion which arises when the repulsive aspects of the human body are considered. Lust is neutralized by disgust. Sumedo said there was no need to make the body artifically repugnant. A close examination of it as it is was always sufficient.

'Take for example the five outer elements of the body, the hair of the head, the hair of the body, skin, teeth and nails. This is all that we see. Often we find these elements quite attractive, yeees. Long black hair brushed back over the shoulders, light golden hair on the arms, smooth warm skin, delicate white teeth and little pink painted toenails. All this is quite attractive. But now imagine all these attractive elements if they are just sitting in five piles in front of us. This pile for hair of the head, next one for body hair, third, a bag of skin, this small one for teeth, and here all the little pink painted toe and fingernails. It's not very attractive any more, is it? So we must ask ourselves where was desire if it doesn't lie in any one of these five piles.'

The teacher went on to describe another common practice for overcoming lust; meditation on corpses. Sumedo recounted his visit to a Bangkok city morgue. He was permitted to visit the room where unidentified corpses were kept.

'Inside they showed me a young man's body. It had been found in the river. The corpse was bloated. The skin had turned black. It was hideous. The stench was so bad it was difficult to stay in the room, even for me. Finally, I touched the body, recognizing that it was no different from my own. I have not gone beyond death. This will be my condition too, some day.'

When exhorting the benefits of repulsion, the Ajahn spoke with ardour. He was nowhere more eloquent than when discussing the inner elements of the body.

'Take excrement. In the West we like to pretend it doesn't exist. Unless you are a farmer you probably haven't spent a lot of your time looking at excrement or handling it. It makes us feel uneasy, yeees. We don't like to think that it's part of us. Yet everybody in this room has intestines full of faeces.'

An especially apt teaching for those of us living on a diet of sticky rice.

'There's blood in my stool' said Richard to me the next day before alms round. He still looked miserable, but ate a full bowl of food at the morning meal. It was hard to fault him. There were over forty plates served to us that Wai Phra day. It was a big celebration. Families came up from as far away as Bangkok, bringing Thai delicacies with them. I had little restraint for the rich meat dishes, none at all for the sweets, the sticky rice and coconut milk goodies wrapped in banana leaves, the pressed dried mangos, or the sweet bananas in purple sauce. Even *durian* was becoming irresistible. There should have been a precept against sugar.

After such a meal, meditation was next to impossible. I sat down in my *kuti* with the heavy load in my belly, lolled sideways and began to doze. I tried to stand and walk it off. My legs dragged in the sand. Finally I decided to lie down for twenty minutes. Hours later, Jim's voice called up at me from beneath my hut.

'Earth to Bhikkhu Bob, do you read me?'

'Bob to Boomer, roger, I read you. Presently orbiting the third *jhana*. Estimated re-entry in ninety seconds. Stand by.'

I straightened my robes and staggered groggily to the balcony. 'So what's the occasion, Boomer?'

'Bob, there's a dozen teenage Thai high school girls who had me cornered in the *sala* . . . '

'Boomer, did you break your third precept? And I thought I had trouble resisting sugar.'

'Not on your life. That kind of *samsara* I don't need. They said they wanted to interview me for their English class assignment. They have to ask *farang* why they became monks. It's the sort of thing you like. Thought I'd invite you along.'

The half-dozen girls were shy. They sat in respectful sitting posture, waiting for us in the *sala*. As usual they looked about thirteen years old when in fact they were high school seniors. A male student with them ran the tape recorder while they took turns reading questions to us from their notes. Since Jim spoke Thai, they talked with him in their own language first. Instinctively they called him Ajahn. He turned red. When they sat down in front of us in the *sala*, they bowed to us three times. I laughed. Jim squirmed.

'Don't do that!' he said to the kids with distress. 'We're not even monks. Just *pahkows*. Damn it, Tim, don't laugh.'

Thai young people display a discomforting amount of respect towards those they perceive as worthy elders, always preferring to err on the side of courtesy. High status foreigners in religious robes must have been doubly intimidating to them. They spoke so softly at first that their questions were inaudible when we played back the tape. We began again, after much fussing. They seemed frightened of offending us. Speaking in Thai, Jim gradually helped them relax. Still, they were easily flustered and mixed up the order of their questions. All six of the girls sat together in a cluster, protective arms on one another's knees, half hiding, half supporting each other as they passed around the question sheet. Like many Thai women they were already tending a bit towards fat. Their teenagers' cosmetics coated mild cases of acne. Four of them had dark Laotian complexions typical of the northeast. The other two were fair-skinned, from the central plains. The questions lacked inspiration. They were standard tourist questions. How many brothers? How many sisters? What did we like about Thailand? What did we think of the King? Jim was well informed and answered the questions in good detail. They seemed oblivious to our answers. Only rarely could we get a giggle out of them.

'What your favourite colour?'

'Red' I said.

'Purple' Jim said.

'Purple?' I said. 'You like purple? It's your favourite?'

'What's wrong with purple? My college room is purple. It's a lot more original than red, Bob.'

'Nothing wrong with it, Boomer. If you like purple you like purple. Really you like purple?'

The students played this section of the interview back three times. They were more amused by Jim and me laughing at ourselves than by anything we actually said.

Before they left, they bowed to us again. Jim sat through it as if he was in a dentist's chair. To them we were worthy of respect because we wore robes and because we were *farang*. But they really didn't seem to know why either of those things made us so worthy. It felt like a reflex from them, an instinct to seek safety in humility. It kept us at a distance and helped them categorize us so that speaking to us would not be unbearable. I wondered what would happen when this generation was in control of the country, after growing up in an age of plastic toys and Rambo movies. How long would unthinking obedience to tradition last against the demands of a prosperous, westernizing society?

CHAPTER EIGHT

What Is and Isn't
Bat Shit

For a full year they had tried to get Tan Bodhipalo out of his cave and back to Pah Nanachat but he had refused to leave. Some people are recluses because an inner fire drives them into solitude. Tan Bodhipalo just didn't like people. He did not seem happy in our community. He used to be a gospel singer, according to Tan Casipo. He had travelled with a church group from town to town, winning souls for Jesus throughout northern England. One day he realized he didn't believe any of it. Like many others, he escaped by drifting to Asia, ending up in Ajahn Chah's care. He seldom talked. If he had to speak it was always with much effort and a strained look of discomfort. His words were as terse as possible.

One day shortly after the recluse had returned to Pah Nanachat, the Ajahn noticed small sticky black spots on the floor during the early morning sweeping of the *sala*. He and Tan Bodhipalo bent down to look at them. The cave monk touched one of the tacky spots with his finger and held it to his nose.

'It's bat shit' said the Ajahn.

Tan Bodhipalo pressed the little black smear again with his fingers and shook his head. We all crowded round the spot. 'No, bat shit is dry' he said.

'Probably it's bat shit' said the Ajahn.

'I lived two years in a cave' said the monk. 'I know what is and isn't bat shit.'

On Wai Phra evening the Ajahn gave permission for laymen and *pahkows* to come to his *kuti* for a *dhamma* talk while the villagers performed their chanting in the *sala*.

'These days I feel there is little need to say anything concerning the practice' our teacher began when we had settled. A single candle lit his face as he spoke to the silent circle of hairless figures gathered on his balcony. 'But since there are so many new faces, and since the responsibility falls on me as the senior monk to give a talk on Wai Phra, I guess I should say a few words. Perhaps you newcomers find it a bit difficult adapting to the discipline here. Some people come expecting to be given a course on meditation. We don't give courses here. There is no need for all that. Many people come looking for something instant to solve their problems, like a ten-day *vipassana* retreat. There are such courses in other *wats*. People go to them and say the experience was really powerful. Then you look at them afterwards. There is no practice in their lives. "What happened to this great practice?" you ask them. "I don't have time for that now" they say. They get dragged back down into sex, drugs and success. Their practice disintegrates as soon as the course is over. For them it is just another experience. They are still trapped in their own ignorance. Here in Wat Pah Nanachat, things are different. Our practice lies within the daily routine. It's a twenty four hour a day practice. Meditation isn't something you do separate from other activities. Here it is your way of living. Sometimes foreigners used to complain to Ajahn Chah that there wasn't enough time for them to meditate during the day. "Do you have time to breathe?" he'd say to them. "How can you find time to breathe all day long if you're so busy with other things? If you have time to breathe, you have time to meditate." So if you feel there is no time to meditate during a work day, remember this is just where meditation can begin for you. Be mindful of your work. This is meditation. Follow the rules and precepts of the community. The rules are the teaching we give you. We don't teach with words but with our behaviour. For everything we do there is a rule. For this reason a monk is not distracted or confused about life's details. He follows the rules to gain calm and peace. Suppose he is not certain about what is right according to the rules. Then he asks a senior monk. This increases humility as well as awareness. It helps us to remember that we are not individuals, we are a community.

'The rules are our source of harmony. For example, they bring harmony to how we eat. You new laymen probably don't know this but it is forbidden to scrape your bowls or make chewing noises. Recently it's been getting pretty loud down at the far end of the food line. I notice a lot of food is being swept up from your mats. There's nothing more pleasing than silence and good manners while we eat. Also watch how you bow. Don't just flop down on your faces. There is a proper way. When a monk asks you to offer him something, do it sincerely. Don't tower over him. Kneel, and offer it with both hands or at least supporting the right hand with the left. Be obedient at all times. Be mindful of resentment and aversion when it arises. This is just ego, just personal desire. The rules will reveal your ignorance to you. When I was first ordained it really used to bother me that I couldn't play my guitar any more. I was once a jazz musician. I was always tapping my fingers. I resented not being able to make music in the *wat*. This revealed my attachment. The rules show you what you need to renounce. Obedience is part of the cure. You learn not to cling to personal preferences. Then you can see things as they really are.

'Buddha laid down the rules over twenty-five hundred years ago. It's probably the longest unbroken tradition in the world. Remember that the tradition is much greater than you are. Submit yourself to the rules and the monks and eventually you will learn that the path of discipline is not only the path to enlightenment, it is enlightenment. They are one and the same. The practice is enlightenment. Some people find this idea not to their liking. They want to get enlightenment in a flash. This way they become attached to something that doesn't exist. Enlightenment isn't a thing you get. So give up your desire for it. I've been a monk for ten years and only recently have I come to see this clearly. Only the practice is the true guide.

'Well, I've said a lot. All that's important is to remember to be mindful and follow the rules.'

We bowed three times to our teacher in the darkness, then shuffled down his wooden stairs and back through the jungle to the *sala* where the villagers still chanted their praises to the Triple Gem. When we arrived, the Ajahn climbed into his ceremonial seat. There was a large crowd for the big celebration. The Ajahn gave them an appropriately long *dasana* while we munched our pickled olives.

Jim pulled at the end of my robe before the *dasana* was over. He motioned me to follow him out of the back door of the *sala*. We sat down together just around the outside corner. There was no moon this night due to the clouds. We could barely see each other's faces.

'So what do you think of our Ajahn now?' Jim's voice bristled with anger. 'Just why is it we call that man our teacher? This is the closest thing to a teaching we've ever been fed by him. "Obey the rules and be mindful" he tells us. "And after thirteen years of following the rules, you'll see that the rules are enlightenment!" Does he think he's enlightened?'

'I don't think he was trying to convince us he's enlightened. He's not conceited.'

'He feels little need to say anything about the practice. Little need for whose benefit? He meant there is no more need for him to talk, he's gone beyond all that. He gives a *dasana* only for the sake of tradition, not for our benefit. You think it's not conceited to say other retreats are no good, only here in Pah Nanachat do you get the genuine tradition passed down from the Buddha over twenty-five hundred years ago?'

'He believes it.'

'Does he believe in the rules? Then why do we have all the loopholes like chewing tobacco and Coffeemate? He doesn't care about the spirit of the rules. He's mindful about how to get around them. He's more like a lawyer than a monk. So we can't drink milk after noon, but we use non-dairy "milk". So monks can't clean the water cisterns, but

119

they make it clear we've got to do it. By the rules he's right.
I don't sense any compassion towards the poor mosquito
larvae though. Monks can't cut plants but look at all the
cutting and clearing he's authorized in this place. When he
decided to clean out the leaves in the compound, he knew
that action was going to cause a lot of suffering to creatures.
But as long as he didn't personally kill anything he thinks
he's obedient.'

'We killed a lot of ants ourselves in that water tank.'

'But we're not preaching the rules to others.'

'We took vows not to kill.'

'Do you think anybody minded that we unpolluted the
drinking water?'

'The ants.'

'I don't mind killing. But I do mind hypocrisy. I mind
manipulation of a set of rules for your own personal ends.
He says the rules teach you how to renounce personal
desires, but he uses the rules to fulfil his own. I guess ten
months of Thai Buddhism and culture is too much for me.
All this hierarchy and structure is too oppressive. The monks
don't use it for mindfulness; they use it to stay on top of the
status heap. They tell us there is no difference between
people, then keep us in a rigid line at meal time. They say
it's to avoid confusion. But why do they sit on a platform
while we sit on the floor? All our *bindabhat* goodies go into
the common bowls before we eat but then the bowls go by
the monks first.'

'That's pretty trivial, Jim. The monks are all sick of the
sweeties they get on alms round.'

'You think so?' His eyes flashed in the darkness as he
leaned close to me. 'Do you know what I found in a monk's
spittoon after breakfast yesterday? A Mars Bar wrapper.'

'I haven't seen a Mars Bar for a whole year' I whispered.

'And it wasn't the first. Do you think any bars will ever
make it to our end of the line? But if we get one on *bindabhat*,
we are supposed to surrender it to the common bowl.'

'You may be onto something really serious here. If news
of this got out we could have a revolt of the laymen against
the oppressors in the *sangha*.'

'So maybe I've been in the country too long. But you should admit it, Tim, the *farang* at this *wat* who call themselves monks are nothing but a bunch of social rejects who have found a place where they can get free food, free shelter and free respect. They are complacent and their only concern is their perks at the top end of the hierarchy. They use the rules to fool the Thais, to fool us and to fool themselves. Nobody here is a strong meditator. Nobody here practises compassion. They say following the rules makes them noble. Look at them. Do you see nobility. It's an act. They couldn't make it on the outside and they have come here to hide. If they were really practising, they wouldn't be talking about the rules.'

'How about Ruk? How can you judge? You're too cynical.'

'I don't know Ruk. But I think the whole place encourages the practice of mediocrity, not meditation.'

'I feel it too, Jim. But I don't like to admit it. You know who we should watch as a litmus test?'

'Who? What do you mean?'

'Percy. If he fits in well here, decides to stay and be ordained, if he makes it, then I concede the point to you and I for one will get the hell out fast.'

He laughed. 'You call me cynical?'

'One other thing we could do is test to see if the monks are really striving for the Buddhist ideal or just acting, find out if they are holy or if they are moral slugs. A friend of mine once said it's hard to tell if some people are spiritually advanced and in blissful harmony with their environment or just "no-minds", too stupid or lazy to bother showing much ego. She said if you scratch hard enough, a no-mind's ego will rise up spitting. It's usually pretty nasty when you find it. So maybe we should scratch somebody hard. Do something downright malicious to see what kind of response we get, something really embarrassing. If the monks get upset, we'll know their calm is just a lack of wind.'

'Bob, you're revealing a whole new side of yourself tonight.'

'I'm just trying to be clinical.'

'You be clinical, I'll be cynical. I admit, the thought of

something like hitting the Ajahn with a bucket of cold water as he's coming out of the toilet appeals to my baser nature. But I don't think I have enough nerve to do it.'

'It would be good training for them, Boomer. A great opportunity to watch anger arise. Then they could overcome their personal preferences.'

'Like a preference for skinning us alive?'

'It would be a great teaching.'

We sat back in silence, two white robes against the dark *sala* wall, imagining scenarios for our test. It was rebellion. Although from the moment we arrived at Pah Nanachat we had been made twins by the community, our judgment of the *sangha* created an us-and-them situation. We both knew this. Our collusion in malicious fantasy drew us together – and apart from the rest.

'It's easy to forget that we're in this hierarchy too' I said.

'It's not the same. We've only been here a few weeks.'

'We're *pahkows*. We've taken vows without honestly believing in them. The Thais feed us on *bindabhat* and bow to us. The laymen watch us and obey us. We don't have to do morning sweeping any more. We've got our niche and we've accepted the perks that go with it. Couldn't all we've just said against *farang* monks be directed against us too?'

'We're not losers.'

'If we stayed you'd be considered a college drop-out and I'd be a shiftless wanderer. I've thought a lot about what you said about the monks stuffing their faces at meal time. I cram mine just as full.'

'It's happening to me too, Bob. That's why I complain about it so much. I'm doing it myself. Food was always just food for me before. Now it's my only chance to eat, so I stuff myself like a turkey. I can barely stay awake to meditate through the morning. Drink time is even worse. Coffee really hypes up my system. Sugar makes me frantic. Normally I never drink coffee but here it feels as if it's my right. I can't have it at any other time and I'm hungry so, hey, bring me two big mugs of that delicious black drug to get me through to breakfast.'

'Maybe we've got the purpose of this *wat* all backwards.

It doesn't protect us from temptation. There are just fewer enticements. That makes temptation stronger. We feel justified in indulging because we are disciplined the rest of the day. That just reveals craving buried within. The Ajahn's right. When we eat anything we want any time we want, we never stop to watch our desire and greed. Here it's all focused on one meal and we really feel it. Pah Nanachat is no refuge from *samsara*, it's full of it.'

'*samsara* is in our minds.'

'Right. Being in a monastery doesn't make any difference. There will always be temptation as long as there is inner desire.'

'So why are we here?'

'To watch our breath.'

'To follow the rules.'

'Maybe the rules are only a beginning. Let's forget the mindfulness crap and just follow the eight precepts we've vowed to keep, in the spirit in which they were meant. The whole point of vowing not to eat after noon is that we eat to live. If we stuff ourselves like gluttons before noon, we break the spirit of the rule. My eating is out of control. I'm going to go back to a strict vegetarian diet and only one sweet per meal. I think maybe together we should fast. Skip one meal each week.'

'That's forty-eight hours without food!'

'We can do it. We don't tax our bodies at all on an average day. I used to fast regularly.'

'I've never done it. Okay. I know it will do me good. When? Tomorrow?'

'Morning after Wai Phra with no sleep is a rough way to start. Let's make it the day after. We don't want to do this as a show. We don't tell anybody. We go on alms round just the same.'

'You like to make this hard, don't you?'

'It's the natural ascetic in me. Why not? We supposedly go on *bindabhat* for the sake of mindfulness anyway, not because otherwise they won't feed us. So we'll sit in the line and just pass all the food by us, stare at our empty bowls

123

through the meal and help wash the spittoons afterwards as usual.'

'Do we wash our clean bowls too? What about the other precepts?'

'Don't kill – not even ants any more. The spirit of the rules means no destructive thoughts and no anger. Maybe we'll have to reconsider the scratching experiment. It's a form of killing just thinking about it. Don't steal. That means don't be greedy, don't envy. Not even Mars Bars. No erotic behaviour, no lust. No incorrect speech – Jim, that means no more lying to ourselves as if we were better than everybody else; no pride. No high or comfortable bed. That means no laziness, no sloth, no mid-morning naps, even on the floor. Jim, do you notice – these precepts seem to fall right in line with the seven deadly sins? Gluttony, anger, envy, lust, pride, sloth . . .'

'What about "NAGAGITA VADITA VISUKADASANA"?'

'No singing and dancing, perfumes, garlands and shows? That means no vanity.'

'Watching a show is vanity? Singing is vanity?'

'Self-distraction. No shows and music because those distract you with the vanity of life. They fill your mind so you can't meditate. Think of what we do with TV back home. The mind never has a chance to be empty. There's your seven deadly sins.'

'But Ajahn Bob, there are eight precepts and only seven sins. What about refraining from drugs and intoxicants? Can we skip that one or does it mean no coffee for me?'

'It makes you agitated? Then drugs make your mind unstable and you break the other seven.'

'I think we've talked for a long time.'

'How do you feel?'

'Not tired.'

'Me neither. Must be past two. Maybe we should go back inside and meditate awhile before morning chanting starts. It's the first Wai Phra I haven't dozed off in.'

'It's been better than three cups of coffee.'

We grinned at each other, and rose stiffly to our feet. Inside, the hall was almost empty. Percy snored softly against a pillar. Tan Bodhipalo's severe form paced slowly back and forth along the rear of the hall. It began to rain.

I could not find my red cup on the way to coffee break. I took the chewed white one instead. From time to time this happened. A new layman or guest occasionally used it, not knowing it belonged to me. I had to tell the offender, whenever this occurred, that it was my personal cup. Then I would ask him to use another. If coffee had already been served, it was a good chance for me to practise not clinging by letting another drink from my red. I loved this little cup dearly. Newcomers must have scratched their heads over such possessiveness in a *pahkow*.

This time Herman had it. I headed him off before he reached the Ajahn's *kuti* where coffee was waiting. The Netherlander, a tall craggy-featured man in his forties, was apologetic. Percy walked behind him. He heard Herman's apology. As he passed us, he raised a cupped hand to his mouth and whispered in a tone too loud to be confidential, 'Yes, whatever you do, don't take Tim's red cup. It's the only material possession he has.'

I laughed. I could hardly believe it. Percy had made a joke, a real joke that nailed me justly to the wall. Obviously I had underestimated his capacities. There was of course the faint chance he had meant it seriously, but from the mischievous look he gave me just before he spoke I concluded there was much hope for him. It was a look free of malice, yet brave enough for a good tease.

The heat of day dissipates in the late afternoon, allowing the tin roof of my *kuti* to cool. This is my favourite time of day. Robe washing finished, my wet *sabongs* dry on the line above my balcony. I rest, waiting for the call of the bell to evening chanting. For some reason mosquitoes can never be bothered to fly up to my porch at this hour, although I hear their hungry swarm below. They make walking meditation impossible. I sit on my straw mat and stare out into the jungle as dusk creeps upon it. I do not try to meditate. As I watch, my eyes become the trees, the branches, the scattered leaves and the squirrels chasing one another. My ears become the falling of twigs, animal chatters, the patter of rain. Occasionally a bird with a bright red breast and electric blue wings comes and sits on the small broad-leafed sapling near the *kuti*. He has a long dark tail plume which bobs up and down as he balances himself on the bough. Sometimes he whistles as if calling for a mate but he never sings his song for very long. He too seems to enjoy simply waiting for the night. Once I watched a snake chase a toad across my meditation runway. I thought of coming down with a stick to protect the victim. But then would I feed the predator as well? The snake was faster on the path but the toad gained ground when it hopped through a muddy puddle at the side. The serpent slithered and lost traction. I cheered the toad onward. The foolish creature took three hops past the water, jumped sideways and froze. The snake soon cleared the mud and followed the toad's trail back into the leaves. It stopped, suddenly, just where the toad changed his course, testing the air with its tongue. Toad smell everywhere. The toad looked like a rock, immobile. The reptile raised its head and peered around, then lowered it again to the ground and slithered past, less than four inches away from its prey. When it had disappeared into the brush, the toad turned and hopped rapidly back across the path to safety.

I sit on the porch and watch. A toad, a snake, a bird, a branch, a jungle enveloping and penetrating all of us. Light does not leave the jungle gradually, but in sudden dramatic darkenings. Suddenly the trees dim. Then twilight falls. The jungle loses its complex features as vines, ferns and leaves merge into blackness. Over the whine of the mosquitoes, the elephant bugs begin their deafening thrum, sounding as if a symphony string section is hidden in the bushes. The music swells into a deep harmonic hum, fills the jungle's fading forms with its vibrations. It sustains and unifies the indistinct shadows. Slowly the sound decrescendos to a single violin note, barely audible, quivering. A pause, a hush of silence between each movement. Then the symphony begins again, loud and throbbing, filling the evening air. Fireflies come out and flit between the black branches. They drift like stars unmoored from the sky, dancing freely below me, as if my view from the porch was a porthole into space. It is rapture just to sit, not conscious of meditating, not conscious of breathing, freed from the chattering of my monkey-mind. I let myself be absorbed in the greens, browns and blacks, the curve of a snake spine, the glitter of blue feathers, a blotch of toad. Slowly the colours blend together, lose shape and form, fade to black except for irradiated dots of glowing life, all united and intertwined by the thrum of the unseen elephant bug.

A bell sounds, far away in the darkness. At first it seems so distant, a clear sound as if made by striking a silver bowl, not an iron bell. The sound is sweet, yet makes me sad. It calls me to the *sala*, to human chanting, away from the jungle I have become night with. In the black air I stand, re-wrap my white robes around me, gather flashlight and bag, umbrella for the rain, and begin the walk to the temple. On this walk, if it is dry, my feet feel light and sure. I want to go barefoot and leave my torch at home. But red ants and scorpions use the path as well. The light is necessary to keep us out of each others' way. I walk slowly and with great care. Toads scatter in the beam of my torch. In confusion they often hop against my legs, frightening me. Sometimes I glimpse Jim's ghostly white form coming through the jungle from his own *kuti*. I wait for him and let him glide ahead when we meet. In the *sala* other dark forms join us. The Ajahn sounds his little gong and we drone our own song into the night. No mating call, the halting rhythm of our Pali chants. The Bhaddekarat-tagatha (Verses on a well-spent day):

Let not a man trace back the past
Or wonder what the future holds:
The past is but the left-behind,
The future but the yet-unreached.
In the present let him see
With insight each and every instant
Invincibly, unshakably,
That can be pierced by practising.

127

The morning of my fast with Jim, Richard did not come on *bindabhat*. Ruk and I went alone. I was glad for the break from the Texan's metaphysical banter. It fed my ego and destroyed my calm. Conversation with Ruk, however, came as gently as the dawn. His smile was always full of joy sufficient to refute all of Jim's pessimism. I wanted to put to him some of Jim's tough questions.

'Ruk, everybody says the monks at Pah Nanachat are very strict and dedicated to the tradition compared to other *wats* in Thailand. People come all the way from Bangkok just to feed us breakfast.'

'It's a lot stricter.'

'Does that make the monks better?'

'It does to the Thais.'

'But does it really make any difference?'

'I think so.'

We reached the lotus pond, a small lake on the side of the road filled with green lotus pads. The flowers rose above the surface, folded open to reveal brilliant pink, purple or white interiors. Ruk stopped and gazed at the lake. When he was a layman, he used to come to this spot and play a flute. Now his vows forbade him. He sensed his answers were not satisfying me.

'When Ajahn Chah was still teaching, this *wat* was a powerful place. He was a real example to us. He had a rare talent for teaching the *farang* monks. He was hard on us when we needed it. I remember having to sit for six hours without moving while he gave a *dasana* in Thai. Sometimes before meal he would talk with the villagers while we sat staring into our bowls until the food went cold. He knew our defilements and he knew how to break them. Sometimes he would yell at us. I remember one morning he threw a monk's bowl out of the *sala* window. He got really angry it seemed. But if you looked closely, there was nothing but calm inside. He wasn't disturbed at all. It was for our benefit. Inside, nothing.

'Since he's stopped teaching there has been nobody to take his place. Many senior disciples disrobed after his stroke. The personal master-student relationship had gone for them. He has sixty four monasteries now but the monks who are teaching in them aren't doing it with the same experience or wisdom he had. They are teaching what they were taught. Ajahn Chah taught what he knew. Some of them are still depressed about the condition of the master. We try to live up to his example but we can't. Even Pah Nanachat is much more slack than it was three years ago. Our reputation is perhaps better than we are.

'The previous Ajahn flew to Bangkok once a month to give a *dhamma* talk at the World Federation of Buddhists. He's very popular in Bangkok. Maybe you have seen his picture in a magazine? They treat him well down there because he was the Ajahn at Ajahn Chah's famous *farang wat*. They think we are all *arahants* up here. After a few days in the city our Ajahn used to come back and get irritated when he saw the monks being lazy instead of practising. When he got angry there was nothing calm about it. He couldn't change us. Sometimes he tried sitting and talking with the villagers about his plane reservations while our food got cold. But then the monks said he was just copying Ajahn Chah. This Ajahn got a lot of funding from Bangkok for building projects which caused some conflict with other senior monks who didn't want to build in the forest. It's costing eight hundred thousand bhat to build the new *bhote*, if it stays on budget. It will be in the new Thai style, all shiny paint, glitter and coloured glass. I don't like it. We did have an ordination hall before, just a tin roof with no walls. It kept out the rain. I liked it. It was a good way to enter the homeless life.'

'Homeless life' I interrupted, 'I haven't had so many possessions since I started travelling.'

'It was also his idea to get more land for the monastery.'

'Good grief, we're not buying land are we?'

'No. But he dropped many hints that donations of land would be a most appropriate offering. He will be coming back here, you see. The present Ajahn is temporary.'

'Ruk, that's not even an honest business practice, asking for land donations. It must go directly against the precepts. And this *wat* is supposed to have a reputation for excellence and renunciation? Tell me, is it this bad all over Thailand?'

'Actually, the northeast is considered the one place in Thailand where Buddhism is still purely practised. All the great teachers of this century have come from this region. Maybe it's because it's also the poorest and most economically undeveloped.'

'The *Dhamma* Belt?'

'Whatever else you may say, at least you will find that here the monks keep the precepts.'

Ruk slung his bowl over to his right shoulder. We had reached the village gates. Our conversation ceased as, heads bowed in humility, we begged for our rice. When we had passed the soaring village *wat* on the far end of the route and were again back in fertile rice paddies, Ruk told me about the age old division in Thailand between forest *wats* and village *wats*. *Wats* like Pah Pong and Pah Nanachat are usually founded by monks who want to meditate. Village *wats* are for more social *bhikkhus*. They have an easier life, and usually become lazy. The people know that a monk who lives in the jungle is serious about the practice. So they will search out these monks in order to do services for them. They will build *kuties*, bring food, even donate land believing that their merit will be greater if the monks are holy. In this way the devotees of the forest monks bring all the temptations right into the jungle.

'That's insidious' I said.

'It's generous. But it does make the village monks jealous, and it sometimes works out badly for the monks who want to be ascetics. But there must be plenty of Thais inhabiting the *deva*-realms because of it.'

'What?'

'Because the Thais are so good at making merit.'

'Ruk, do you honestly believe the Thais go to *deva*-realms for giving us rice-flour sweets? Let me ask you a riddle.' I told him the riddle of the king and the false *arahant* and watched him ponder over a reply.

'With a selfish attitude like that, I think the king gets no merit.'

'No, he sincerely wanted to give to an *arahant*.'

'Then since there is no real *arahant* involved, I suppose he doesn't get the merit for giving to one but – wait, of course, the merit is the same. Beggar or *arahant*, there is no difference between people.'

'Right!' I was pleased that my favourite monk had given the correct answer. 'But if merit is the same, why do Thais prefer to give to holy monks rather than their own poor? If it's the *sangha's* fault for misleading them, isn't that just plain immoral?'

'Perhaps they wouldn't give to the poor.'

'We should tell them to.'

'It isn't so simple. The Thais have their own customs. We are fortunate that involves feeding monks. We must live in harmony with them. They take care of us.' Ruk seemed defensive.

'I sometimes feel we're a zoo for the villagers to come to and gawk as they feed us' I said. 'I suppose the *farang* monks are the only entertainment they have, but the *sangha* should be teaching more than merit and obedience. It seems the villagers give us their precepts to keep!'

'Do you remember Edgar, the English novice? He was here when you arrived, I think.' Ruk spoke distractedly, as if he was unsure of what he was telling me. 'The villagers became upset with him because he had a funny habit of staring at things for long periods of time. He used to come on *bindabhat* with me.'

'They said he was a *pee bah*' I said, recalling Michael's coffee making from my first day.

'I was sorry to see him transferred to another *wat*. Fear of ghosts is very strong in the Thais. When I came back they told me fewer people were bringing donations for the morning meal. They are up again since he went.'

'Ruk – are you telling me the *sangha* had him transferred because he spooked the villagers? If the monks won't stand up for one of their own against superstition . . . '

'We respect their traditions.'

'You mean we compromise the *Dhamma*.'

'I'm not certain that was why he was transferred. Maybe he left on his own.'

'Or he really was a *pee bah* and just disappeared.'

131

There was a loud bellowing moan on the track ahead of us. Two Thai women had stopped their buffalo and cart to kneel in the wet earth as we passed. The beast panicked at the sight of Ruk. It veered and ducked away. The women jumped back to their feet, scrambling to control the buffalo and keep the cart from tumbling as the lumbering animal charged into the paddy, eyes white with fear.

CHAPTER NINE

Mind Over Menu

'**H**ungry?'
    'Not today, Bob. I'll just eat air.'

I took my place next to Jim in the morning food line. Our bowls were set before us. At the head of the line, a villager offered the first basin of rice to the Ajahn. He received it silently, filled his enamel alms bowl, and passed it to Tan Bodhipalo sitting on his right. Bodhipalo passed it on down the row of ochre monks and novices seated on the platform. Since Richard had missed alms round, Mark was last in the upper row. The Fan Man took the basin from him, and offered it to me, lead *pahkow* of the lower tier. He looked faintly surprised when I handed the basin straight on to Jim, taking nothing. Quickly he turned to the bowls of curries coming down the line, each of which was passed on in turn, untouched by either of the two *pahkows*.

'Pineapple-tomato-tofu, Boomer?'

'No thanks, Bob.'

'Fish in sweet curry sauce? Bean sprouts and egg? Baby corn and peas? Diced squash? Fried noodles and chicken? Sausage roll? Mushroom and bamboo shoot soup? Boomer, you're not taking anything. Mangos? You usually eat two or three. No? Rambutan? Pineapple slices? Sticky rice sweets? Coconut cream sweets? Pressed mango – holy *pahkow*, Jim, banana bread. Dukita baked banana bread this morning. I haven't seen or tasted banana bread in over a year.'

'It smells delicious, Bob. We can fast any day.' He offered

the tray of warm yellow bread back to me. 'Why don't you take just one piece?'

'Get thee behind me, *bunte*! No banana bread for this would-be *bhikkhu*. Lust of the belly begone!'

We sat through the meal in silence, watching the others feeding at their bowls, fully absorbed in their mastications. I had my regrets about the banana bread.

After the meal, the Ajahn declared another work day on the leaves would commence at noon. He also requested a few volunteers to come to his *kuti* for a special project at eleven. I decided to take the earlier job so I could sit uninterrupted through the last half of the day. On my way to the mid-morning assignment, I stopped to check on Jim at his hut and found him sitting on a bench on his porch, head held in one hand. He did not notice me approach.

'How's your stomach?' I asked.

'Empty. I feel pretty light-headed too. I'm not so sure fasting was a good idea.'

'How's the meditating?'

'Lousy. The last five days have been pure hell. As soon as I sit down I get these strong thoughts and desires about going home. All the old memories are dragged up from inside me. Maybe I've just been away too long. I'm ready to go back. I keep asking myself why I'm staying here. The more I do that, the more miserable I feel.'

'So are you just missing home or do you think it's the effect of this place?'

'Both. You know how I feel about the hierarchy here. I can tolerate it, sure. Alone in my *kuti* it's not so bad. But the Pali chanting is starting to drive me crazy. Do you know what we chant every day? I read the English translations beside the text. "Homage to the blessed one's disciples who have practised faithfully, purely, steadfastly, worthily. . . ." I can't say that any more. My knees, they've had it too. They hurt so much I can't even sit crosslegged in my *kuti*. I had to go and get this bench. I don't think they can take another Wai Phra.'

'You really sound low. Five days? Are you sure it's not just lack of food?'

'It's lack of life. I wonder what I'm doing with these losers, just sitting and trying to watch my breath all day. I don't see that it is doing me any good. I feel like I'm suffocating in a vacuum. It's funny though, there were times at school when the pressure got so heavy I just longed for a place like this. It's the perfect zero-stress environment. All basic needs taken care of, a nice little hut alone in the jungle. Yet I'm as depressed and miserable here as I ever was at school. Weird. I think it's teaching me something about myself. In school I blamed the pressure – the assignments, the deadlines, the teachers, my classmates. But if I feel just as miserable here where there is no pressure, I can't really blame the conditions back at college, can I?'

'Sounds like you are having an enlightening depression.'

'It's so wonderful I could cry. There's one other thing. All these desires for home I'm feeling, I know they aren't real. They are just a reaction to the *wat*. It's not sensible desires about home that come up in me, it's strange isolated things, like for a McDermitt's pinwheel pizza, or shopping for a new pair of ski boots. These cravings spring up whenever I settle down to meditate. When I look at them, I know I don't really want them. They are useless to me here and now. Once I do that they go away. If the same desires come up again, all I have to do is say "ha, you again" and they disappear. They lose their power over me.'

'Maybe you should fast more often. It sounds like productive interior work.'

'It feels like diarrhoea of the mind. It just keeps coming out like there's no end to it. It's exhausting. Thanks for listening.'

'Dump on me any time, Boomer.'

I left Jim to evacuate his brains in peace.

The Ajahn had marked out a section of jungle directly behind his *kuti* which he wanted cleared of plants and leaves, all but a few sapling. He had plans to level the area and turn it into an extension of the marble patio beneath his quarters so he could receive larger groups of visitors. Nimalo and Tan Casipo were already raking the plot clear of leaves. Herbie hacked at the plants with a small machete. The monks, of course, could not cut them, according to the *Vinaya*. The Ajahn gave me a hoe and led me through the site. It was against his precepts to actually tell me 'cut this down' so he couched his instructions in direct hints. 'In that whole area, nothing needs to stay. Just leave this bush over here. Go over that section one more time with the hoe.' It seemed like a tight loophole. The Ajahn was using a lot of grease. I slashed at the brush in frustration. Nimalo and Tan Casipo loaded the debris into a pushcart. They hauled the cart down the trail to dump it. Herbie's face was black as he hacked away at a thick root. 'We don't need that stump' the Ajahn had told him. Some well-dressed Thai visitors arrived, and the teacher was called away to greet them. I worked my way closer to the teenage layman and spoke to him.

'So you don't like it either?' I asked Herbie in a prison whisper.

'I've done too much killing for monks in the past four months' he said, scowling. 'The Ajahn before this one was worse. He was always clearing spaces and cutting the jungle. This is supposed to be a forest *wat*. Soon there won't be any forest left. Monks are supposed to live in harmony with their environment, not kill it to make courtyards. I've *koppied* more plants since I came here than I've ever had to kill in all my life. Next time someone asks me to destroy a tree or bush or even a flower for him I'll tell him to find another assassin.' Herbie threw his machete into the ground and walked off towards the *sala*, back rigid and tense. It was the first time he had spoken his mind to me. It was the first time I began to suspect him.

'Where's Herbie?' said Tan Casipo when he and the Australian novice returned with the empty cart.

'Gone' I said, picking up the fallen machete.

'I see' said the monk. He began loading the cart again with freshly slaughtered plants, but stopped to watch me swing the blade through the air.

'You were fasting today, weren't you?'

'Yes' I told him. 'So was Jim.'

'You didn't tell anybody.'

'No.'

'I thought you went on alms round.'

'We did.'

'And you stayed through meal.'

'Yes.'

'Why?'

'Jim and I talked about it. We decided we had both developed a lot of bad food habits since we came to the *wat*. We wanted to break them. To skip the meal itself wouldn't have broken anything.'

'I can't fast' said the monk. 'I get weak and go to pieces by the afternoon.'

The Ajahn returned from his audience with the Thais. Tan Casipo turned to him.

'Tim and Jim were fasting today' he said.

'I thought I saw them in the *sala*.'

'They were there but they didn't eat. Tim says it's for discipline in their food habits.'

'I practised discipline in my food habits today too' said the teacher. 'I forced myself to eat two big pieces of Dukita's banana bread. I'm still suffering for it. We had a Thai monk here once, a special disciple of Ajahn Chah's. Do you know what he did for food discipline when he fasted? He sat in line and filled his bowl with food. Then he brought the first mouthful right up to his lips, opened his mouth and then put the spoonful aside. He did that for every mouthful of the whole meal until his bowl was empty. He sent his discarded food back to the kitchen. That was good discipline, all right. I think maybe that back section could still use a little more work, Tim. Where's Herbie?'

'Gone.'

'Gone where?'

'He didn't say. I think he's trying to wash the sap off his hands.'

Later, while raking the far end of the area to be cleared I uncovered a baby snake, no bigger than a worm. It writhed and jerked as if in agony. I thought perhaps I had hurt it. I called the Ajahn. He came and crouched over the wiggling little creature. We watched it together for a few minutes.

'It's too small to bite' he said. Then he gently picked it up in one hand and placed it back further into the jungle, outside the work area. He bent down to watch the relocated snake. I returned to my raking, soon disturbing a colony of big black ants. They scattered in all directions, carrying white translucent eggs in their mouths.

'He's fine now' said the Ajahn. 'All he needed was some leaves around him. I suppose he didn't know what happened when suddenly his leaf-cover was removed. I put him down and he just slithered happily off into the jungle.' The teacher smiled at me.

Once a week we had a sauna. It was a small brick room with a wood fire stoked on the outside that had been built next to the wash pump. Inside, a dozen people could sit on wooden benches in the darkness, and sweat. The monks liked the temperature hot. They poured water from a bucket onto the hot rocks piled above the heat of the fire. It steamed and hissed and perspiration rolled down our wet and skinny bodies. Our skulls glistened. Salty sweat filled our eyes. Half baked, half blind, we would push our way through the heavy curtain back to the sunlight, dousing ourselves with cool water from the great washing cisterns. On sauna days there was no evening chanting. The heat left us drained yet relaxed as day turned suddenly into dusk.

'Jim's roof creature attacked my *kuti* last night' Richard told me one day in the sauna's gloom.

'Aha' said Jim's voice in the darkness.

'I even saw it, sort of' said the Texan. 'I got it with a flashlight. It had green eyes.'

'Sounds like a *pee bah*. Or a hungry ghost. Did it have an English accent?' I said, still an unbeliever.

'It had a bushy tail and sharp black nose. Stripes, I think.'

'It sounds like a chivvy cat' a fourth voice spoke gently out of the gloom. It was Ruk.

'A cat?' said Jim.

'It's not a real cat' said the German. 'It's a tree-badger. You have something like them in North America. They have black circles around their eyes.'

'Raccoons?' said Jim. 'In Thailand?'

Less than a week later Jim, Richard and I caught our first glimpse of a chivvy cat in daylight. Three villagers brought one to our *wat*. They placed it in a wire cage which they hung from a tree branch behind the *sala*, near the bowl washing area. The chivvy cat hid on the cross piece of the cage roof, terrified. The villagers said it had a bad paw. It looked more like a cross between a large monkey and a rat than a cat, with a long body like a weasel, too skinny to be a close relative of the American coon. Are even our animals overweight? It cried out for hours in a high-pitched wail.

Nimalo took it upon himself to clean the cage every day. He fed the little animal with scraps from our morning meal. The right hind leg was always kept close to his body as the chivvy cat hopped about his cage. Sometimes the other back leg seemed weak as well and after several days there was some concern that the creature might never recover well enough to be set free. Fearing perhaps the damaged leg was infected, Mark and Nimalo decided to give it a check-up. The rest of us looked on while our bowls dried in the morning sun. The Australian novice put on a pair of stiff rubber gloves, then a pair of industrial rubber mitts on top of them. When he reached into the cage, the patient screamed like a child. It bit through both layers of Nimalo's protection. The novice cried out but he held tight and removed the animal from the cage. Mark covered it with a cloth, then gently pulled the wounded leg out to examine it. He looked it over like a loving physician.

'It's broken, but healing without infection' said Doctor Mark, loud enough for the rest of us to hear. 'But it's crooked. I guess he won't get much use out of that leg. He should be able to survive without it though. He hops around well enough in the cage. The other one was cut, but seems to be recovering.'

Nimalo the zookeeper smiled and agreed. He gently placed the creature back into its cage. The two novices grinned at each other as if they had just performed successful surgery. Nimalo took off his gloves and examined the marks on his hands.

'No blood. His teeth were too small to break through the skin. Lucky I had two pairs of gloves. Poor fellow, you must have been really frightened. Sorry little one.'

Compassion towards all living beings is *karuna*, one of the four great Buddhist virtues. Seeing Mark's tenderness and Nimalo's steadfastness in caring for the chivvy cat, I was gladdened. Buddhism is not navel-gazing. Inherent in it is concern for all living things, a willingness to ease whatever suffering lies before one. Yet watching this scene left a sickening feeling in my stomach, just as I had felt when I saw the Ajahn with the baby snake. The image arose of a rich woman feeding candies to a fat, ugly dog. She loves her precious one, but ignores the poverty at her door. Secluded away in the jungle, these two men in the prime of life lavished attention on a sick coon. It developed their *karuna* and benefited the coon, no doubt. But outside our jungle was a world that suffers. It seemed they had fled from that. Perhaps, as Tan Sumeno argued, the outside is incurably insane. Perhaps healing this chivvy cat was the best and most productive thing these two would ever do in their lives. But in coming here, they placed themselves on the other side of a wall built to keep most of the suffering out. When that wall is erected within us as a safe place to hide from the misery of others, we become imprisoned in delusion just as surely as those bound by suffering in the outside world. In the tranquillity and safety of Pah Nanachat there seemed to be a separation from reality, *karuna* performed for the sake of discipline. Refusing to feed a beggar unless he wears an *arahant*'s robes. Yet the chivvy cat gets better.

'I'm going back to the *wat* where I was ordained' said Richard.
    'What about the gay monk?' I asked as we sloshed through the flooded muck of a rice paddy during alms round.
    'I have to take my chances. He should still be in the south. I won't stick around there for long anyway.'
    'Then where will you go? Back to Sri Lanka?'
    'Maybe. Or maybe I'll go to New Zealand and join the

Ananda Margi group. They send supplies to Africa for famine relief. I know they can use all the help they can get.'

'So you'll disrobe and put on the turban?'

'Disrobe, yes. But no turban. I've been wearing too many costumes lately. Knowing me, a turban would be even more trouble than these robes.' The novice's outer garment was again slipping loose around his neck and trailing into the water. 'I may even go back to the States for a while first and work until I save enough money to stay in India a long time. I didn't see much of it the first time.'

Poor Richard. I knew everyone would be relieved to see him leave Pah Nanachat. He did not fit his robes, did not suit his niche in the hierarchy. He knew it too. That at least was good. We had not spoken much on alms round in recent days. I had been downright rude to him. I told him I didn't want to talk while I walked. I just wanted to stay in line and keep up with Ruk, who was always well ahead of us. When he asked me why, I told him it made my feet sore to walk slowly. Since then we had not spoken.

Most likely he will travel, I thought. Richard could spend his life roaming India. He's not a devotee. He's a wanderer, still searching for a conceptual framework for his dreams and drug trips, his fascination with the mystical and the compassion which is genuine inside him.

I found Percy scratching at the leaves with his broom all alone by the back entrance of the *sala*. Although there were four other laymen and two guests staying at the *wat*, he was the only one following the morning sweeping rule. He looked discouraged. His sweeping seemed particularly futile. The section he had just passed over was littered with leaves and berries.

Giving me his courage-in-the-face-of-the-insurmountable smile, he said 'I suppose that's enough sweeping for today, isn't it?'

'There are still leaves all over the compound' I said.

'A few. I like to let them pile up a bit, then clear them all at once.'

'Actually, the reason sweeping is done every day is to

141

prevent them from piling up. Centipedes and scorpions often hide under the leaves. If the paths aren't swept daily we'll be stepping in them. The nasties don't like an open path so much and a black scorpion is easier to spot on the sand than beneath a dead leaf. That makes sense, doesn't it?'

'Yes, I can see that' he said looking around at the debris. 'It's quite reasonable. Don't know why I hadn't thought of it before. We wouldn't want to all go around stepping on scorpions every day. I can see that, yes.'

'Is nobody helping you today? Where are all the new laymen? Where's Herbie?'

'I don't know. I'm all alone. But never mind.'

'Perhaps the new ones just don't know this is their responsibility. Nobody gets told anything directly around here. I'll mention it to Julian and the others. Meanwhile, I'll get a rake and join you.'

I had an ulterior motive. Fetching the largest, best-bristled broom in the pile, I began sweeping close to the Englishman.

'Percy, don't be offended, but why don't you try this broom for a change? Look how well it sweeps.'

'Actually, I always use this broom' he said.

'I noticed that. But such a little broom isn't the most efficient tool for such a big job. If you use a bigger broom and broader sweeping strokes the broom creates a wind, like this. That blows the leaves right off the path. Here, you try it.'

We traded brooms. Percy took a couple of practice sweeps. Leaves fluttered in all directions. He looked as if he would topple over and fall.

'It's a bit heavy' he told me, biting his lip.

'But see the difference it makes. With those big strokes you'll be able to sweep up twice as much in half the time. I'll go and trade in your model for another big broom for myself. You keep practising. Remember to be mindful.'

When I returned with another, Percy was leaning on his broom handle, talking with the Malaysian monk, Yenaviro.

'Yenaviro has just given me a new pair of white trousers to wear, Tim. The ones I'm wearing have a hole, you know.'

The monk gave me a smile, then disappeared back into the *sala*.

'I suppose I had better go now and try them on' said Percy.

'Why now? They'll be the same size when we finish sweeping.'

'That's subtly put.'

'Subtlety is my speciality.'

We raked for a while in silence.

'So Percy, how long do you think you'll be staying on at Pah Nanachat?' I decided to check my litmus test.

'Maybe two more months. I quite like it here. My breathing is coming along quite well, although I still wish I could get more teaching. I'm frightfully keen on the tapes.'

'How is the congested *chakra*?'

'I think it's getting better. Hard to tell. Certainly I feel much less sinful being here.'

'So when will you be ordained as a monk?'

'I don't think I could do that!'

'Why not?'

'To be honest with you, man to man – there's a girlfriend involved.'

'Ah. She'd be heart-broken if you turned *bhikkhu* on her?'

'Definitely. Perhaps she misses me already.'

'Do you think about her a lot?'

'That's a rather personal question.'

'Sorry. I didn't mean to intrude. I was asking for the sake of your *chakra*. It's a difficult choice, having to choose between women and the holy life.'

'Was it difficult for you?'

'No.'

'Yenaviro, why do Thai women kneel or crouch down whenever monks pass by?' I asked the Malaysian one afternoon while water hauling with him.

'It's so we won't be tempted by the shape of their figures.'

'You get tempted by the old women in Bung Wai village? How long have you been a monk?'

'It's easy for you to laugh. You haven't even been in for

a month. Just try it for a few years. There's a saying an old monk used to tell his disciples. He said "I can give you charms and *mantras* to ward off all enemies who would do you harm, but there is nothing I can give to protect you from the beast with soft horns on its breast."'

'The creature with soft horns on its breast? That makes me want to disrobe right now. Don't say it again.'

'Imagine it after two years.'

'I admit, I can't resist temptation. Soft horns. Okay. Hide them when we pass.'

'It's really not so bad. After all, it's the first pair a man loves the most.'

'Yenaviro! That's quite a remark for a young monk to make!'

'Be honest about it. It's the truth, isn't it?'

'Let me try to remember . . . '

'You can't remember. But there's no comparison. The first pair fed you, didn't they?'

'You, Yenaviro, are a trickier monk than I thought.'

'I had a dream. I was running from a horrible monster' Richard told me on his last day at Pah Nanachat. We were on *bindabhat*. I was glad he had broken the silence between us that had existed since I told him walking slowly made my feet sore. There was a light drizzle in the air. We had not brought our umbrellas. Our robes clung to us with a warm dampness. 'He was like a great gorilla with a hideous face like a devil. Suddenly I realized it was only a dream. I was making it all up. Even the creature chasing me was just part of my mind. I turned around and started running towards the monster. I jumped right into its hairy arms that reached out to grab me. I hugged it close. I wanted to kiss it full in the face. But the face changed. It wasn't hideous any more. It was my own face staring back at me. I realized this creature was just me. I woke up loving everything. Everywhere I looked I only saw my own face. I was happy for days. I knew that everything in the world was perfect just as it was.'

'So you do believe in the Hindu form of pantheism?'

'Of course. But it's Buddhist, too. It's all one, all perfect . . .'

'No. Buddhists don't say all is perfect. There's suffering.'

'But suffering is just illusion.'

'It still hurts, so the world isn't perfect.'

'It's perfect all right. You just don't realize it.'

'I know what is and isn't perfect, and I don't buy the logic of perfection in a world full of pain.'

'Maybe I'm not explaining it too well. Love means accepting everything.'

'Love means accepting everyone. And responding to that actively.'

'You don't seem to understand what I'm trying to say.' Richard was getting frustrated. We reached the tiger gates of our *wat* and walked on barely noticing the wet, hard gravel beneath our feet. We argued about the negative side of *kamma*, or *karma* in Hindu Sanskrit, the doctrine that a being's present suffering is caused by evil actions committed in a past life.

'The law of *karma* means a being is free to do evil, but it will always be done back to him eventually. This keeps nature in a perfect balance' said Richard.

'If *karma* is a law, then I want to violate it every chance I get' I said in a rage. 'It's an excuse for the fortunate to ignore the suffering of the unfortunate and then live with an easy conscience in the face of a need which God, if you bother to believe in him, created us to meet.'

We reached the footbath in front of the *sala*. Richard stepped in and I followed him. It was a small pool. We were forced to stand unintentionally close.

'What I hear you saying, over and over again, Tim, is that you are right and I am wrong.'

We looked into each other's eyes, inches apart. I dropped my gaze to the mud on my feet. 'At least you understand me clearly' I said, stepping back out of the pool and drying my uncleaned toes on the mat.

'It's okay' said Richard. 'I feel a lot of love coming from you sometimes.'

'I hope that makes up for some of my words.'

'I'm glad I found a guy here who wasn't so into his own trip he noticed that some of us need to talk. Nobody else ever really spoke with me here.'

'Good luck, Richard, in your cave up north. Or New Zealand, Sri Lanka, Texas, wherever.'

'I'll come back and visit you sometime.'

'Here at the *wat*? Richard, don't take me for a lifer!'

I needed to send a telegram to my parents. In some other world, their wedding anniversary was about to take place. Julian the layman asked if he could come to town with me since he needed to cash some traveller's cheques. After drink time I wanted to ask the Ajahn for permission for the two of us to make the trip in to Ampher Warin on the following day. But the Ajahn first wanted to speak with Mark. I remained at the back of the marble patio while the two men in ochre conferred. It seemed the teacher had a stomach ulcer. He told Mark he was still in considerable pain. Perhaps this accounted for his tight-lipped manner and the worn expression on his face. He spoke as if the novice were a doctor. After receiving permission for my trip, I found Mark and asked him about his training.

'I just finished my internship this past year' said the New Zealander.

'And you wanted to set up a practice in a Thai *wat*?'

'Not at all' Mark grinned. He was the most emaciated member of the community. His head seemed large and bulblike, accentuated by small eyes and teeth. His complexion seemed to be turning grey. 'I was really in a mess when I finished my internship. I was completely disillusioned with the whole medical system, depressed about it all. I became a doctor to help people, but I didn't feel I was doing anybody any good. All I was doing was patching up bodies. Inside, most of my patients were still emotional wrecks when I sent them out. I couldn't do anything for them. It was worse with the ones I couldn't send home. Hospitals don't know anything about dying people. Doctors keep up this game of saving lives. We don't like to admit it, even to ourselves, when a patient is going to die. There's no real support for dying people in a hospital. I didn't know anything about death and here were people dying right in front of me. It depressed me so badly I had to get away until I found some answers to help me deal with it. That's really why I am here. I wanted to find some answers about death so I can work with dying people. If I want to do it as a doctor, I need to understand it myself first.'

The more I learned about the monks and novices in Wat Pah Nanachat, the more I tended to reject Jim's assumption that they were all losers. Mark's motives for coming to the monastery were probably the most noble I had heard. Certainly they were better than Jim's or mine. He was a doctor and intended to return to the hospital after some tough personal questions were resolved. Yet he was the one easiest to dismiss as a failure on the basis of his bumpy skull, skinny frame and little chin. These things tended to fade when I looked at the steadiness of his eyes.

Julian and I walked out of the jungle into the mid-morning sun. I had forgotten how hot it was in Thailand in June. I had ventured out of the cool shelter of our jungle at dawn. The sun seared our bare heads as we walked towards the highway. We waited in the shade of a wooden bus shelter until a small red truck with two rows of seats along the inside of the back picked us up. We climbed into this local bus and took our seats among half a dozen fat village women on their way to market in Ampher Warin. They grinned and chuckled to each other over the two *farang* passengers, Julian in his white shirt and trousers, me in my robe. Our clumsy pale bodies must have seemed incongruous in Thai religious costumes, especially mine, since the white robe is normally worn only by women.

'Tell me, Julian, what did you think of the Ajahn's Wai Phra *Dhamma* talk?' I asked, curious about the layman's response. 'Do you agree that the practice is enlightenment?'

'I don't have much faith yet. I need more faith for my meditation to progress.'

'Did the *Dhamma* talk give you faith?'

'A little.'

WHAT THE BUDDHA NEVER TAUGHT

'It didn't give me any faith at all. Do you believe that if you just follow the rules you have *nibbana*?'

'If you do it purely, I suppose.'

'The Buddha said the *Dhamma* was a raft, a vehicle to carry you to enlightenment. But like a raft on a river, once you have crossed over to the other side, you are finished with it. You don't carry it on your back. An enlightened person isn't bound by the teachings, according to Buddha, so how can rules and enlightenment be the same thing?'

'It was quite clear to me that the Ajahn was right. If you can be completely mindful of the rules, distracted by nothing, then that's enlightenment, isn't it?'

'It would be perfect concentration. But wouldn't you develop the same thing no matter what you were following as long as you did it mindfully? Mindfulness, not obedience, is the key.' I had to speak loudly to make Julian hear me. The truck roared and the wind battered against the canvas roof. The women were delighted with the show. They hugged baskets full of produce to their bosoms. 'Going to town can be just as much an occasion for mindfulness as following the rules in a *wat*. Everything is a means. You just have to use it with skill. If you use the rules poorly, you can sit in your *kuti* and never break your vows, but you will only get fat and lazy unless you are also striving for meditation.'

Julian put his face to my ear. 'I don't think so' he yelled.

The truck arrived in town more quickly than I had anticipated. We jumped down at a busy intersection, went first to the post office and then to a bank. It was my first sight of civilization since entering the monastery. Buses and cars honked and screeched in the streets. A blind beggar, crouched on a corner, played a bamboo hand organ. We each put a *bhat* coin in his cup. The tellers in the bank stared at us, but they offered iced tea and smiles. I was glad to see city women again, ones who did not crouch when we passed by them on the pavement.

We wandered from the business centre into the crowded produce market. There familiar foods mixed with strange Thai delicacies. Well known to us now were the spiny rambutan, the sweet segments of yellow jackfruit, red lichees, pur-

148

ple-skinned mangosteens, the rough green scales of custard apples and the spike-like armour concealing the stench of the once-dreaded durian which I had come to love. I sniffed its delicate garbagey odour above the rest. The fruits were heaped on tables and piled high in pyramids. They overflowed from bamboo baskets. Further into the market we saw bowls crawling with beetles (cockroaches, I maintained). There were pots full of wiggling black eels, a dozen different kinds of fish, wet and flapping, dried squid, shrimp, unidentifiable shrivelled sea creatures coloured pink and green. The next few stalls contained bushels of black-shelled clams and mussels. Hundreds of live baby crabs struggled to scale the smooth walls of their boxes. Larger crabs lay sedately on top of one another, claws bound tight with twine. Nearby were bowls full of baby frogs – a Thai speciality, peeled and deep fried whole. Larger relatives hopped futilely in baskets, keeping their legs in good tone, since those were their selling point. In another section we found chickens, fresh and clucking, legs bound together. Satisfied buyers carried their birds by the feet. The hens hung upside down, staring with patient stupidity. For a quick meal they could be bought split and roasted on wooden spits. We watched a child gnaw a deep-fried rooster head on a stick. A popular snack. Deeper into the meat section blood and sausage and piles of grey-green animal organs surrounded us. Pig heads for sale, sheep eyes, buffalo tongue, liver, kidneys, hooves and jowls. Steel cleavers sliced thin strips of fatty bacon and dirty hands cut to order pieces of flesh for the customers. This was a food market full of the reality of life and death, both for sale this morning. Behind us, radios blared from a dozen noodle shops and rice stalls wedged up against the side of the market. Mekong whiskey and Singha beer were both displayed on every counter for shoppers with a thirst. We rushed through to the vegetable section at the far end. It was a blaze of colour. Corn, cabbage, green geodesic whatnots, horn-like purple bamboo shoots, fiery red chillies, ginger fingers like leprous hands, lettuce heads, a dozen varieties of leaves, carrots, cucumbers, wrinkled green pumpkins, squashes, gourds and baskets of sweet

149

baby corn. We squeezed out of the other side of the market dizzy with smells and kaleidoscoping colours, the petty struggles for life left behind us.

We retreated to a quiet restaurant. Julian ordered a Sprite. I wanted a glass of Mekong whiskey, but drank orange juice instead. The bottle was full of chemical additives. In Thailand, where everything is available fresh, they don't need sweeteners, colourings, preservatives or artificial flavourers. But that's not what the consumer wants. He wants it in a plastic bottle, with plenty of additives added. If it's fresh squeezed, nobody will buy. The markets will soon be replaced by supermarkets. They will wrap all this ugly life up in plastic and freeze it.

Julian and I returned to Pah Nanachat in time for a cup of tea at the end of community drink. We arrived to hear the Ajahn announce that the rest of the afternoon would be another work day on the leaves. I went back to my *kuti* to drop off my white *pahkow* handbag and some new thongs I had bought. I felt frustrated that a whole day would pass without time for a concentrated sit.

'Piss on it' I reflected quietly. I sat down under the cover of my mosquito net and promptly fell into the second *jhana*. Whatever it is that clicks, suddenly clicked. My breath came through clearly, easily. It sustained itself with a perfect concentration never before achieved. Thoughts arose from time to time, but they could not intrude. I was aware only of balance, of ease, and of the steady flow of air through my nose. It seemed odd to locate that sensation in an external place. It was a surprisingly active state of mind, neither automatic nor trance-like. Only moment by moment concentration could sustain it. It required energy but produced no stress. When my knees began to ache, I noted the feeling without the usual temptation to shift and relieve the pressure. I knew that to move would end the *samadhi* and I had no desire to do that. I felt I could sustain the state indefinitely. Still, for the sake of my knees, after forty-five minutes I returned and opened my eyes. I hadn't expected it would come so quickly. Yet it was the reason for which I had been sitting and trying to focus for near to a month. Perhaps something was grasped, or something shaken free by the marketplace. I did not know. What I cherished was the feeling of ease. I thought I could recall it at will.

CHAPTER TEN

What the Buddha Never Taught

I went early to the wash pump, still a little shy around the others for skipping yesterday's work duty. Already I had heard one or two indirect remarks about it. I didn't like it when others skived off, yet my own irresponsibility led me to my best sit of the season. I felt justified in following the spirit – but not the law – of the *wat*. I am here to meditate, not rake leaves, I thought, mindful of my disobedience.

My robes were grey and sweaty from the trip to market. I added a little bleach to the wash bucket and began to scrub. I remembered Richard on his way back north. He had left quietly that morning before alms round. I was sad the monks could not accept him for what he was. Not pleasant to see anyone pecked off the roost, especially in a Buddhist coop. True, without his enticing conversation, I would have peace on *bindabhat*. Our bizarre discussions would no longer reverberate in my skull whenever I sat down to meditate. Richard had found in me a source of support, a sounding board for his need to vocalize. But I was only half a friend and he knew it. Our talks were always painful to me, an addiction I couldn't resist, until I told him I didn't want to talk.

Richard may have resented my intimacy with Jim. Every word with my twin was to me an insight shared, an experience enriched by our complementary perspectives. Jim kept me exposed to a view of the *wat* which was often negative, but definitely valid.

The tall *pahkow* arrived with his own laundry while I was

thinking nice thoughts about him. I watched with fondness as he pumped a bucket full of water, added suds and crouched down next to me. His skull was beginning to grow a little fuzz on top. We had shaved each other's heads last week. I cut him so closely he said I must have taken the roots off. He doubted his hair would ever grow back. It was an act of mutual trust. A little blood had been shed between us but the ritual made us bald brothers.

'I'm glad your hair's coming back now, Jim' I said affectionately.

'It's at the velcro stage. I can't get my undershirt off without it sticking.'

'I know. My head keeps getting stuck on the mosquito net. That first millimetre of hair clings to everything. Would you like me to sandpaper you down smooth again?'

We laughed. I felt light-hearted to be able to share these little things in an environment which could have been so isolating. Suddenly Jim stopped. He looked away from my eyes and into his soaking laundry. When he looked back again his smile was gone.

'I've decided to leave' he said.

'Before you attain perfection? Give it a few more years.'

He held my gaze. He was serious.

'When?' I asked softly.

'In a week. Maybe two if I stay for Buddhamas. Don't get quiet on me, Bob.'

'So you'll be staying barely a month instead of three?'

'It's this system. I can't put up with it any longer, all the bowing, the hierarchy, the exploitation of the villagers. I see them working in their fields when we set out on alms round each morning. It's not for me to live on their backs. You know I've been miserable here. It's no reflection on you. I know you are getting a lot out of it. That's fine. I finally realized I just didn't want to be a part of this. I realized I can go home any time I want. Suddenly all the desires that had tormented me left. My miserableness just dropped away. I don't feel bad any more. It wasn't missing home that was the problem, it was being stuck here, suffocating where I don't belong. Now that I've made the decision to leave, being here doesn't bother me. Do you know what was keeping me in Pah Nanachat?'

'What?' I asked dully.

'The thought, "What will I tell my friends in America and the people I lived with in Chiang Mai? Everyone will be disappointed with me." It's the same old ego trap, worrying about what other people think. It's ridiculous. There's no sense in staying if I'm unhappy, so I'm going home. I feel it from the gut. This is the right decision for me.'

I stared into the grey water of my laundry pail. 'I really want to argue with you, Boomer, to convince you to stick out the next two months with me. But I know the only real reason for it is that I'll miss you when you go. That's not something to argue about.'

I grabbed my wet *sabong* from the bucket and vigorously scrubbed at a spattering of red mud on the hem.

Richard gone, Jim going. They were the ones on either side of me in the hierarchy. Pretty soon there will be nothing left for me but to sit in my *kuti* all day and meditate. If Jim does leave, I will try ten days of solitude. Herbie can bring me scraps from the kitchen. I'll sneak out to the washing place mid-mornings when it is deserted. I will empty my *kuti* of books, the bowl, the lantern, throw all the junk accumulated in my homeless life out of the door, live without tools, strip the psyche bare and pry that crack in the ego open so wide that the whole ghost disintegrates back into dust. . . .

In daily meditation my mind wanders through the same familiar fantasies. I travel through China to Tibet. I return to university in Canada, teach courses and write a brilliant book. Always dwelling in a non-existent future, again and again I struggle to bring my mind back to the simple present, to walking and breathing, away from the voice which cries in my head, 'I, I, I'. I know I can survive here alone despite my distractions. Richard has left. Jim will leave. I came here to live alone. 'I can put up with hierarchy, with complacency, with exploitation. As long as they give me a chance to meditate' I say to the bird on my branch, 'and let me breath through the little crack opened through that first touch of *samadhi*.'

At morning meal Jim told me he would leave in just a few more days.

'I thought you said you were staying two more weeks, at least until Buddhamas.' Buddhamas was the name Ajahn Chah gave to a major festival held each summer in honour of the Buddha's birth, death and enlightenment. It was a time of great excitement at the *wat*.

'I thought I would too, then today on *bindabhat* I realized that would be spending two weeks waiting for something I didn't really care about. I have better things to do with my life. I could be home in less than a week if I want. I could leave by Monday. I don't have any reason not to leave by Monday. That's four more days. I decided I'll go to Bangkok, change my air ticket, then travel to Chiang Mai to say good-bye to the family I lived with. They will be disappointed, but it doesn't bother me. I'm going home. I'll spend my last few days back in Bangkok with a stewardess friend of mine who works for Thai International Airlines.'

'So it's a stewardess that makes you so eager to chuck your vows!'

'Don't worry about me, Bob. I don't have any plans to break that third precept until I'm back in America. It could cause too much trouble in Thailand. A lot of women want to marry a passport – another reason for me to get out of the country. I've been a good boy for over ten months – don't look so surprised. Remember, I'm just a tender sophomore, not a hardened world traveller.'

'What a waste of dedication for you to throw up the robes. Ten months? That's renunciation. I've been thinking, if you go, there's no one left for me. It's a chance for me to try isolation meditation. I want to do it for about ten days, just staying in my *kuti*, not seeing or talking to anyone.'

'That's heavy stuff. Are you sure? You don't want to go any crazier.'

'What's the difference? Once you leave, I'll have no reason to talk to anybody. I'm here to meditate, not follow the rules.

Don't worry, I spent five days in a cave in the Himalayas. I've wanted to do a longer spell for some time. Besides, my alternative is to spend my life sweeping leaves with Percy in a *wat* full of work days.'

The Malaysian monk, Yenaviro, would often sit at the robe-dyeing shed near the wash pump and whittle long thin sticks into strands like wicker. He would be there most days when I came early to do my washing. I liked to avoid the late afternoon rush. Intent on his work, his brown face would concentrate on smoothing the sticks into delicate wooden tubes. Often the two of us would be alone. We talked while he worked and I scrubbed at my stains.

'Being a monk is not easy' he told me.

'It seems easy to me' I said. 'You don't have any work, you don't have any responsibilities, any causes to fight for or enemies to fight against. All you have is your little monk duties and meditation to fill up your day and give you some self-esteem. The homeless life seems pretty cushy to me.'

'You're just a *pahkow*. It is an easy life for you. Don't assume you know what it's like for us. There's no pressure on you. If you break a precept it doesn't matter. You can do as you please. If a monk makes a mistake he can really suffer for it. In a community this small, everybody knows everything. You don't keep many secrets. The smallest things make you miserable for weeks. There's no escape. Sometimes the other monks make you want to quit. If you break a rule they look down on you. It can drive you crazy.'

'I guess you *bhikkhus* don't even have anything strenuous to work off the anger on.'

'It's an offence even to get angry! We have to respect each other. Harsh words are forbidden.'

'I worked on an oil rig once, Yenaviro, and there we had only two kinds of relationship between members of a crew. You tolerated each other or hated each other.'

'We can't hate. We can't even think bad thoughts about somebody else. If I do, I feel terrible.'

'So you can't take a swing at a brother even if he needs

to be kept in line? A fight's not always a bad thing. It helps to let off steam.'

'It's a serious offence for a monk to hit another monk.'

'What if he provokes you?'

'To provoke a monk is also a serious offence.'

'Sometimes these rules make sense. I admit, I feel the pressure inside myself already. Not that I'll hit anybody.'

'Try it for three years. We're not even supposed to feel resentment. We're supposed to cultivate shame. We're taught to be sensitive to what others think about us. That's why the rules were laid down, to develop our shame.'

'It would drive me crazy. Shame just keeps you tied to your past bad acts. How is that a virtue?'

'It will prevent you from repeating them. But shame isn't the worst part of a monk's life. The worst part is the boredom. You can't meditate all the time. Year after year, the same thing every day. Nothing new, nothing new, sometimes it makes me want to scream. For the first few years you can learn the chants. It's all kind of fresh and exciting. Well, maybe not exciting . . . '

'If you feel this way, why be a monk? Doesn't it seem like you're wasting your life?'

The monk put aside his sticks and spoke directly to me. 'Out there in the world it's even worse than here. Everyone runs around trying to make money, trying to buy happiness. They only end up miserable and in debt. Running and running; after a while you're not even running for happiness any more. You end up running to pay the bills. At least here, when you are bored, that's all there is to it. Boredom is just boredom. You live with it. You don't run around trying to change it into happiness.'

'What did you do before you became a monk?'

'I was an accountant.' Yenaviro turned again to his bundle of sticks. One by one he held them to his eye, checking the length for straightness.

'Yenaviro, can I ask a personal question?'

'I suppose so. But don't pick on me any more.'

'Pick on you? I wasn't picking on you.'

'What about the easy life you said we monks lead?'

157

'It's just the way I talk. I'm glad I mentioned it. You showed me how difficult it really is.'

'You can ask.'

'What are you doing with those little sticks of wood? I think you are doing a fine job on them, getting them all round and smooth. I notice you've been doing it for a long time.'

'This is my second batch. I made the first batch too thin. Last week I had to start all over again.'

'You wouldn't want them too thin. I can understand that. Too bad.'

'Not really.'

'So what are they for?'

'A bowl stand. I'm building my own bowl stand.'

'But you have a bowl stand.'

'Not one I've built for myself.'

While we were talking, Ruk came out of the jungle with Sun Tin. They were pulling a cart loaded with deadwood. Ruk was soaked with perspiration. Sun Tin's crooked grin stretched wide across his face. They placed the larger logs on two sawhorses and began to cut the wood with a two man saw, stacking it at the woodpile under the tin roof of the dyeing shed. The Thai and the German breathed heavily. Sunlight glistened off the sweat on their bodies. When they had finished, Ruk came over to sit with us. Sun Tin cooled off under the water pump.

'Ruk, what does a monk do while waiting for his five *pansa* to pass?' I asked.

'There's plenty to do' he said with a smile. He wiped his glasses with his drenched ochre sash.

'But what do you do most of the time?'

'Watch boredom arise.'

In my *kuti* I had fallen prey to sleep again, lulled into it by a false sense of confidence. I had been wrong. *Samadhi* did not return with ease. It was as fleeting as ever. I awoke when the bell called for evening chanting, the thrum of the elephant bugs already fading into the night. I rushed through the dense jungle air, arriving late. Dark forms had already filled the *sala*. I joined the silent walking back and forth, trying to concentrate on the touch of the cool tile floor on my bare feet. I tried in vain to attune myself to the wavelength of bliss which had been so calming. Something inside me felt heavy like an undigested lump of sticky rice. The dull dread of separation. Jim could go. I would survive. I could learn to watch boredom arise. Yet there was more than that. I walked out of the hall and stared at the waxing moon through the tree tops.

The silent voice questioned me.

'Why so sad?'

'I feel bad about Jim leaving.'

'Separation from the liked is suffering.'

'But there's something else. His reasons for leaving are sound, but a good reason isn't always a true answer. I sense he's not being honest with me or himself. He told me he thought Pah Nanachat was the ideal no-stress environment he had always dreamed about whenever he was miserable at school. He said his present misery he couldn't blame on the conditions here. Yet now he says he's leaving because he isn't happy. He says the system repulses him. Is the system in America any less exploitative? Where will he go to find a perfect system? He won't be happy at home either and he knows it. Then why run away? I think life here is depressing Jim because he can't do anything. He can't even build a bowl stand. There's nothing to distract him from the fact that he's suffering and he can't stand knowing that there is no external cause for it. It's not environment, it's him. He's running away from something wrong in himself. I feel I should tell him so, force him to acept that it won't be any better in the States. Wherever he is, he'll suffer.'

'And you?'

'I'll still be here.'

'And you?'

'What about me?'

'Will you still be suffering?'

'Me? Suffering?'

'You, suffering.'

'Because Jim is leaving?'

159

'Because with nothing to distract you, you will know . . . '

'I'm not suffering. Not like Jim. There's nothing wrong with me.'

"Then where is your *samadhi*?'

'Distraction is natural.'

'What happens when you sit to meditate? Your mind runs from one fantasy to another. You forsake the present by travelling in the future. You busily write books about that which you have yet to experience. You cannot keep still. Do you have peace?'

'Some.'

'From whom do you run?'

'It's not wrong to dream a little.'

'Did you come here to dream? You trade reality for that which does not exist. Why?'

'I don't know.'

'Why?'

'I don't know.'

'Why?'

'Because, because, damn it, I can't stay alone with my breath. My mind runs wild, out of control. I panic. Is this what you want to hear? Alone with my breath, I suffer.'

'Then what will you tell Jim?'

'That he – that I – that we are running. Does everyone run from himself?'

'All is suffering.'

'When I was in Nepal, I dreamed about India; when I was in India I wondered about Bangladesh. In Bangladesh I longed for Burma; in Burma I yearned for Thailand. Always running. The present never satisfies me, never gives me what I want . . . '

'The present is just your environment.'

'And there is nothing wrong with the environment. It's me. There is something wrong with me.'

'Who are you?'

'Illusion.'

'Bob? That you?' Jim's voice whispered behind me in the dark. Moonlight cast our shadows back through the doorway into the *sala*. He looked like a great white *pee bah*, his robes glowing dimly. I grabbed him by the sash and pulled him around the outside corner of the temple to the place we had sat and talked last Wai Phra eve. He seemed wary of my vehemence.

'Listen until I finish' I said. 'You say you are leaving because you're unhappy here. But you are not suffering because of the place. You are suffering because of you. Here you just can't hide from it. It's true for me too. In my meditation time, I run from the present and live in my fantasies. All our complaining about Pah Nanachat just distracts us from the real problem: our dissatisfaction is on the inside.'

He grabbed my clenched fist which still held his sash. His hand was like ice. 'That's exactly what I came to tell you' he said to me.

We released each other and slumped back in a daze against the outer wall of the *sala*. Neither of us moved. Inside the hall, chanting had begun. The clouds began to smother the moon, dimming the pale light. Fireflies zigzagged through the trees and danced beside the metal water tank.

'You came to tell me the same thing?' I said to my twin.

'It's not the place I wanted to run from. It's me. I was even going to warn you, if I had the nerve I think you are running too.'

'So all *samsara* is suffering? Every one of us suffers. Wherever we go, whatever we do, we are running to avoid the suffering that sits inside us.'

'Even living in a monastery is suffering' Jim said.

'Living in America is suffering' I said.

'Living in Thailand is suffering.'

'Living is suffering.'

'If it's all suffering, Bob, what do we do?'

'I don't know. It's depressing to think about it.'

'Do we kill ourselves?'

'I don't know. Maybe we just get reincarnated if we try. It solves nothing, just adds more bad *kamma*. Life rebounds at you.'

'I don't believe in rebirth.'

'Me neither. Maybe the concept was invented to keep all Asia from self-destruction.'

'Death is a great pain reliever.'

'But suicide can't make suffering any better if there's no one left to feel relieved.'

'You feel relief knowing you're about to die, knowing there will be an end.'

'We're all going to die anyway. That should provide relief enough.'

'Suicide makes it shorter.'

'But if you know it will end eventually, you can endure.'

'Why endure? Why not simply die, or run away and hide, keep up the fantasy, keep busy, keep high, stay stoned, lie to yourself that you're happy and hope to God you burn out fast.'

'Stay pretty, die young, you mean? It's illusion, Jim. You still know you are lying to yourself.'

'Do you suffer any less with knowledge?'

'A reckless life hurts others too.'

'They suffer anyway' said Jim, falling silent beside me.

The question of suicide had become deadly serious. My mind probed possible refutations to Jim's logic. But this was no longer strictly philosophical. The clouds had fully blotted out the moon. I could see only the dark outline of Jim's face. A firefly landed on the hem of his robe, creating a small green-white glow. Gently he brushed it off.

'Tell me one thing' I asked. 'Why didn't you load a second cartridge?' The question hung in silence.

'I don't know.' Jim rested the black shape of his head on his knee. 'It's something you build up to. When it was a dud, out of all the cartridges made in the USA, that fact shocked me. I couldn't do it again.'

'How did you feel? You were deprived of relief. Why not simply say "even bullets don't work for me in this life" and load up again?'

'It's difficult. There was a moment when I was ready to do it. Afterwards – same thing the second time with the train. It was twenty minutes late. But I was still there when it came. I stood on the bridge and watched it pass. Something changed. I couldn't do it any more.'

'Why not? What in you wanted to live?'

'Nothing. It just felt futile. There was no purpose to it. I suppose suicide is the supremely egoistic act. You judge yourself worthy of death and appoint yourself as executioner. It's a self-righteous fantasy. I never thought of it like that before. At the time I just wanted to get it over with.'

'So you're alive because it was futile to try and die?'

'It doesn't make me feel any better. Sisyphus just rolls the rock, but he's not happy.'

'Why Sisyphus? Why not Buddha or Jesus? What about your professor-guru and my meat exporter? Maybe they suffer too. Still they make their lives worth living. I have more to learn from them before I say suicide is better. Maybe that's what faith is, hanging on to the belief that the *arahants*, saints and *bodhisattvas* have found something genuine. We just don't know it.'

'You're telling me to hang on faith?'

'Faith is just patience. Jesus and Buddha, I think they actually did advocate suicide. They said die to yourself. The thought "I am" is to be eradicated. It's the ego, the self, the monkey-mind that does the suffering. What wants happiness? Not the body. The ego wants happiness. But what the Buddha taught was that ego was an illusion.'

'I sure believe in it.'

'So do I. We've all created an illusion, a thing we want to believe in so much we let it torment us all life long.'

'It causes a lot of suffering for something that's not real. Is suffering illusion?'

'Suffering is real. But it's caused by wanting something that's not real. We want a stable sense of self, but the world doesn't support it. That's what suffering is. Do you remember the story the Buddha told about the mangy dog? Buddha saw this mangy jackal running from place to place, into the bushes, then into the field, then over some rocks. It lay down, stood up, ran around, stopped again. Everywhere it went it was suffering horribly from mange. But the poor dog thought the itching was caused by its position, so it ran round and round trying to escape its suffering. It was senseless. The jackal's problem wasn't the environment; it was the mange. He carried it with him.'

'So we've got the mange? Is that why we shave our heads?'

'We've got mange as long as we've got ego.'

'Then how do we kill it?'

'I don't know. Meditation? *Samadhi*-suicide? My stomach hurts. If I could kill my ego right now just by putting a gun to it, without hurting my body or whatever lives besides the "I am", I couldn't do it. When I became a Christian I thought I died to my old self so I could be born again. I still believe in that, but the old self still isn't dead. It doesn't want to die, either. It just became a Christian-type self.'

'So you still suffered? It seems kind of pointless.'

'Pointless, pointless' I mumbled. 'No, there was a point. I really wanted to become Christian. Maybe that was the problem. I wanted to become something. The ego lives by pointing into the future, and making its points stick. This is how we shore up the illusion that the self is real. We try to make something solid out of the points we make in life – even through the self-righteous judgement of suicide.'

'Then if we stop trying to make points, we cut off the ego.' Jim spoke slowly, working over each word before speaking. 'That would force us to stay in the present, kill our fantasies. Law school is pointless, going home is pointless, meditating is pointless. . . . ' Jim's voice droned in unison with the monotone chanting of the monks which floated out from the temple.

'Writing books is pointless, travelling is pointless' I took up the new litany.

'Living in Pah Nanachat is really pointless.' Jim giggled in the darkness.

'You're pointless, Boomer.'

'You're pointless, Bob. That's all we've got to remember. There's no point in making points. It sounds too easy. But I feel something changing just knowing there's no need to struggle for what I can't have.'

'I still feel sick. It's depressing. What's the point of being pointless if you don't make any points at it?'

'Don't repeat that.'

'If I don't make any points in life, then my ego will wither and die. But then there will be no one to take satisfaction in how good a job I'm doing, or even to enjoy not suffering. If you act without ego, then there is no pay-off. You just do it. You don't get any points for not making points. There's no reward. There's no happiness, because it's the ego that gets happiness. If I stop making points, no more suffering and no more happiness. I could give up happiness if I thought I was getting something from it, even something mystical beyond words. But giving up making points means even if there is something beyond, the ego which is me can't benefit from it. It is pointless.'

'How do we practise pointlessness?'

'Sit in a *wat* for five years. Isn't that what these monks are doing? They just sit around bored, watching youth and career and marriage pass them by. You said yourself you feel suffocated here. That's their goal. Suffocation of the ego. They bore their selves to death. Here there's no place to run. They give up all distracting activity. The ego stops breathing, like a shark caught in a net. That's why our minds get so frantic and restless. They are struggling for air, struggling for a point to make. That's why we are just supposed to passively accept the rules. Even our attempts to follow the spirit of the precepts are just our egos asserting themselves. They are desperate. Look at your misery, look at my fantasy – our egos want out where they can breathe.'

'But these *farang* monks, Tim, they aren't suffocating. They just use the monastery and the rules to make points. They call themselves blessed disciples and allow the Thais to bow down to them. All I see here is ego. They think they're holy. Do you think they believe they are here to be bored into enlightenment?'

'Some, yes.'

'This place is full of ego. I go to the Buddha, I go to the *Dhamma*, I go to the *Sangha*. I'm a novice, I'm a *bhikkhu*, I'm part of a tradition that's twenty-five hundred years old and comes straight from the Buddha. I follow the precepts, so I'm a noble being. Can you think of a better way to make points than by coming to a *wat* so that your little ego can get itself enlightened?' He started laughing and I thought he might disturb the monks inside. He didn't seem to care.

'You're so hard on the poor monks. They don't want to be worshipped.'

'You are wrong. You remember the Thai schoolgirls who interviewed us? I never told you, but often Thai visitors would start talking to me because I could speak their language. They would ask me what I thought of Pah Nanachat. You know how I feel. I don't like to lie, but I couldn't just tell them I think the place is full of complacent losers. I went to the Ajahn to ask how I should deal with visitors according to the rules. I said it was a distraction. "The best response is to maintain a noble silence" he told me. "If the monks talk to the lay people too much and get too friendly, then respect will begin to disintegrate. We should preserve a proper distance. Otherwise there will soon be joking. They will stop bowing to us. Things will start to break down." Do you believe this is from a man who teaches impermanence? "Things will start to break down." Our teacher is mighty concerned that the villagers may some day stop worshipping him and the *sangha*. The *sangha* here is all ego, dedicated to making points along the noble path.

'Do you know what is craziest about my bad feelings towards Pah Nanachat? I can only see complacency and manipulation here, and I hate it. But I think it will change my life. No matter what happens now, if I get depressed, I can't blame it on the conditions. I know I can't escape. Even suicide is just ego. There's no way out. If I can accept that, maybe I'll stop trying to run. It won't make me happy. Happy or unhappy doesn't seem to make a difference any more.'

'You mean it's pointless? I always feared there would come a time in my travels when suddenly it would all be futile, when I'd understand there was no purpose to the journey. Then I'd just go home. Now there is no purpose. Do I go home?'

'Dummy. You don't have to go home. You can still go to China, still write your books. Or you can go back to Canada and maybe write better books about ice and snow than you could about Asia. Either way is pointless. It doesn't make a difference, and it won't do you any good. That's all we have to remember: nothing will do us any good. There are no points to make along any path you choose.'

'Boomer, do you suppose this is enlightenment?'

'What difference does it make?' He laughed.

'My ego wants a structure to hang this on. It wants some defined goals for a pointless life. It wants to score points out of pointlesness. My ego still wants to think it's getting enlightened.'

'You don't "get" enlightened.'

'The light comes in when the ego goes out. Nobody's left to get it.'

'What's the point in making it into philosophy?'

'No point. No difference. It just feels empty inside, like a hole's being carved out of my stomach. Will you still go?'

'It doesn't make any difference. No point in leaving. I'll leave. Monday. You?'

'No point in staying. I'll stay. No point in missing you.'

The chanting stopped. Dark robed forms shone beams of light out into the trees. Carrying their flashlights to ward off scorpions, the monks glided out of the *sala*. We sat in silence until the last of the lights disappeared into the jungle. Jim rose to return to his *kuti*. I walked into the dark and empty temple.

Two altar lights had been left on low, causing the Buddha images to shine with a tarnished glow. I took my place on the mat and gazed at the giant serene forms, their lips closed in the all-knowing smile. I had come to Pah Nanachat prepared to root out that which separated me from the knowledge behind this smile. I was prepared to right a balance in my psyche, as long as the gain was worth the sacrifice. But when the ego is given up, there is no gain, no satisfaction even in knowledge. From where I could see, only darkness.

'I go to the Buddha for refuge.' What teaching can induce one to enter darkness? You cannot teach a bird to fly, only how to let go his branch and begin to fall. The night felt awful and empty inside. 'Trust only your own experience.'

It seemed safe enough. Sacrifice yourself, and gain nothing. You never taught us that.

The vacant hall suddenly fills with a loud and penetrating thrum, the thundering swell of an elephant bug somewhere in the *sala*. It decrescendos. I hear the creature fly from place to place. In flight it buzzes like a two-cylinder engine. I stare around in the dimness, trying to follow its path. Startled, I see a black human figure crouching near the monks' plat-form. It has been in the *sala* with me all along. Prickles rise on the back of my neck.

'Hello?' I call.

The bug thrums again, deafening. A flashlight clicks on. The dark figure scans the wall with the beam, following the hum. By the light he casts, I see it is Sun Tin, the Thai monk with the crazy smile. His light catches the insect. It flies. He tracks its lumbering flight with the torch until it lands on the floor of the *sala*. He creeps toward the bug as silently as a cat. I want to scream, but I move from my mat to squat beside him. Sun Tin gives me his crooked grin, accepting that I am a little strange to be sitting here in the dark after everyone else has gone. He points to the insect and utters incomprehensible syllables. I nod. The elephant bug strug-gles to free its front pair of legs from several strands of gossamer spider web. The sticky webbing covers its head and feelers as well, perhaps explaining its unusual late night activity. For the first time I see one close up. It is the size of a mouse, shaped like a beetle, with a hard silvery green metallic cover for its wings. Sun Tin grabs it by the ridge of this cover between his thumb and forefinger. He turns the insect over and gently begins tugging the gluey strands from its kicking legs. His face grows serious and intent while he works. The smile disappears. When he finishes he grins at me again and places the bug back on the floor.

'Dee-ma' he says to me, the bug and himself. That's better. The bug seems to agree. As soon as the monk lets go, the silvery green covering opens and the wings spread. We hear the engine-like roar as the elephant bug flies straight up between us, through an open window and out into the night.

Sun Tin looks at me with a smile I think will crack his face. Then he shrugs, tilts his head in a way that means 'I'm going now' and leaves me alone in the empty temple.

'He knows, doesn't he?' I say.

But the Buddha tells me nothing.

CHAPTER ELEVEN

A Perfect Place to Hide

The stones still hurt my feet on *bindabhat*. Farmers in tattered shorts shout abuse at their water buffalo ploughing the rice fields. Ruk is sick so a young Thai monk, Tan Wee, leads me through the village on our morning begging rounds. Old women chat with their neighbours and spit red betel juice before kneeling down to put rice into our empty bowls as we pass. We are part of the rhythm of their day. A little girl helps her grandmother donate coconut sweets wrapped in greasy banana leaves. She puts three into my bowl and I smile at her, risking offence. On the long walk home, I feel hungry. Tan Wee is far ahead of me. I dip a hand into my bowl and pull out a small lump of sticky rice. Although the sun is up, and by the rules I am permitted to eat until noon, a monk would never munch food from his alms bowl while walking on *bindabhat*. I eat the lump. It tastes chewy and a little sweet. I never relished glutinous rice before and often wondered why the others liked it so much. Secretly I eat a second handful, taking care not to be seen by six women planting new green shoots in a paddy. I roll the rice on my tongue, enjoying the added tang of sacrilege. Puddle crabs scuttle out of the way as I pass. The ground is wet with flood water. My feet sink into the path, red mud squirting through my toes. I laugh and walk on the grass and paddy dykes. My mind wanders to the future. I have filled my life with enough plans to keep three people working overtime. The fantasies drop away into the wet, fresh fields. I leave them there and follow Tan Wee's trail back into the monastery.

The teacher had gone to visit another temple that morning. He had been invited there to give a special *dasana*, since it was Wai Phra. Villagers had already arrived at our *wat* to prepare our meal. Several cars were parked at the edge of the compound. More visitors were from Bangkok. We of the community tended to shun these crowds, but when a mini-bus full of Thai monks arrived, it stirred much interest. A famous Thai Ajahn, a disciple of Ajahn Chah's, had come for breakfast. He was ushered into the *sala* and given the seat of honour. Even our own teacher would not sit in it. With him had come half a dozen monks and a few female Thai *pahkows*, old women who would be staying several days in the fenced-off far section of the *wat*. We took our places in the food line while the hall filled with guests, most of whom had already donned their white clothing for the day. They brought fifty-three dishes of food in to us, including the banana and coconut milk dessert usually served only at ordination ceremonies. 'Bhote bananas' Jim called them. Tan Casipo warned us that we must take some food from every dish when many villagers come to feed us in order to avoid offending a donor. Never ever sniff at a bowl and pass it on, the helpful monk advised. Our bowls soon became a jumble of tastes which suited Jim well. Since our decision to fast, he had decided not to crave taste in his food. He religiously dumped fruits, curry, vegetables and sweets on top of one another, mixing them together with his hand.

We gloomily expected the substitute Ajahn would follow our own teacher's practice of giving a long *dasana* in Thai on Wai Phra morning. It was a way of thanking guests for their contributions, teaching us to renounce our appetites at the same time. It was also customary before breakfast for the Ajahn to give the eight precepts to outsiders planning on staying for the evening vigil. The visiting monk did none of this. He gave a perfunctory blessing after the food was served, then munched right into the feast. Perhaps our guest did not know he was required to sing for his supper. It should have fallen on Tan Bodhipalo to give the precepts. The dour monk was doubtless relieved when the holy visitor took his place. Once the meal had begun, there was no graceful way for the number two monk to recover the normal order. The white-clad villagers left, once we were served. Having been denied the precepts, they did not stay for their morning chanting.

'You see Jim, without the Ajahn, things break down' I said as we dug into our loaded bowls. The food was delicious, despite the mix, and despite my early start on the rice. I ate swiftly and without restraint.

'Bob, Bob, take a look at yourself' said Jim, reprimanding me. 'Where is your mind?'

'All over the place. I know what I'm doing.' I laughed. I felt giddy, like sliding on a roller coaster. 'It's not how fast you eat, it's concentration, knowing what you are doing. This morning on *bindabhat* I felt hungry. I started eating rice.'

'On alms round?'

'Why not? We've made eating into such a big deal but that's going in the wrong direction. It complicates life with rules. Keep it simple. As the song goes:

> I eat when I'm hungry, drink when I'm dry
> If the sky don't fall on me I'll live till I die.
> Whiskey, rye whiskey I've known you of
> old,
> You've emptied my pockets of silver and
> gold.

'Go back to your bowl, Bob.'

'If I could put my head inside it, I'd do it. And scrape the bottom with my teeth. That's not forbidden in the *Vinaya*.'

After we had finished feeding, the visiting Ajahn permitted first the higher, then the lower ends of the hierarchy to bow before his pudgy figure and cherubic face. When we finished, he gave us a *wai* which caused Jim to gasp.

'Did you see how high he held his hands? They were halfway up his nose. The higher the *wai*, the more respect is shown. He did us a great honour.'

We washed our bowls and the spittoons as usual, then sat in the sun against the *sala* wall to watch them dry. Both of us had eaten too much. We were content to sit, lazily watching a purple butterfly flit around the water tank. There seemed no point in hurrying back to our *kuties* to meditate. Jim turned and noticed the body of a small lizard dangling from the shutters of a *sala* window. It was limp, bent over backwards, hanging upside down by one foot which clung to the wood with suction-cup toes. It looked ridiculous and sad.

'Must have had a heart attack' I said. 'One minute catching flies, content as a lizard can be; the next, reincarnated as a human being.'

'Now that's a teaching' said Jim. 'Too bad nobody else is here.'

We left it hanging there, a new reminder of mortality. When the sun had soaked up the last of the moisture from our bowls, we slipped the orange wool covers back over them and began lacing up the straps.

'When will you tell the Ajahn?' I asked.

'Today.'

'That's not much notice.'

'I don't think he'll have to close down the *wat* until they find a replacement. I can't wait to see the look on his face when I tell him I'm leaving in two days. Of course, if I never see his face again it won't bother me either. It doesn't make a difference.'

'Do you mean either way you'll suffer, or either way he'll suffer? This doesn't feel very spiritually gratifying, Boomer.'

'It's not supposed to. Why should he suffer?'

'You said you'd stay three months.'

'By his rule I'm allowed to leave any time I choose. Even a monk just has to tell another monk three times that he quits and he's released from his vows.'

'I think the Ajahn will be disappointed.'

'I doubt he really cares. How much attention has he given either of us since we've been here? None. Do you think he'll be concerned about me when I go? No way.'

'If he feels bad, that might be a good thing. I wish he had a chance to hear the things you told me about this place.

Maybe it would have helped the monks to get a better perspective on some of their own problems.'

'It's too bad there wasn't anybody here who could tell it as it is to these guys, Tim. Someone who didn't play the game or fall for the twenty-five hundred year tradition. Someone who could be himself. Don't you get any ideas.'

'I guess that used to be Ajahn Chah. He's back from Bangkok, you know. Tan Casipo told me he was driven to Wat Pah Pong in his special van last week.'

'What's his condition?'

'Stable, according to Casipo, whatever that means.'

'I think they keep him alive like a vegetable so they can keep building branch monasteries' said Jim with sudden anger. 'Since his stroke over twenty new monasteries have been built affiliated with Wat Pah Pong. For the Thais it's a sure way to make merit, giving to Ajahn Chah, an *arahant* if ever there was one living. This happens all the time in Thailand. Once an *arahant* is dead, you can't make merit off him, so the donations stop flowing. They keep him alive in a two million *bhat* air-conditioned *kuti* near his monastery. When he dies they'll build some great memorial to him so that some money will keep coming in. I saw the mausoleum of one teacher from Bangkok. His disciples gilded his body and set it on display. How's that for impermanence?'

'I'm glad you haven't lost your cynical edge.'

'I'm still suffering, with or without it.' We grinned at each other, and went our separate ways in the jungle.

At drink time, my beautiful red cup was gone. I searched all over the kitchen. I thought perhaps one of villagers had taken it. Separation from the liked is suffering. Transience. The objects of our thought are unstable. After drink I asked if anyone had spotted it. No one responded. Tan Casipo helped me search the *sala*. All we found were ants. They had moved from the concrete water tank into the shelf at the rear of the hall.

'Material objects just dematerialize sometimes, don't they, Tan Casipo?'

'Then maybe it will rematerialize as well' said the sympathetic monk. I remembered he was an applied physics student in his pre-*bhikkhu* days. 'Try not to think about it' was his sound advice.

Without the Ajahn, Wai Phra was dull. There was no *Dhamma* talk for us. Tan Bodhipalo set up a taped *dasana* for the villagers. There were far fewer this evening than there were in the morning. We didn't even get medicine with our evening coffee. Jim gulped down two cups of caffeine. I drank three. The night passed swiftly. My own sit was calm but full of mosquitoes. I wrapped my feet and my arms in a blanket and covered my bald head with a sitting cloth. There was no thought, no concentration, no wandering, no energy.

'This isn't meditation, it's suffocation' I thought. 'Death through inertia, that's the goal.'

'You flatter yourself with death' came the silent voice.

'You again.'

'You think you have achieved something? Are sloth and slackness freedom? Have you ceased striving because there is no gain for you? You forget those you held up as examples. Have you done that which has yet to be done? You have only taken a little step along the way. Now you sit inert as a stone.'

'I'm trying to avoid the ego.'

'Who is avoiding?'

'Self, I admit. But I'm not trying to make points. I can't meditate on anything without it being self.'

'Meditate on the non-self. This is freedom.'

'But everything is non-self. Self is only illusion.'

'That should make it easy for you.'

To be or not to be, that is the question.
Neither to be nor not to be, that is the answer.
Avoid extremes.

'Just what is the point of staying up all night on Wai Phra?' I overheard Percy say to Herbie in the dark. I strained to hear the little layman's response.

'There's no point to it' Herbie answered, as if stating the obvious. This was the second time I suspected him.

Making cocoa that morning before dawn, Jim told Herbie that he was leaving soon. No one else knew of Jim's departure, except me. His intent was to draw Herbie out a bit about his own background and future plans. The teenager had indicated from time to time that he didn't have much money. Jim still thought he was a runaway.

'A *wat* is the perfect place to hide' my twin had said. 'Nobody would ever find you. You get food and shelter for free. Look how secretive Herbie is about everything. He hardly eats at all, there's so much tension in him. I'm worried about the kid.'

Despite his inner struggles, Herbie had remained a model layman. Although he seldom did morning sweeping, he was always in the *sala* before *bindabhat*, helping the monks put on their outer robes. He knelt at their feet every day, fastening the clasps inside their robe linings. After alms round he assisted the novices in sorting the rice and goodies into separate basins. He worked silently, without pretension, grateful if nobody took any notice of him. He seldom complained and never asked for more than unwanted olives on Wai Phra nights. He was an example of service and humility to us all, except for the secret smile which sometimes crossed his lips. After the smile, he would laugh, as if surprised at its presence on his face. For an instant his tension would dissolve. Then he would fade into the background again. Otherwise he appeared as flawless as a robot.

Jim's information succeeded in drawing the little layman out of his shell. Herbie confessed that he too would soon be leaving.

'I thought you didn't have any money?' said Jim.

'I wired my mother in Canada. She's sending me some.'

'Where will you go?'

'Peking. I want to take the Siberian express to Moscow, then go to Europe. I have relatives in London. They will put me up for a while.'

'Any plans to go home?' Jim's question betrayed a lawyer's technique, but the concern was genuine.

'No.'

'I'll bet your mother was glad to hear from you.'

'Not really.' He shrugged. 'I just called and asked her to send money. We don't talk a lot.' Herbie turned back to the kettles. He added cocoa to the steaming water and stirred. I could see he was an expert, well trained by Pahkow Michael, long ago.

At dawn there was good news. Mr Chicago was back in town. He had returned from Bangkok with Ajahn Chah and had spent the last week at Wat Pah Pong. Since Ruk was not feeling well and decided to fast through Wai Phra, Mr Chicago went in his place on *bindabhat*, with little Tan Wee wedged between us.

'So, kiddo, how are you progressing?' he asked as we began our walk out towards the gates. Tan Wee was already ahead of us. The older *bhikkhu* seemed in no rush, content to chat with me as we did our morning round. 'Any pretty girls in the villages?'

'There's one who's a real honey, even when she kneels' I said with a grin. 'She's out there with the rice every morning. Pretty, but wedding ring. Some day before I leave I'm going to walk around on *bindabhat* in my civvies just so I can smile back at her.'

'That was a trick question, you know. You're not supposed to look at them.'

'You caught me. I confess, Mr Chicago, I'm glad I'm not in the robes for life.'

'It's Sumeno, Tan Sumeno. You should call me by my Pali name. I remember you from before. I want you to know I've been a monk for over twelve years so you should listen carefully to what I'm going to tell you. This may be the most important conversation in your life. Maybe you haven't considered this seriously. You're young. You have your whole life ahead of you. I was middle-aged before I even heard the *Dhamma*. Remember that it was 27 May 1985 when a monk named Tan Sumeno first said to you, kiddo, "why not throw it all over? Cancel your travel plans. Write to your family and friends and tell them you're not coming back.

177

Get yourself ordained as a novice and become a monk." I'm getting old. This body will soon wear out. You, you've got everything on your side. You could attain enlightenment in this very lifetime if you devoted yourself to the practice.'

I was excited at Mr Chicago's words. At last, a hard sell job, a monk who wanted to convert me. This was familiar territory. After so much indifference from the rest, I loved it. It was something I could argue with. I pondered the monk's words in silence until we had safely crossed the paddy dykes and were on the wide track to the village.

'Why can't I attain enlightenment without becoming a monk? Can't I do it out there in the real world instead of locked up in a *wat*?'

'Kiddo, out there you'd just be swamped by *samsara*. There's no time to meditate.'

'It's *samsara* in a *wat* too, Mr – er, Tan Sumeno. And just as swampy. The temptations may be fewer, but they are more intense. Inside or outside, everywhere is *samsara*. The *Dhamma* only teaches about *samsara*. *Samsara* is what we need to learn about.'

'You don't learn about it by drowning in it. You've got to renounce and restrain, or it drags you under.'

'But I learn best when I'm in the middle of things, when I'm so thick in *samsara* it scrapes against me on all sides like sandpaper. The most productive meditation period of my life happened while I was falling passionately in love with a German woman I met in India who had agreed to be my lover. She was a foreign student in Varanasi. It would have been very bad for her to have been seen with a man. I spent days just watching my desire rise, accepting the complications, letting it pass away. I had to live without expectations that it would ever work out. My lust taught me a lot of patience.'

'Alone you'll never make it' said the monk, shaking his jowls. 'Why not stay? It's much easier.'

'I could stay. There is no real reason for me to go. Either way, I will suffer – I have learned that much here. I guess some people are better suited to one environment than to the other. For me the monastery is a very seductive form of *samsara*. It's tempting to think you are progressing just because you're here. The market place keeps me on the razor's edge.'

'A monk's life is not so easy. Just the other day I was sewing my robe in the *sala* at Wat Pah Pong. The robe was ripped. I had to use an old machine to fix it. The needle always sticks on it and it's impossible to stitch straight. The thread kept breaking. The room was full of mosquitoes, all biting me. It was hot and sweat kept running into my eyes and stinging so I couldn't see. Some Thai people started arguing on the far side of the hall. I wanted to throw my hands in the air and quit, give it all up and just walk out into a new pair of blue jeans. But I persevered until the robe was finished. I struggled with aversion all the way along. After all, I am happier with only three old robes to my name than I was when I used to buy a new suit every other week.'

'Let me tell you how I came to be here, kiddo.' He smiled at me and continued as we passed the lotus pond. 'I was a millionaire before I was thirty-five years old. I ran ten companies out of Chicago. Not little ones either. One of them had over a hundred employees. I was a name in real estate. I had one wife, one ex-wife and a string of girlfriends. I had to be careful because I didn't want the girls to find out about my wives. I had a new car every season and every headache and hassle you can imagine. My businesses were all making money and my friends all looked to me to bail them out of trouble. Some days I felt I was running the world – without any help. Then the IRS and FBI started getting on my back for some small thing. Just another headache. One day I called all my girlfriends and said goodbye. I went to all the directors of my companies, told them they were in charge as of then, and that I was sending over legal papers to put everything into the hands of the employees. I told them to share profits in any way they agreed upon. I came home early in the evening, which surprised my wife because usually I was out late or with a girlfriend. I told her to pack a suitcase. "I have bought two round-the-world tickets for tomorrow, honey. I've sold the house to the agency. Anything you can't take in the bag, give it away." She thought I was crazy. Then I

went out to play mini-putt with three old friends. We hadn't
been together in years. I called them up for the occasion.
We played for a quarter a hole, just like in the old days.
They all loved it. When I told them I was saying goodbye,
they said I was crazy. They said in two months I'd be back
in Chicago. My wife cried. Then they offered to drive us to
the airport. I knew when I left I was never going back.'

'Did you ever go back?'

'I did. Just last autumn, still in my robes. They were surprised to see me, all right, after fifteen years. They were
pretty interested in what I had to say.'

'What about your wife?'

'She went back to the States without me. She's an artist
somewhere in Maine, I think.'

'So how did you eventually find Theravada Buddhism?'

'Theravada Buddhism found me.'

Mr Chicago slung his bowl strap over his right shoulder
as we reached the village gate. The monk frowned and told
me it had been a long time since he had been through this
particular village. He wondered if we had changed the old
route in the last five years. Little Tan Wee was waiting for
us. He stepped into place, looking ridiculously small
between two tall *farang*. Tan Sumeno bowed his head in
quiet humility. Then the ex-millionaire, who still talked like
a real-estate racketeer, led us through the village to beg for
our daily rice.

We started off well, but at the first crossing where there
were no kneeling devotees to indicate the way, the monk
faltered. We could not just wander aimlessly through town.
Our alms givers expected us to pass by their houses. I waited
for Tan Wee to direct, but the little Thai remained silent. We
hovered indecisively.

'Left' I hissed, with as much decorum as possible. Sumeno
turned down the correct road. Although the route had
become part of the pattern of my life, I had always been a
follower, keeping my head bent and my eyes to the ground.
I knew how quickly word would spread through the villages
if it appeared the *farang* monks were lost. It would truly
humiliate us. So I directed our way from the back of the line,

trying to remember in advance which way we would turn, searching for any landmarks to guide us through the rough stilt houses, litter and buffalo dung. Mr Chicago responded to my commands without ever looking back. The only cause for concern among the Thai villagers that morning would have been the constant muttering and peering around of the rude *pahkow*. I was sweating by the time we reached the village *wat*. We came out of the far gate of the village and passed the two giant trees at the edge of the paddy fields. Tan Sumeno suggested I offer to carry his alms bowl back to Pah Nanachat. A more mindful *pahkow* would have done so without having to be asked. When Tan Wee once again walked ahead of us, the elder monk resumed his attempts at conversion.

'If you don't become a monk, what do you want to do with the rest of your life?' he inquired.

'I want to write books.'

'Write books?' He sounded dismayed. 'Don't you think there are enough books in the world already? I remember bookstores from my days in Berkeley, books stacked past the windows. Too many books. Burn the books! That's what I say. They don't do anybody any good. Better to let the paper stay on the trees.'

I couldn't speak. I looked at the mud on my feet. I wanted to argue that the *Dhamma* is also written in a book. Did he want to burn the *Dhamma*? But I knew real *Dhamma* is not a book. His point seemed strangely valid. Especially from the perspective of the trees.

When we neared the shelter of the monastery's jungle, I showed the senior monk a short cut Ruk used which avoided most of the gravel road inside the tiger gates. It led along a slippery mud dyke, across a paddy which was now flooded.

'I remember this field from ten years ago, when Pah Nanachat was first started' said Tan Sumeno. 'Ajahn Sumedo and I used to come out here for walks every evening. I remember he came back here from England for a visit a few years ago. "Sumeno" he said to me, " when you get old and can't get around on *bindabhat*, you'll retire and come to

Chithurst monastery. We'll stay together and just watch the seasons roll by.'''

'And feel your teeth growing long?'

'Meditate on that, kiddo. "Watch the seasons roll by" he said to me. What could be better than that? Remember, I'm telling you this for a reason. Once I thought I had it all: money, business, women, cars, success. Now I have only a nice little hut in the jungle, a twenty second walk away from work. I eat one good meal a day, served to me by beautiful and generous Thai people. I sew my own clothes and spend my days in quiet contemplation. In the end, the body will grow old and weaken. It will return to the earth. But before I die, I will sit on a porch and watch the seasons roll by. . . . '

The monk began to slip off the dyke. Before he overbalanced, he leapt across a little channel of water, landing neatly on a dry section near a clump of bushes. From there, the path led back to the *wat*.

'You still seem pretty spry to me, Mr Chicago. How long did you say you've been here?'

'Twelve years. Twelve years of peace and satisfaction.'

'And you're still not enlightened?'

At the footbath outside the *sala*, I jumped in first, carrying both bowls around my shoulders. Even after weeks on *bindabhat*, my feet were still painfully tender. Mr Chicago looked at me with reproachful eyes.

I knew what I had done. 'Come on in' I said, moving over to the side of the square little pool.

He shook his jowls at me quietly.

'Is it against the precepts for us to take a bath together?'

'That's right. The senior monk should go first.'

'That's a precept? Sorry. I didn't mean to break the law.' I stepped out of the bath with my feet still muddy.

'It's only a rule for convenience in case there is any confusion about who should go in first. It's not that I mind.' He stepped into the bath.

'If you don't mind, then why do we need the rule?'

'Just to avoid confusion.'

'If neither of us minds, then there's no confusion. We

were both pretty confused for a minute. It was the rule that confused us.'

'The rules are so that you can be mindful and control your desires' said the monk, stepping out of the bath.

'The desire to follow the rules just controls other desires' I said stepping in.

'You didn't understand me. You should meditate on what I just said to you.'

'I do, I do understand you' I said to Tan Sumeno's wet footprints. The monk had disappeared inside the *sala*.

I rubbed my hands with glee at the thought of Jim's reaction to my morning conversation with Mr Chicago. The story of riches to robes would disgust him. Yet I was glad the evangelical monk was back in town. I liked having somebody try to convert me. It would give me something to scrape against once Jim had left.

After drink time I helped my twin with the special chores he usually did with Nimalo instead of water hauling. It was their daily responsibility to empty the washing cisterns by the wash pump and fill them with fresh water. Nimalo had gone to Wat Pah Pong for a few days so Jim had taken me on to help with the task. He fumed as I recounted Tan Sumeno's tale. He told me the monk was just like the rest, he had given up on life and settled for comfort and personal peace, sponging off the 'beautiful and generous' Thai villagers who worshipped him.

'But you're a dipshit for that crack "not enlightened after twelve years."' my friend said. "Why should you insult him?'

'Suddenly you're sympathetic to the *sangha*!' I said, surprised and a little hurt at the criticism.

'So he's a failure at his chosen vocation. So he's complacent. So he's living a lie. What points do you make rubbing his face in it? What were you doing playing with him like that?'

'I like him better than you like the Ajahn. I just found some loose links in the armour of his logic I wanted to open up.'

183

'For whose sake, Bob?'

'Ego, Boomer. I'm a slow learner.'

'You're a dipshit.'

I pumped water into the buckets in silence. Jim emptied them into the last of the cisterns to be filled. We walked together past the mango trees, back into the jungle to a well near the furthest *kuties*. There was one more cistern to fill at the toilet nearby.

'Have you seen the moss-aphids?' said my twin, stepping off the overgrown path. He turned up a leaf to reveal a clump of white moss or fungus on its underside. I looked closer. They were insects, each with a delicate feather-like tuft rising from its back.

'It's a perfect disguise' said Jim. He released the leaf. 'I told the Ajahn this morning. I said I'd leave tomorrow.'

'What did he say?'

'He said he didn't have much to say, so he didn't say much. "Lots of people come here" he told me, "but the ones who stay are the ones who are really fed up with the world."'

'Like Mr Chicago.'

'I suppose so. I told him I guessed I just wasn't fed up yet.'

'That's all?'

'It's all he said to me. But I should pass this on to you if you want to know more about Mr Chicago. He came by when I was finished with the Ajahn and wanted to talk with him about a visa problem. The Ajahn said to him, "This is the third time you've come to Pah Nanachat and you've never paid proper respect to the Ajahn. Whenever you arrive at a monastery you know you are supposed to pay respect. You haven't done this once since I came here as abbot. I know I have only one *pansa* more than you. That is a personal matter which doesn't make any difference." Mr Chicago got flustered. He went to pieces like a little child scolded for being bad. "I'm sorry, I'm sorry" he almost whimpered. "I know I still have a lot of aversion inside me. I admit it. But I do like to bow. I know it's good for me. It humbles me. I love to bow. I'll do it now if you like. Next time I won't forget." He kept on talking, but I never saw him bow. No wonder he gave you the hard sell, Tim. He's totally insecure himself. When he heard I was leaving, he asked me to help him with his visa problem. What could I do for him? He wanted me to speak to the embassy. He seemed incapable of doing anything on his own. I said I didn't have a phone where I was staying so it would be hard to get in touch. It was true. Suddenly he changed. "That's okay, we'll probably just bump into each other on the street" he said in a cheerful voice. "That's the way these things work."'

'And I wanted to bully this man, Jim?'

'Like I said, you're a dipshit.'

CHAPTER TWELVE

The Lone Pahkow

I sat near the pump and watched Jim wash out his robes for the last time. Losing him was difficult. No one else would tell me when I was a dipshit. He gave me all his leftover *pahkow* supplies, mosquito repellent, flashlight batteries, a spare cotton belt. I was to pass them on to others when I left the *wat*. Together we hung his dripping *sabongs* and sashes on the clothesline. I promised to return them to the communal cupboard when they were dry.

'The village girls will be sad when the tall *farang* with the big bowl disappears' I said.

'Take my bowl and go in my place. They'll never know the difference.'

'Are you Tim or Jim?'

'Doesn't make a difference.'

'Didn't there used to be two of you?'

'The other one was just a figment of my imagination.'

'Is that what I am?' I laughed.

'What else would a suicidal pseudo-intellectual law student imagine as a jungle companion other than a mystical macho-roughneck world traveller?'

'I've enjoyed being a figment of your imagination, Boomer. Without your perspective I'd probably be complacently on my way to the *bhote*. You cut through my optimism and gave me balance.'

'Without you, Bob, I'd have nothing but loathing for this place. But I learned a lot. You kept me sane.'

'So now we split the twins into their separate insanities.'

'Practice mindfulness, *bhikkhu*, and obey those rules. Write me when you get to *nibbana*.'

'Don't you fall too deep into *samsara* with that stewardess.'

'No way. And if I ever get a letter telling me you're going to be ordained permanently, I'll come back and drag you into the nearest Bangkok brothel.'

Jim looked peculiar dressed in trousers and a blue shirt. Only his baldness seemed normal. I couldn't remember what he had looked like the day we both arrived. We returned to his *kuti*. I helped clear it out and carry his mats, kettle, blankets and mosquito net back to the *sala*. Then I followed him to the Ajahn's hut. The teacher came down to receive him for the last time. Jim dropped his blue day pack beside the stairs and knelt in front of the Australian. I sat demurely at the rear of the marble patio, legs folded respectfully to the side.

'I don't really have anything much to say' said the teacher. He looked detached and pale.

'I just wanted to say goodbye to you sir, and to thank you and the *sangha* for my time here. I learned a lot about myself. I've been given something solid to work with and I will definitely continue to meditate.'

'The important thing is the practice.'

'I'll practise, sir. And if you don't mind, I'd like to wish you good luck.'

'I don't wish for luck, only *Dhamma*.'

'Just a gesture, sir.' Jim laughed a little nervously. He bowed.

The Ajahn rose and started slowly back up the stairs. The two of us headed for the front gates.

'I'm not sure what we went through that night will last, Tim. I want it to stick. I want to find some way of hanging on to it so it will be there when I need it, but it's like quicksilver in my mind.'

'I think that's good. It doesn't stick because it doesn't make points. It teaches us not to stick. It is quicksilver. Remember, even that night won't do us any good. It won't end suffering.

Whatever we do, we will suffer. No particular choice will make us happy. That gives us our freedom from desire.'

We left the cool of the jungle and walked out into hot afternoon sun, following the path between paddy fields to the nearby highway. The grey strip was empty. We stood in the shadow of the large wooden Pah Nanachat signpost and waited. The heat made our scalps sweat.

'What will you do now?' Jim asked.

'Suffer.'

'Tell me how. Will you do your isolation meditation?'

'No point. I was trying to prove something with it, trying to get somewhere.'

'Will you stay the full three months?'

'Probably not. I haven't thought about it. Nothing holds me here. I could leave this afternoon or stay until the rains retreat ends in October. It makes no difference. I won't wait around for enlightenment. I'd like to visit Ajahn Chah before I leave, since he's back in Wat Pah Pong, just to pay my respects.'

'If you quit soon, you can visit me in Chiang Mai.'

'Thanks. I'd like that. My life is hard to predict all of a sudden.'

Vipassana wisdom suddenly sensitized me to highly complex empathetic fluxions manifested as the *kammic* formations of a passing car. I stuck out my hand and flagged it down. It slowed and Jim ran for it. The Thai driver poked his head out of the window. I saw he was pleased my twin could speak his language. Jim threw his little pack in the back and climbed in after it. Spinning wheels kicked up gravel. I waved as Jim sped off towards Ampher Warin and the railway station.

Slowly I wandered back down the path. Water buffaloes lazed in the flooded fields. Above the pools, farmers and their families rested out of the sun in little bamboo and palm leaf huts raised on stilts. Ploughing would resume when the sun was lower. They watched the white-robed, white-skinned figure dawdle. Crazy *farang*, he was frying in the sun. He stopped at the entrance to the Pah Nanachat jungle, not entering its shade. He stood by the gates and stared down the road for a long time.

It was a good five degrees cooler in the jungle. That did not seem like much of a reason to go back. I went to the *sala* and searched through a shelf in the sewing room where the books were kept. I found a copy of the *Vinaya* in English translation. If I was going to follow the rules, I should learn what they are for myself, I thought. I was not searching for loopholes, just slipknots to untie. Ruk was sweating over a new robe on the sewing machine.

'Ruk, what's this?' I interrupted. 'It says here in the *Vinaya* that monks are only allowed to eat medicine if it's been pickled in cow urine.'

'Indian civilization used cow urine for many medical treatments' he said.

'But if the monks are concerned about following the rules, what about the olives we eat on Wai Phra? If they're not pickled in cow urine, this so-called medicine should be forbidden.'

'What do you think they're pickled in?'

'What are you telling me!?'

'That we hold to the *Vinaya* more strictly than you think.'

Evening meditation had been cancelled for the weekly sauna. I arrived late, after most of the others had left, and found Percy alone in the little brick hut.

'I'm finding a lot of inspiration from sweeping leaves these days' he told me when I sat down next to him in the gloomy hot house.

'Tell me your inspiration, Percy' I said. It was time to re-appraise this Englishman.

'You see, it's like this. The universe is always either expanding or contracting, getting more orderly or more disorderly. It's just like the leaves. That's why you sweep them every day. Otherwise it's like the universe. If you aren't mindful, it piles up. Everything increases and gets out of hand. It can give you a headache.'

I heard a splashing noise. Percy had his leg in a bucket of water.

'What's the bucket for? Are you running another *chakra* test?'

'This isn't for the *chakra*. It's for the leg.' He pulled it out of the pail. 'I can't stay in here much longer. Do you want to look at it?'

It was my first chance to look closely at Percy's bad leg. I followed him outside into the fading light. All around the ankle it was mottled purple and puffy from knee to toe. Veins crisscrossed the limb like ugly blue rivers. It could have been dead flesh.

'What happened to you?'

'Broke a leg, that's all. I fell off a mountain. It broke in two places, here and here. They didn't have much in the way of medical facilities in Crete. That's why it looks like this. It didn't heal very well. Back in England the doctors had to strip the veins. They said I was lucky not to lose the leg. I get around on it alright now. Last week in the sauna it suddenly opened up and started to bleed. Mark told me it was the heat. He said I should keep it in a bucket if I want the sauna. He's a doctor, you know. I'm afraid it was quite a scene with my blood all over the place.'

'What were you doing on a mountain in Crete?'

'Climbing.'

I was awed and irritated by Percy's story. This man should definitely be spending middle age in a failing backyard garden, tending dying flowers. He should be miserable in a clerking job and dominated by a fat and shrill-voiced wife. Instead he's been climbing mountains in Crete and puttering through the *ashrams* and monasteries of mystic Asia. I felt a deepening respect for him, even though it seemed natural that if he climbed a mountain, he would be destined to fall.

'You've travelled a lot, haven't you?' I asked.

'On and off since I was twenty four.'

'Do you have a career or trade back in England?'

'Not exactly. I did bits here and there, working in restaurants and shops.'

'You work to save money for travel?'

'That's it.'

I looked at him in wonder. Here is a man who defies his *kamma*. Everything about him decrees he should be in a suburban garden, waging futile wars against the dandelions. But he was living the life of an adventurer, undaunted by the mountains he fell from, heroically scraping leaves around the *sala* in a valiant attempt to keep the universe in order.

'You've been to Crete, haven't you?' he asked.

'Never.'

'I recommend it. The mountains are marvellous. A bit tricky though.'

Soon after Jim left, Mark's mum arrived. From what he told me, this was not just a vacation trip. Mum came from a 'good Christian family' which apparently was deeply concerned about Mark. He said he was surprised at the number of letters he had received from relatives after he sent word of his decision to be ordained. Suddenly his mum decided to come for a visit.

'I didn't think anybody at home really cared about me. It's good just to know they bothered to write, even if they don't understand at all. I think part of the reason mum is coming is to find out if I've been brainwashed. She may want me to go home.'

'I hope you didn't send her any pictures' I said.

I saw her at breakfast. Mum had ruddy cheeks like a farm girl. Her shyness was common for people coming to the *wat* for the first time. Her hair was greying and her whole conservative dress and manner seemed well suited to my concept of what a rural New Zealand mum ought to be. Doubtless, she was very pleased when her son became a doctor. She must have been totally at a loss when he apparently threw it over and left the country; bewildered to have him join a Buddhist monastery. Mums don't generally know a lot about Buddhist *wats*.

A few days later, when Yenaviro asked me to come with him into Ampher Warin to have some passport photos made, Mark asked if he and mum could come along. Mark

191

explained to me that the *Vinaya* forbids him to travel alone with a woman.

'She's your mother' I said.

'Others don't know she's my mother.'

'If others are watching you, you're not alone then, are you?'

'They might think we are going to be alone.'

'Any monk who really wanted to be alone with a woman wouldn't travel to town with her on a bus.'

'It's just a rule for mindfulness.'

'It's a rule for mindlessness, Mark. Besides, you're only a novice, not a monk.'

'Don't pick on him' said Yenaviro, timidly.

'I'm not picking. Heck, I really would be glad to get to know your mother, Mark.'

'Perhaps you could take her through the market.'

'We can all go through together.'

'No. Monks are forbidden' said Mark.

'I see. But since I'm a *pahkow* I can go into the market, alone with your mother, and soil us both in heavy *samsara*.'

'That's just the rules.'

'Stop picking on us.'

In town the conversation worked around again to monks in the market place. Yenaviro said he hated going to town, that he would prefer it if he never left the monastery.

'It just exhausts me. All the noise, all the rush. People yelling and selling, all the hostility, greed, anger, crime. It takes me two days to recover.'

'But the market place is the ideal spot for a monk' I argued. 'It's his destination. A monastery is just a place he passes through on his way to *nibbana*. Once he's attained it, he goes back out into the streets.'

Yenaviro stuck out his tongue as if tasting bitter durian.

'Look at what happens in a busy street when a monk walks through' I said, imagination catching fire. 'Wherever he goes, a true *bhikkhu* is surrounded by an aura of peace. The city's hassles don't penetrate him. His tranquillity penetrates them!'

'I suppose that's right' said the Malaysian monk, wary of

my conversation. 'If some people are fighting and they see a monk, maybe they will feel ashamed and stop.'

'It's much more than that, Yenaviro. The townspeople will feel the cool in the air. Hot tempers will suddenly drop and nobody will know why until they spot a monk. If there is an accident, he will be the first one to offer assistance, the first to tear his robe to make a bandage or a sling. He'll stand between combatants to stop a fight. The partisans will know he is impartial in his judgment. Little children follow him just because he is good to be near. They know he shares their childlike joys. The suffering and the joyful alike are all just waiting for a monk to walk around the corner. They know he is a potential for spontaneous goodness wherever he goes. Without speaking a word he brings comfort. Without raising a hand he brings peace. Compassion and friendship flow from him. People hear *Dhamma* in his footsteps. Isn't this right? I'm not picking on you. Even without his robes an *arahant* is recognized simply by the effect his *metta* has in a crowd. This is why a monk meditates, isn't it? This is why a monk spends five years in a monastery, just being bored. He knows self is an illusion and he wants to live his life in full contact with all beings, free of that delusion. He wants to walk in the streets, sleep in the alleyways, live the homeless life and bring *Dhamma* right to the heart of those who need it most.'

'We're not allowed to preach *Dhamma* on the streets, only to those who come to the monastery. It would be unseemly, throwing it away.' Yenaviro was becoming agitated.

'Casting pearls before swine? Don't preach it, live it. Who needs *Dhamma* the most? Not the ones smart enough to come to a *wat*. What benefit are you if you only speak to those who kneel at your feet and humbly ask for it? People in ignorance don't know how to ask, but they can still receive generosity and compassion, justice and joy. These are a monk's wares for flogging in the market, the four cardinal virtues taught by Buddha. How will they spread if you lock yourselves in a monastery?'

'You should be giving the *dasanas*, Tim' said Yenaviro. 'You make it all sound so easy and wonderful.'

'So why aren't you becoming a monk?' Mark asked.

'Maybe I am. I just don't want the robes, that's all.'

'I thought you said a true monk doesn't need to speak a word' said the Malaysian.

'I did. I guess I'm too busy preaching to practise.'

Yenaviro looked at me with a combination of timidity and hostility. I felt my face turn red. Mark and mum went inside a shoe store to buy sandals. Yenaviro wiped the sweat off his bald head with his hand.

'Are you sure you aren't picking on me?' he said.

Mum was duly impressed with the market. I told her all the interesting stories I knew as I guided her through the jungle of fruit and into the living maze of the meat stalls. I explained that since Thais are Buddhists, they don't like to kill animals. It brings bad *kamma*. But they do like to eat meat, so certain loopholes have been devised. They skin baby frogs alive. Flaying is not actually killing, they reason. Live shellfish they dump into boiling water. This way the water, not the cook, is to blame. Fishermen don't kill their catch. They merely lay them out in the air to suffocate. When it comes to larger animals, there are, fortunately, a minority of Thai Muslims, whose God does not believe in *kamma*, allowing them to perform butchering services for their Buddhist neighbours. Mum declined my offer of a deep-fried rooster head on a stick. I told her it was past noon, so I couldn't have one. She also turned down a small bag of crispy cockroaches to munch. Before I could offer anything else, she suggested a soft drink with the monks once we squeezed clear of the vegetable section.

We made a strange foursome, sitting in the little store, sipping Fanta Orange and Mountain Dew. Mum with her ruddy cheeks, a Malaysian and a Caucasian *bhikkhu*, and a *farang* in a woman's *pahkow* dress. The pudgy shop girls giggled, covering their mouths and whispering to each other in Thai. Their dark eyes danced at us. We sipped our drinks and tried not to stare at the glossy posters of voluptuous nude women plastered all over the walls. These ads for Mekong Whiskey are found in almost every corner shop in

Thailand. Nobody seems to take any notice of them, or gawks like I first did at such blatant and repulsive sexism. They accept it as a fact of life. How this nubile blonde woman with the soft horns relates to whiskey, I never knew. Maybe the ad promised that if you get drunk with Mekong, you will dream about her. Or perhaps when Thai men see the picture, they realize they will never touch a woman like her in their lives and the thought drives them to the bottle. We sucked our soft drinks quietly, glad that Mark was not here alone with his mum.

Without Jim, I had to provide my own cynicism. As a twin I could always adopt the optimist's position, knowing the dirty truths would still be aired. Alone, my thoughts began to grow increasingly negative. In conversation with the monks I became antagonistic. I had assumed Jim's afternoon chore of helping Nimalo empty and refill the bathing cisterns. Jim had admired the Australian novice as the calmest and purest of devotees. I knew he had recently returned from Wat Pah Pong, home of Ajahn Chah. The more I learned about the teacher's paralytic condition and the massive monastery building campaign his disciples had underway, the angrier I became. I wanted to talk with Nimalo and gain a positive perspective.

It was my turn to man the hand pump while the novice filled and carried buckets to the jars. Our conversation was fragmented, spoken in sentences broken by his trips across the washing area.

'Nimalo, you visited Ajahn Chah last week?'

'Yes, and several times before.'

'What's it like?'

'It's very peaceful.'

'I plan to go in another week to pay my respects. Can you tell me why they keep him alive?'

'It's against the precepts to kill. You don't expect monks to kill their teacher, do you?'

'There's no evidence the teacher is within his body any more. He can't even move. They don't have to kill him.' I waited while the novice hauled two full buckets away, and continued when he returned. 'Just unplug him from intra-venous feeding. His body will do what it is ready to do. They could just *koppy* him.'

'They tend for him out of compassion.'

'Compassion for a body with no function left except to die? I can't believe Ajahn Chah wanted to grasp his last few breaths after teaching impermanence and detachment all his life.'

'He's not clinging. He clearly told his disciples before his stroke that if he got sick they should not artificially prolong his life.'

My mouth dropped open. Nimalo left me sputtering alone at the pump handle.

'After the stroke' he continued, back with empty buckets, 'the senior disciples decided they couldn't just let him die. All Thailand would be angry if they did. It would cause division and disgrace. How could they let a holy man die?'

'Nimalo, I can't believe the disciples ignored their teacher's wishes out of fear of the crowd. Who do they believe? Who do they follow? The Ajahn's not even dead and they've forgotten every word he ever taught them. They are clinging to a body and collecting a fortune in donations from his name. Are they just weak or are they despicable?'

'It's not like that. There's no proof he's not inside his body.'

'I hope to hell he's not. Would you like to be stuck for three years inside a breathing corpse? All he could do is wait for death and watch his monks disobey his instructions. The teacher hasn't even left the classroom and the students have forgotten what he taught. If there's any of Ajahn Chah left, I hope he's enlightened enough to laugh at what his devotees have done to him.' Water overfilled the buckets and splashed onto the flagstones.

'I don't think he'd laugh' said Nimalo, walking away with a load.

'I hope he can laugh, or the suffering would be too much. How would you like to spend a lifetime teaching non-cling-ing and transience and then watch those closest to you ignore the message in the way they treat you?'

'But he's still giving a teaching.'

'How?'

'By letting them tend him.'

'So they can observe suffering and decay?'

'Caring for his body is the practice of *karuna*. It's beautiful to watch the compassion and tenderness of the monks who look after him. Monks and novices rotate every week, so everyone gets a turn as the Ajahn's nurse. We are all still learning from him, you see.'

'A fine argument, Nimalo. But it smells rotten. It's incense to cover up a stink. I bet I know what goes on in that two-million-*bhat* bungalow. Tending the Ajahn is like serving a helpless god. They are all scoring points for their own merit and petty holiness, using him as an opportunity to practise their *karuna* when real *karuna* would let him die. They feed off him. They gain identity and prestige and self-importance through keeping him alive. It's an ego-builder, just the opposite of what a monk's practice is all about. When he dies, you watch, they will all be devastated. Why? He's as good as dead already. But the whole rotting system gets its meaning from his presence. Being his disciples is the mean-ing of their lives. When he dies they'll have nothing left but a hundred monasteries which nobody will want to join because there is no longer a living teacher. I know some of his senior disciples have disrobed already because they aren't getting their personal Ajahn Chah fix. Most of them, you say, are satisfied just to push around his wheelchair? Tell me, what will they do when he dies? Will they build statues of him and place them on altars like they do with other holy monks? This goes right against the spirit of all he taught. It's attachment and craving and identification of ego with another – even though that other taught only non-self. I'll bet they build a temple for his ashes, or a park, some tourist attraction so everyone in Thailand can still come and worship him. I smell it in the air. Have they printed up brochures yet? I think Ajahn Chah's body is kept alive for the sake of emotional gratification and profiteering amongst the *sangha*.'

'It's only a skilful means . . . '

'Bullshit. They ignore the teaching and turn the teacher into a lifeless god.'

'I wouldn't say that' said the novice quietly.

'Of course not. You're on the inside. I'm speaking as an outsider. But what I've seen in Pah Nanachat is no different from the worst stories I've heard about Buddhist monks in Thailand. The few monks with any real talent – except the Ajahn Chahs – they compromise with the lay people's notion of religion and call it "skilful means." Their skilfulness in compromise permits merit-craving Thais to spoil rotten every monk in the country and to corrupt any teaching true to the *Dhamma* by smothering it with gold leaf. Why don't the monks let Ajahn Chah die? That would be a real teaching to the lay people. That would teach them that Buddhism is about suffering, impermanence and not-self. Death teaches that. But it's not what the *Sangha* wants, is it? It wants to encourage the lay people to believe Buddhism is about making merit by giving to pious monks, about bowing reverently, about depending on them for fortune readings, holy water, winning lottery tickets and good luck. That's what the Thai people want, so the monks give it to them. But why call it Buddhism? Call it Thai-ism. Why drag Buddha into it? It has nothing to do with his teachings. Look at the way Pah Nanachat, supposedly one of the best monasteries in the country, is run. We spend all our time observing Thai rules and customs, feeling so pleased with ourselves for belonging to a twenty-five hundred year old tradition. But we'll transfer a novice if the villagers disapprove . . . '

I stopped. Nimalo had been standing in front of me, patiently enduring my tirade. Although I had stopped pumping long ago, I was still perspiring. Water ran down the sides of my head and dripped from my chin.

'The jars are full' said the novice.

'Nimalo, it's nothing personal. Don't mind my being so critical.'

'I don't mind' he said, emptying the buckets beneath the pump spout and turning them upside down. 'I don't agree with you, that's all.' His voice was gentle and undisturbed. It made me both angry and glad.

'I don't ask you to agree with me' I said.
We exchanged timid smiles.

Before the meal I practised walking meditation on the concrete pathway which encompassed the *sala*. The far side,
behind the sewing room, was a good place in the morning.
There one could be isolated, yet not lose all sense of time
and miss the morning meal. The Ajahn walked by me with
a glance at my meditative pacing. It felt good knowing he
was seeing what a good *pahkow* I was, practising so early in
the morning. He stopped and turned around.
'How's it going?'
The question took me by surprise. This was the first time
since ordination he had asked me anything remotely concerning my practice.
'Very well, thanks' I said and took a few steps toward
him, indicating further questioning would be welcomed.
'I hope you're not thinking like Jim' he said, turning his
pale eyes on me. I thought he looked thinner now than he
had at first.
'Actually, Ajahn, our thinking and our experience here
have been quite similar. We shared our perspectives with
each other occasionally. It helped both of us stay balanced.
Jim had a good point of view. I miss him sometimes.'
'You're not planning on leaving, too, are you?'
'Not now. I may leave in a week or two. I don't know.
That would be much sooner than I expected when I came
here. What I came here intending to accomplish – establishing a grounding in *vipassana* – that's happening much more
quickly than I thought it would. Jim and I made some interesting discoveries together which will take me a long time
to sort out. As for my other reasons for being here, they
have dried up. I have enough to work with on my own for
a long time.'
I could tell by the pinched look on his face that this was
all wrong. I tried to revise.
'Not that I'm saying I have reasons for leaving. My reasons
don't make a difference any more. That's just it. I came here
for reasons. Now reasons have no more hold over me. So

stay or go, I can't tell. I can no longer say I'll be here until September. At least, this is my thinking. Not that I follow it because it's me that thought it. Actually, speaking in terms of "me" at all is starting to make no sense, I think.'

'That's what happens when you listen to your thoughts' said the teacher. 'They only delude you.'

'Well, maybe they do. I've lived my life with my thoughts. I know what it is like to be dominated by them, if that's what you mean. For a long time I thought meditation was to help me get rid of them. They are the cause of suffering and delusion, I know. Poor thoughts, they know it, and we suffer more because of it. At last I can feel a little compassion for them. I'm beginning to think they have a place in my life after all. Not the place of domination I once permitted them to have. The "I" itself has to learn not to be in control. . . . '

'You see? Thoughts will only confuse you.'

'I'm sorry if they don't make sense to you, Ajahn. I admit, they aren't very clear to me right now, either. But I don't want to abandon them yet. If I decide to leave, I'll be sure to give you at least a few days' notice. For now I can only take it one day at a time.'

'That's what I've been doing for over ten years' said the teacher, making a sound that might have been a laugh. He gave me a look near to a sad smile, if only his lips had moved. 'Some days I still think maybe I'll go back to playing jazz guitar.' He turned. I watched his tall stick-like figure, clad in its mud-brown robe. It jerkily walked into the jungle, down the path which led to the senior monk's teak *kuti*.

Aversion grows within. Morning meditation stretches intolerably before me. I find myself checking my watch, which I once kept untouched on a shelf in my hut. I sit on my straw mat out on the porch and try hard to concentrate. Mosquitoes bite my feet and my head. I slap at them and wipe the blood on the railing. I don't want to smear blood on my robe. One morning, I unroll the mat to sit and a dizzy Gonzo lizard lands with a plop at my feet, too confused to move. He has been sleeping in the open space in the rolled mat. It's my first close look at my hut mate in daylight. He's bumpy and ugly but the flecks of rust and red give his blue-grey skin a certain panache. I can no longer be choosy about my friends.

'No more pounding on the roof at night' I tell him with a prod of my toe. Aware again, he skitters up the wall in a zigzag, into the rafters. I hope he takes no offence. I feel very alone.

'Who are my companions?' I ask the jungle, its leaves dripping with rain. I give up my meditation, go inside and write a list of the ordained members of the hierarchy, from top to bottom.

> The Ajahn – ex-jazz guitarist
> Tan Bodhipalo – ex-gospel singer
> Tan Sumeno – ex-real estate tycoon
> Tan Casipo – applied physics drop-out
> Ruk – mechanical engineering drop-out
> Sun Tin – ex-Thai farmer
> Tan Yenaviro – ex-accountant
> Tan Wee – village boy turned monk
> Meow – Cheshire cat
> Nimalo – professional novice (joined a *wat* in Australia while unemployed)
> Mark – resident *wat* doctor (searching for the answer to death)

An educated group, the *sangha* of Wat Pah Nanachat. Dedicated to mindfulness, obedience and following the rules. May practice be fruitful for them. May all beings be happy. But I doubt they will. Strange, that I describe the monks by the negation of what they used to be. Jim called them failures, losers, drop-outs. Yet, if our own conclusions are valid, then dropping out is exactly what a monk needs to do. To silence the monkey-mind, the ego must be put away, not simply improved or developed. It must be eradicated, suffocated through following the rules for no gain. No wonder they are not sparkling personalities filled with zest and enthusiasm. If sparkle comes from ego, then the enthusiastic are stil trapped. Through emaciation of mind and body, in passive conformity to the rules, they work out their enlightenment. Their egos starve. If this is true, it justifies all I see. A Bodhipalo or a Percy are as capable of that death of self as a Ruk or a Nimalo. When all *kamma* is destroyed, only the One Who Knows will survive.

The question which remains is, does it work? Has the training of Pah Nanachat borne fruit in any of the *farang* monks? Ajahn Sumedo is held up as the best example. His *Dhamma* tapes were throroughly uninspiring. The Ajahn, Bodhipalo and Mr Chicago are the only senior monks that I know. I'd rather be a *samadhi*-suicide than turn out like any one of them. The only life with any of the joy of liberation in it is Ruk's. But his gentleness and laughter could be due to his natural disposition just as well as to following the *Vinaya*. I hope his beautiful soul does not suffocate. There is no convincing evidence so far. I still do not even know what could be convincing. Ajahn Chah? I dread my visit to see him. Searching for answers there will only lead to disappointment and anger.

All I have learned is that enlightenment won't do me any good. The perceiving ego won't feel any of it. Whatever peace *nibb ana* offers seemed discontinuous with the suffering self, which is what 'I' am. To end the suffering is suicide of the ego. No need to rush the process. I am better prepared to give up my desire for attainment and live with the chattering of my monkey-mind. At least I will not be so easily deluded by it. This home away from homelessness, it has no more attraction for me. I'm not particularly happy here, but at least I've learned that a search for happiness is futile. I look to the jungle. What to do?

> Breathe in, calming the mind.
> Breathe out, calming the mind.
> So taught the Buddha.

CHAPTER THIRTEEN

The Water Tank is
Made of Metal

A large yellow-backed spider lay before me on the ground, belly up, as I walked to the *sala* for evening chanting. Her black legs stretched upwards into the night air, curling slowly. Her body was larger than a hen's egg and her delicate legs spanned thirty centimetres from tip to tip. My flashlight disturbed her. Quickly she climbed an invisible thread up to a web spread across the low branches above my head. Near her belly, a tiny spider, clinging. A male. Celibate half-monk, I felt sorry to have interrupted them. I ducked beneath them with a blessing. Especially for him. This would be his last act in the dance.

Buddhamas was coming. Tan Casipo told me hundreds of Thai visitors would soon arrive for the festival, all bringing food, ready to stay and celebrate the birth, death and enlightenment of the Buddha. Buddhamas was the affectionate name Ajahn Chah used for the ceremony when he spoke about it to his Western followers. In preparation, the Ajahn declared it a work day to polish the Buddha statues at the front of the *sala*. A dozen of us worked for three hours at the job, emptying five bottles of Brasso. As well as the four large figures – two of Buddha and two of kneeling devotees – we also put a high shine on the dozens of smaller images, on candlestick holders and incense bowls. Our task involved more than mindful attention to detail. It demanded constant awareness that these were Buddhas we were polishing, not

203

just hunks of brass and bronze. We were told not to grasp them by the head or hold them upside down. That would violate all Thai sense of propriety. Still, I was permitted to take a black rag and burnish up the large Buddha's eyeballs.

I worked with Herbie on the lower of the two giant Buddhas. He seemed absorbed in his polishing and smiled as if the holy day was one he had long awaited. I mused out loud while we rubbed as to why there were two idols in the centre. To my surprise, Herbie had the answer ready.

'The front Buddha represents the *Dhamma*, the back one represents the Buddha.'

'You mean this Buddha is really the *Dhamma*?'

'Yes, and the two kneeling side figures are the *sangha*.'

'I understand' I said, illumination dawning. 'The altar sets up Buddha *Dhamma sangha* – the Triple Gem.'

'That's right. But this altar is set up in a funny way. You see how the *sangha* are bowing to the rear Buddha only? Usually they pay homage to the front Buddha, the *Dhamma*.'

'So here the *sangha* ignore the *Dhamma* and worship the Buddha? What do you make of that?'

'Me? I don't make anything of it.'

At drink time, mum caught my attention and pointed to a small black object crawling near the edge of the marble patio where we all sat surrounded by mosquitoes.

'It's a scorpion' I told her, 'a needle-tailed scorpion. There are a lot of them around here.'

Several monks and laymen craned their necks to see.

'It's not a scorpion' said the Ajahn.

'What is it then?' I asked, with all the humility I could muster. I hated to lose face as a reputed arthropod specialist.

'It's something like a scorpion, but it isn't one.'

We watched the little non-scorpion crawl slowly back into the leaves. It seemed unconcerned about the nature of its true identity.

Mum seemed to be relaxing. She was getting used to the monastery and to seeing her son bald, emaciated and wearing an ochre shroud. Mark told me it was a strain having her there. He had spent very few hours with any of his family for the past ten years. Renewing the relationship with his mum was taking up most of his time. His mat was always empty at evening chanting and he complained that he had little energy left for meditation. Likely, whenever he closed his eyes, *kammic* formations of mum would appear. Difficult to practise the homeless life when your mother lives in your *wat*.

Still, Mark was happy she had come. He said the time was well spent for both of them, despite their different perspectives. They were getting to know each other again. Mark felt she was beginning to accept that his coming here may have been best for him. She confessed he seemed happier than he had been in years. Soon she began helping out in the kitchen. She baked goodies for the morning meal. She had brought a jar of home-made jam for Mark which was passed around in the mornings along with fresh bread. She lived in the women's quarters with Dukita, who had become her good friend. Dukita's natural cheerfulness and near-fluent English helped mum through her initial days at the *wat* when the monks must have seemed cold and devoid of personality. It must have been a shock at first, to see her child as a part of this environment. Especially Mark, whose small frame and nobbly skull made him appear severely malnourished. Not the easiest conditions for family reunion.

'Mum seems to be taking a real interest in the place now' the novice told me some time after our trip into town. We had met with our kettles at the base of the large concrete water tank. 'She's even starting to ask questions about Buddhism and *vipassana*. She said she thinks maybe she and the family reacted against my ordination without knowing enough about it. She thought it was a cult at first. Now she wants to know about the *Dhamma*.'

'I suppose her concern was understandable' I said. 'Robes and a hairdo like a Hari Krishna, chanting at three every morning, one meal a day, sleep deprivation once a week – maybe we are a cult. How soon do you think it will be before we can shave her hair?'

'She'll soon be one of us!' cried Mark, eyes bulging in mock-sinister fashion. He flashed his little white teeth, but then frowned. 'On second thoughts, maybe it would be better to leave her to the Methodists. I don't know if I want to live the rest of my life in the same monastery as my mother.'

'The rest of your life?'

'Possibly.'

'I thought you were going back to be a doctor?' Looking up, I noticed black dots gliding over the top rim of the tank. Already the ants had returned to their home. I shrugged and filled my kettle.

'That's not certain now. Please don't mention this to mum. I haven't told her about it yet.'

'You think you may stay?'

'I don't know anymore. I never thought I would until recently. Now I feel I have much more to stay for than to go for. There's no point in upsetting her by it. Funny, I think she came to persuade me to go back with her. She'd never admit it, but it's what I think. Seeing her again and thinking about the life I have left has helped me to feel prepared to make the decision to stay. I had some aversion to what I left behind. It's gone now. I'm not running from anything any more. It just seems that a monk's life is the only one which makes sense, the only place where I can do something that can give my life meaning.'

'I thought you were going to help dying people? Doctors can do a lot too.'

'I don't think so, not now. The whole system is crazy out there. I wanted to be a doctor so I could help people. But medicine doesn't really touch the root of human suffering. What actual good was I doing in a hospital? Why should I put myself back into a system that is basically inhumane?'

'Mark, *vipassana* gives rise to wisdom wherever it's prac- tised, in a hospital or in a temple. Practise in a *wat* and you'll get insight into your mental processes. Practise in a hospital and you'll get insight into your patients. It doesn't matter what you are doing, giving injections or burning boils, the power of *vipassana* will make a difference in every person you deal with. You can spread calm through a hospital corri- dor, you can be a generating centre for compassion and friendliness wherever you go. I think it's the outside world that a monk has to gravitate to eventually. All this talk of the world of *samsara* as opposed to some *Dhamma*-world inside a *wat*, it just creates artificial boundaries. It's just the collective ego of the *sangha*. That's delusion too. When monks retreat into a monastic "we" they isolate themselves in a holy delusion which is just as bad as individualism. It becomes a wall which only blocks meditation.'

'Stop, stop, Tim, you confuse me. I don't know anything about collective egos and individualism. I'm a simple novice. I came here just to learn about how to deal with death. For that, a monk's life makes most sense. I still don't have any answers. All I've found is a place to start.'

'You came here to learn about death? You came to the right place.' I spoke with a sudden nasty vehemence. I didn't know why. 'Because death is what they teach here in Pah Nanachat. All you're learning here, Mark, is how to die. Buddhism doesn't give answers to death. It doesn't help you deal with it. It tells you to do it. That's the solution: do it.'

'What are you saying? You don't make any sense at all.'

'I'm saying you should stay here until you die. Then go back to New Zealand and be a doctor. Then you can help other people die. That's the meaning of life. Be sure you die here, because it's too easy to just live on forever as a blessed holy *bhikkhu*.'

He stared at me, wide eyed, not speaking. I turned from the water tank and stepped to the mouth of the jungle trail. I wanted the solitude of my *kuti*. I looked back.

'Mark, I . . . I'm sorry. I don't know what it is that comes over me these days. I seem to be picking on everybody, just like Yenaviro says. It doesn't make a difference. Be a doctor, be a monk. You'll suffer either way. It's stupid of me to argue as if I know what's best for you.' I turned again and started walking into the trees, arms hanging limply at my sides. My kettle dangled and sloshed water.

'Thanks for your concern' he called after me.

'I'm sorry, Mark. I like you.' I smiled faintly through the trees, hesitating for his reply.

'I like you too. I wish you were planning on staying longer.'

'Merry Buddhamas' I said to Herbie as I took my seat next to him on the morning of the big festival. Over two hundred and fifty people showed up for breakfast and the Wai Phra vigil, bringing everything from sticky rice to the finest delicacies of Bangkok. I counted the serving bowls at the front of the *sala*. There were sixty-seven of them. In my *pahkow*'s handbag I carried my camera. I had blown the dust off it the day before and removed it from the *sala* safe-keeping drawer. I stood up from my place in the food line and approached the Ajahn, camera in hand. I had asked his permission the night before. He merely gave me a nod when he saw me coming. I stooped as I passed him, careful not to tower over him. I gave a respectful bow of my head and a *wai*.

First I took a few pictures of the monks in the line, empty bowls before them. They seemed solemn and as still as statues. It was an unusual feeling to move through the *sala* while the others were all frozen in place, as if I were invisible. The Ajahn spoke engagingly to the Thai visitors who gathered for the blessing at the front of the hall. I took some shots of the crowd. The lay people watched me with amusement. What I wanted most was a photo with the bowls and silver trays full of food in the foreground and the erect and emaciated row of monks in the background. It was difficult to get both in focus. There was not enough light in the *sala* for a wide F-stop unless I was willing to hand hold shots at a low speed. I didn't want to risk under-exposure. In front of the altar, I fiddled with my aperture, then crouched down on one knee to steady myself. The villagers laughed at the fuss I was making with my camera. When I finished I was glad to be on my way back to my unobtrusive place in the line.

'Be careful how you sit when you get to your seat' Tan Casipo whispered as I passed. I froze in horror. Blindly I stumbled the rest of the way to my mat and lowered myself slowly into place, face burning, looking self-consciously to see who was watching me.

'Herbie' I croaked. 'Did you see me taking pictures up there at the front?'

He nodded.

'Did you see much of me?'

He nodded.

'Was my *sabong* . . . when I crouched?'

'You could tell you weren't used to wearing it.'

I started to giggle. I held my face in my hands in order not to laugh.

'What's wrong?' said Herbie, sounding detached.

'I was so concerned about under-exposure. Turns out my problem was just the reverse.'

A few of the *bhikkhus* grinned at me during bowl washing, but no one said a word until I crouched to dry my pot.

'You're hanging out, Tim' said Tan Bodhipalo as he walked by.

I resented that. You would have had to put your head to the ground to see anything up my *sabong* that time. If you don't like it, don't look, I thought. Damn rules. I should have been a Jain ascetic. They don't wear any clothes at all. There's a precept that wouldn't give me trouble.

Bodhipalo, the cave monk, came back and sat down beside me at the edge of the *sala*. In a voice both genuine and gentle he explained to me the proper kneeling position for drying a bowl.

'That's fine for a monk' I said, 'but if I kneel with my bum resting on my feet, my robe gets too dirty to wear. Nobody notices it on a monk.'

'Then you can sit in respectful sitting posture.'

'How about like this?'

'No, you can't cross your legs.'

'Why not?'

'It's not according to the rules.'

'It's not in the *Vinaya*. I've read it.'

'It's not the way we do it here.'

'In the rules, monks were supposed to sit so the bowls wouldn't break if they dropped them. We don't use clay bowls any more. What difference does it make to anybody if I sit crosslegged?'

'You must remember, the rules are really just the practice of mindfulness and obedience. If you sit properly there is a grace and harmony about it which makes it pleasing to the eye.' His voice remained soft and gentle. 'That's what lies behind all our postures and bowing, the gestures of offering and holding the hands together in a simple *wai* when speaking to a senior monk. They build a sense of care and beauty into a day. Each act becomes a meditation rather than a heedless response to the environment. Life becomes peaceful and tranquil. All this takes time, of course. When you are new you are bound to make mistakes from time to time. That is fine. Everyone understands. Just work on it every day. Soon it will come naturally.'

Three emotions twisted inside me in reaction to this beautiful piece of aesthetics. On the surface, I hated being told yet again to follow the rules, however nicely it was put, especially when they were not even the real rules. Secondly, I still felt embarrassed at my own recent over-exposure. By making no direct reference to that event, Tan Bodhipalo was saving my dignity. In a roundabout way he was telling me not to be concerned about it. His speaking to me was not a chiding, just timely advice which I obviously needed. Thirdly, I was genuinely overwhelmed that the recluse was speaking to me. I knew he hated to talk. This made his words a true gesture of compassion. He had never spoken so much in my presence in all my time at the *wat*. Yet he was taking it upon himself to give me a complete lesson in monastic etiquette. He talked on, melting my resistance. Bodhipalo speaking! It felt like an honour. Or perhaps a measure of how serious an offence I had committed. If I didn't accept all his advice, his sincerity alone touched my heart.

When at length he had finished, he asked if I had any questions. I did not wish to fight with him, but could not pass by the opportunity to ask a tough one.

'Why do we bow to monks?' I said.

'You don't bow to them as people' he answered in the

same calm tone. 'It's the robes you must respect. Especially as a *pahkow*, you must remember you have put yourself under the guidance and protection of the *sangha*. They are your teachers, all of them. You are dependent upon them. Personally, you may not like some monks. You may feel inclined to argue with them. They might be real arseholes. You bow to them all the same. This bowing teaches you humility. If you think you are better than somebody else, then your will is rigid and you are incapable of learning anything. Bowing makes you malleable. Then you will be ready to receive the *Dhamma*.'

'Thank you, Tan Bodhipalo, for speaking with me' I said and raised my hands in a respectful *wai*.

'Thank you for listening' said the recluse. He stood and left me to my bowl.

I realized this monk, the ex-gospel singer, had inadvertently passed the test Jim and I had devised to determine the genuineness of the *sangha*'s calm. We had considered performing a malicious prank, deliberately annoying a *bhikkhu*, to see if we could scratch hard enough for someone to bite. My exhibitionism was undoubtedly more of an embarrassment to the Ajahn and senior monks than to me personally. It reflected on the whole community. The Thais would laugh at the *wat* when they talked of the *farang* flapping in the breeze at the front of the temple, Buddhamas morn. Yet there was no harshness in Tan Bodhipalo's lesson, though perhaps the Ajahn sent him to me for that purpose. I could have been made to feel like a fool. His respect for my feelings seemed an adequate refutation of Jim's total cynicism.

On Buddhamas evening, the monastic community gathered on the Ajahn's balcony for another private *dasana*, while the *sala* rang with chanting Thai voices. The theme of his talk was, as usual, that he didn't have much to say. We should follow the rules and be mindful, especially about not scraping our bowls. *Pahkows* were also reminded to be careful how they sit so as not to embarrass themselves. The lone *pahkow* in the crowd took the advice to heart.

'I also notice many people aren't making much of an effort

any more to stay up all night on Wai Phra' he continued. 'In the old days, everybody stayed in the *sala* until dawn. We didn't even get any Ovaltine. Perhaps there's a relationship there. Maybe we should cut out Ovaltine before *bindabhat*. Tonight is the Buddha's birthday. I think it's as good a time as any to give our best effort to staying awake. I know I've had trouble staying up, too. That's because I have visitors all day long. I don't get a chance to sleep in the afternoons like the rest of you. But that's no excuse. I want everyone to stay awake tonight, even me.'

When the pep talk ended, we all returned to the *sala*. Two hundred Thai devotees sat waiting, all dressed in white. Preparations were underway for the ceremonial walk around the monastery compound. The atmosphere was exciting throughout the temple as we were each handed a candle, three incense sticks and a lotus blossom, traditional offerings to the Buddha. The monks formed a line at the rear of the hall, according to hierarchical order. The rest of the community of Pah Nanachat followed. The crowd of lay people came after us. One by one we lit our offerings from candles at the rear of the hall. Then in single file we walked out into the night and began three slow circumambulations around the central area of the *wat*. As we left the hall, I noticed Herbie behind me. He was wide-eyed with boyish delight. When he saw me observing him, he beamed an unguarded smile.

'This is just pure *metta*, pure *metta*' he said, enraptured.

'Tell me' I whispered as the procession began, 'what do the offerings represent? Does one element stand for each event? The lotus for birth, the incense for death, the candle for enlightenment?'

'They're just sticks, candles and flowers' Herbie said with a shrug. 'They look nice, though.'

The long line of worshippers gradually formed a glowing ring, encircling the dark compound like a march of fireflies. Incense filled the night air, mingling with the delicate fragrance of over two hundred lotus blossoms. Last year's procession had been marred by the chatting of the towns-people from Ampher Warin and Bangkok. They were not as naturally respectful as the folk from Bung Wai. This year the Ajahn included a stern command for silence in his *dasana* to the people. It was well kept, providing the appropriate tone for the solemn ritual. Without flashlights, and holding candles before our faces, we could not see very well where we were walking. Each one merely followed the one ahead. As the march was a holy rite, we were also required to do it barefoot. I wondered for a moment why the monks ahead of me all started stomping their feet as the procession rounded its way onto the gravel road. Seconds later, I knew. Red ants crawled up my ankles, entangling themselves in the hair of my legs. They bit viciously. We had crossed the path of a foraging army. Bad form to swat them with hands full of lotus and incense. I joined in the frantic stomping and shaking of limbs. As we were all maintaining strict silence, I could not even warn those behind me. The line jumped and jerked as ants and devotees continued their intersecting marches. Our procession turned into a candlelit game of 'do the hokey pokey and shake it all about.'

When the third round was completed and the last of the ants brushed from our bodies, the people spontaneously planted their offerings in the ground around the *sala*. Only a few returned them to the baskets. The whole area around the temple was illuminated. Lotus flowers glimmered with the reflected light. The candles were placed round the *sala* with care, while faint wisps of incense hung soft in the air. This was the spirit of Buddhamas. The Thais created these glowing little shrines with delicate artistic sense. Some nestled candles among the dry leaves. Other propped them between tree roots, placed them in the crooks of branches, or even inside knotholes. It transformed the *wat* grounds into a hundred holy shrines full of flowers, smoking incense and tiny flames. Here and there tree bark had already begun to glow like red embers where candles had been laid against them. Leaves smouldered on the edge of the jungle. I joined a few of the monks as we circled the compound a fourth and final time, extinguishing dozens of potential forest fires.

When I returned to the *sala*, I took my seat next to Herbie, ready to begin the long vigil of the night. The Thais had resumed their chanting. I noticed the little layman held an unopened lotus blossom in his hands. It had been detached from its stem, resembling an egg with one end tapered to a point. He cupped the pink flower gently, grinning.

'The water tank is made of metal. A candle burns outside' he said into space. Then he bent his head to the flower, pushed it to his nose and inhaled deeply.

'What did you say? What are you high on? Where did you get that from?' I said.

'What? The flower?'

'No, what you just said. "The water tank is made of metal. A candle burns outside." It's beautiful.'

'It's nothing. I'm just trying to be objective about things, just accept what is.'

I looked at the skinny teenager in amazement. 'Fantastic. It pierces reality' I said. '"The water tank is made of metal." You say it and right away you realize they are just words, they don't tell you anything about anything. The words have nothing in common with what's really there, outside in the dark. Yet the words are all we have to share our experience and remember it by. I watch how you laugh, Herbie. You use words but you don't believe in them. You don't fall for them. I always suspected you, you know.'

'I'm just trying to be objective about things, just accept what is.'

'But you say it like that, and it's poetry. You free yourself from the illusion of things, from attachment and aversion.'

'It's not like that. I just accept what is.' He lifted the lotus to his nose again and squeezed the shut blossom like a little bellows, injecting scent into his nostrils.

'So what do you know?' he asked.

'What do I know?'

'What do you know?'

'You want to know what do I know?'

'Yes.'

'Only one thing.'

'You know only one thing? What?'

'Herbie, don't tell on me, not around here . . . ' I looked around at the other stiff forms. No one noticed our whispering. If I wanted Herbie to reveal himself to me, I had to be willing to be honest with him.

'I won't tell' he said.

'God.'

'You know God?'

'Yes.'

'How do you – No! Don't try to tell me. If I don't know God, then you can't explain it to me. I just accept it. You know God.'

'I guess you're right. What can I tell you about God except "the water tank is made of metal"?'

Herbie took another deep sniff of the lotus and nodded.

'Why did you ask, if you know I can't explain anything I really know?'

'I like to ask. I like to ask everybody, "So what do you know?" Sometimes I ask the monks, "So what do you know?" Then they tell me about the *Dhamma* and mindfulness and obedience and Buddha. I have to stop them. "Let me rephrase the question" I say. "So what do you know?"'

'I see the problem' I said.

Herbie stuck his nose back into the flower. 'I used to think, either I know everything, absolutely everything, or I know nothing, absolutely nothing, or I know some things and not other things.' He looked at me to see if I understood, then dropped his eyes to the lotus. He smiled at it and shook his head. 'But that's all wrong. It's too complicated.'

'It is?'

'So I just accept I know nothing, absolutely nothing. I ask other people "So what do you know" and if they say they know something, I just say "Oh". Maybe they do know something. I don't know that they don't know.'

'That's a pretty lonely form of scepticism.'

'Is it?'

'Yes.'

'Oh.'

'I see how it works.'

'So you know God?'

'Yes.'

Herbie buried his face in the flower.

'I could say lots about Buddhism, Christianity or philosophy in clear conceptual terms, Herbie, if you wanted me to
explain it that way. But the concepts aren't truth.'

'Do you call God truth?'

'I try not to call God anything. Even "truth" is too small
a word to hold what I mean when I say the word "God."
He's what's there if you burn everything else away. And if
you could burn God away, there would be nothing left at
all. The Hebrews said theirs was the God with no name.
He's the one I know.'

'Oh.'

'You're right, Herbie. Better to have no view. Then you
stay open enough to just accept whatever comes along without conceptual prejudices. "Do not search for truth, only
cease to cherish opinions." I learned that here.'

'But I have a view. I think you need a view.' He sucked
air from the flower again. The chanting stopped. The chimes
in the *sala* rang twelve times for midnight. He continued in
a low whisper. 'My view is that I know nothing. I try to be
objective and accept what is. Can you get stoned on a lotus
blossom?'

'I don't know. Let me try.'

Herbie handed me the flower. It felt soft and satiny in my
hand. The creamy white colour near the base of the bud
gave way to pastel pink near the rim of the petals. I put the
point where the closed tips came together close to my nose
and squeezed the middle of the blossom, as I had watched
Herbie do. Sweet perfume seemed to fill me. It felt heady,
like a large mouthful of warm white wine. The fragrance
swirled through my nostrils even after I had taken the bud
away.

'A lotus stone could bring instant *samadhi*' I said. 'Maybe
we should try for it.'

He smiled and reached for the flower.

'Herbie, you were right. Everyone needs a view. Well,
maybe not God, maybe not an *arahant*. But a view is a tool
to help us make sense of the world. As long as we don't get
attached to our views and can remember any view is bound
to be full of delusion, then they can be a great help in daily

living. Jim and I hit on a new view to help keep us from
running from our suffering. We say it makes no difference.
Either way, we'll suffer. Knowing we suffer no matter what
we do, there's no point trying to force life one way or
another. This frees us from the desire for happiness. Without
desire, we can be open to the wisdom of *vipassana*. I suspect
vipassana might be a connection with the voice of God. Keep
it a secret.'

'I think if you say "it doesn't make a difference" that
could offend some people. Maybe to them it does make a
difference.'

'I see your point. How do I know that to them it doesn't
make a difference? Just because it's my view doesn't mean
the theory should be applied to everyone. Herbie, you're a
good teacher. I always suspected you. Pass me that lotus.'

I sniffed and looked around. Most of the monks were still
in the *sala*. I watched Tan Bodhipalo pacing across the rear
of the hall, near to us. It occurred to me we were supposed
to maintain silence. I motioned to Herbie to get up with me.
We took our blankets outside the temple and sat against the
wall on the corner Jim and I used to share. The full moon
shone down on us, casting long shadows from the tree tops.
The jungle was bathed in white light, revealing the details
of every leaf, every creeper, striped with blackness wherever
shadows fell. We could see dozens of lotus blossoms planted
in the ground around us, little stubs of incense sticks, the
dull gleam of wax reflecting the moon. To our right was a
large rectangular shape like a black window cut into the
glowing night. The water tank was made of metal.

Herbie spoke spontaneously. 'I remember Pahkow
Michael and I were making coffee one day in the kitchen.
There was a South African monk here then. The nit bugs
had been breeding and the kitchen store room was full of
them, all fluttering around with their floppy wings. The
South African was supposed to clean out the room. He
started catching toads and putting them inside. They were
eating the bugs and doing his work for him. Michael got
upset. He told the monk he was messing with the toads'
kamma and he was messing with the nits' *kamma*. I thought

217

about this. I realized Michael was just messing with the monk's *kamma*. I was going to tell him so, then it hit me that this was just messing with Michael's *kamma*. In the end, it's best just to try to be objective and accept what is.'

'How long have you been doing this accepting, Herbie? Did you work it out in the *wat* or did you carry it here inside you from wherever you were before?'

The teenager squeezed another shot from the lotus. 'I don't know' he said in his familiar toneless voice.

'Do you know what the Buddha never taught?'

'I told you, I know nothing.'

'I think that you know but don't know that you know. How do you know you don't know? You are the one who knows, aren't you?'

'I don't know.'

'Oh' I said.

We sat in silence for a while, passing the lotus between us. It was becoming limp. The fragrance was beginning to fade.

'You know, I could never talk to people' Herbie said.

'You talk fine.'

'Back home I used to hate going to parties. My girlfriend took me anyway. I would sit alone for hours, not saying a word. If she introduced me to someone, I would just stare at them. I knew I was supposed to talk but there was nothing I could say. I felt desperate.'

'A lot of people are shy with strangers.'

'This often happened with people I had known for years. They used to think I was weird. My mother sent me to a couple of psychiatrists. I couldn't talk to them either. I used to worry about whether or not anything was real. I wasn't sure if anybody existed, even myself. This bothered my girlfriend. Then I wrote to a friend of mine who plays for a rock band in London. I used to sing with him when we had a group together back home. I respected him a lot. He'd done a lot of hard drugs and came out human. I asked him how he handled all these difficult questions that were destroying me. "Try not to think about it" he wrote back. I realized he was right. Thinking about it only messed me up worse. I don't have to think about these questions. Knowing whether or not something really exists doesn't really change anything.

'At that time I wanted to write a play called *The Audience*. It's about a man in a mental hospital. He believes the fourth wall in his room isn't a wall at all. He thinks it leads out into a huge audience. Everybody in this audience is staring in at him, he says. Other characters in the play – doctors, nurses, relatives – they want to talk him out of his delusion. He tries to show them the people sitting out there. Nobody else sees. The audience knows that the crazy man is right. They are watching him. But they also know they aren't really looking into a hospital room. It's only a play. The other actors know they are on stage. They don't really see a fourth wall. But this is just what the crazy man says: "You're just pretending you don't see all those people."'

'Then is it a play about a man who sees an imaginary audience, or about many characters who see an imaginary wall?' I said. 'It depends on whether or not you consider the audience as part of the cast, doesn't it?'

'In the end the man gets up and speaks directly to the audience through the fourth wall which isn't there. He says to them that there is an audience looking in behind each one of their fourth walls too.'

'I hope you write it.'

'I don't know if I can. There isn't much point.'

'Herbie, I'm sure you know anything worth doing isn't done for points. Do you know what I want to do? I want to write books. And do you know why I want to write books?'

He shook his head.

'Neither do I.'

'I like that' said the little layman with a smile.

'Aha, caught you in the subjective.'

Our lotus blossom finished, we sat back and watched the moon in a sad silence that made me want to giggle. Herbie had been here all along, yet this was the first time we had opened up to each other. In a few more days, he too would leave.

'Are you looking forward to going to China?' I asked.

'I don't really look forward. Even when I was back home,

I couldn't plan things because I didn't think about them unless I was in the middle of doing them. I can say that I'm going to China, but even while I'm speaking the words I'm not really thinking about it. I'll probably be surprised when I get there.'

'I wish you could teach me that. I spend all my life in future plans that never exist.'

'Oh.'

'I'm glad you can be objective about it. How do you feel about leaving Pah Nanachat?'

'I haven't thought about it.' He shrugged and began pulling open the blossom of the lotus, unfolding the pink petals one by one. 'I haven't left yet. I like it. Many people are good to me here. When I came I was totally confused. In some ways the monastery made that worse. I used to think I should be ordained as a *pahkow* or a novice. Finally I realized that wouldn't have helped. All that meant was more talk and ideas. That was what I needed to get away from. I'm better off if I'm not messed up in it. I like the meditation and the quiet. It helps me stay objective.'

'What will you miss most about Thailand?' I asked, missing Herbie already.

'I don't know.'

'There won't be any sticky rice where you're going.'

He looked worried for a second, then turned his face full to me and laughed. 'I suppose I should take a case of lotus blossoms too.'

CHAPTER FOURTEEN

Ajahn Chah
Gives a Teaching

A t Ovaltine time, before *bindabhat*, my red cup rematerialized onto its shelf. I waved it at Tan Casipo, who had
helped me search for it. He was delighted.

'Perhaps one of those old Thai *pahkows* took it' said the
helpful monk. 'I know they took some other things to the
women's quarters. They just left yesterday to go back to Wat
Pah Pong.'

'Probably it just rematerialized' I said. 'That's a good teaching for me. If an object dematerializes, just forget about it. It
will spontaneously re-appear in its own sweet time. Fussing
about it just sets up *kammic* formations of goneness which
prevent it from coming back.'

The applied physics drop-out tilted his head at me. He
would have raised an eyebrow if he had one. 'You'll probably
find three or four of them popping up all over the place now'
he said.

Ruk tells me he will fast this Buddhamas dawn. He says the
Ajahn will replace him today on our *bindabhat* route. This
will be my first alms round with the senior monk, the first
time for me to have direct contact with him alone, and a
good opportunity to learn something about the man I call
my teacher.

'Are you still thinking of leaving?' he asks after the two of
us clear the paddy dykes and begin walking along the road.

'I'm not thinking of staying, Ajahn.'

The morning holds a slight drizzle and mist. We have forgotten our umbrellas.

'I suppose I don't have to tell you I'm kind of disappointed in your and Jim's performances here.'

'I hope not. We both learned much from Pah Nanachat. A surprising amount in such little time.'

'To really learn anything, one has to stay at least six months. Otherwise it's all on the surface. It won't last.'

'Can one learn much in six months?'

'Not much.'

'How much time to learn much?'

'These days I feel I'm finally beginning to learn.'

'That's a long time. Tell me, Ajahn, why did you come to Thailand to meditate anyway?'

'Actually, I didn't come here to meditate. I was on my way to Japan, just passing through. I wanted to join a Zen monastery. But when I came to Wat Pah Pong, I had to surrender those plans. That's how my whole life has been ever since: renounce and surrender. In Japan I would probably have been permitted to play my guitar. I still miss it sometimes. Every day self arises and must be renounced. That's the only way to freedom from becoming. One must give up all personal desires.'

'How does that help you cease becoming?'

'Sense pleasures lead to craving. Craving leads to grasping. Grasping leads to becoming.'

'And then?'

'Becoming leads to birth. Birth leads to decay, death, sorrow, lamentation, pain, grief and despair' he recites.

'So you cut the chain at desires?'

'You realize desires are just ignorance. Ignorance is the first link in the chain of dependent causes. This binds you to the cycle of rebirth. The only way to break free is to renounce.'

'Tell me, Ajahn, did you come here from Australia in order to escape the suffering of rebirth?'

'Even the desire to escape suffering must be renounced. I didn't ask to be Ajahn, you know. I don't particularly like the job. But when one becomes a senior monk, tasks and responsibilities come with it. This too is renunciation for me.'

'So you end up spending all your time entertaining Thai tourists and briefing *farang* guests when you could be meditating. It doesn't sound very satisfying.'

'Even the desire to meditate must be renounced. Just follow the rules. That is the key to letting go of self. I say it again and again. All you need do is follow the rules.'

The teacher concentrates on the wet path at his feet as we walk. I study his face. He is a man bent on suffocation of the self.

'Ajahn, were you here when Pah Nanachat was formed?'

'Of course. I had just been ordained as a monk in Wat Pah Pong.'

'Can you tell me the story?'

He gives me a smile. 'Just over ten years ago, a few of us Western monks came into the forest area near Bung Wai. There used to be an old cremation ground near where our *wat* is now. Thai people are afraid of ghosts, so monks find these places best for a meditation retreat. It was quiet and deserted. We lived in umbrella tents. When *farang* monks started coming around the villages on *bindabhat*, there was a lot of excitement. The people guessed we were from Ajahn Chah's famous monastery. They came into the jungle and started building wooden *kuties* for us. They entreated us to stay. It would bring great good fortune to Bung Wai, they said. The monks went back to Ajahn Chah to ask his permission. Then Wat Pah Nanachat was formed as a branch of Wat Pah Pong. It was to be an international forest monastery for training foreign monks. They would eventually be able to set up branches in their home countries. That was the idea. Ajahn Sumedo was our first Ajahn. He was a great inspiration to me. Now he is in England, and Ajahn Chah. . . . There is nobody who can inspire the monks in the same way.'

'You see that as a problem here?' I ask carefully.

'Definitely. Without an embodiment of the ideal, the monks soon get slack. They need an example, someone who can teach them real wisdom. Without that, discipline degenerates from within. It's hard to enforce it from the outside. Soon evening meditation stops, as it did here before I arrived. In some branch monasteries they don't even do morning meditation any more. The monks sleep in until alms round. Once the monks get lazy and sloppy, they start to question the value of what they are doing. Next they disrobe. Many monasteries which were once full have only a few monks left. Caretaker monks, even in plenty of Ajahn Chah's *wats*. Once discipline goes, everything breaks down. That was Ajahn Chah's specialty, discipline. He knew just how to push the monks so they could develop their internal strength. Sometimes he kept us sitting for six hours at a single *dasana*. It was torture. To give you an idea of his style, I'll tell you a story. A long time ago the squirrels in Pah Pong used to be chased by the village dogs. That was one reason why Ajahn Chah finally agreed to plans to build a large wall around the monastery, so there wouldn't be animals running around all the time. A while after the wall was up, everybody noticed the squirrels were getting lazy. There were no dogs around and they knew the monks wouldn't do them any harm. They just made half-hearted attempts to hop out of the way. Do you know what Ajahn Chah did? He told us to leave the gates open and let the dogs back in! Even the squirrels in our *wat* had to stay on their toes. That was his style.'

Tan Wee waits for us at the village gate. The Ajahn steps up to the lead. We fall into place behind him. Our heads bow in humility. He knows our route perfectly, but leads with deliberate slowness. Emerging from the far side of our round, he tells me he would like to return to the practice of reciting the *Vinaya* aloud while receiving alms. I offer to carry his bowl, heavy with rice, balancing his and my own, one strap across each shoulder, on the walk back between the rice paddies. The drizzle does not stop. Our robes are damp and the pathway through the fields is slick and full of crabs. Eager to resume the open conversation between us, I ask the teacher for his opinion on the causes of things breaking down among monks in Thailand.

'For the last two hundred years people have been saying

everything is breaking down, the monks are getting slack and the tradition is degenerating. I suppose they've been saying it from the beginning.'

'You mean everybody thinks it was better in the good old days?'

'Yes. That may just be the flaw of a limited perspective.'

'So you think things aren't really getting worse?'

'I think they are definitely getting worse. The monks are becoming too comfortable. There's too much affluence in this country nowadays. The lay people spoil the monks rotten. These days it's common to see a monk carrying money, keeping tape machines, even music cassettes. Not here though.'

'In Bangkok I've even seen some monks with television' I add.

'Also there is a lot of government pressure for the *sangha* to be involved in social welfare programmes.'

'Do you think that's bad?'

'It's not a monk's job. Some of it is very political. In border areas near Laos and Vietnam the government has the monks teaching villagers to beware of communist groups and obey the king. Whether or not there is a need for this kind of work, it shouldn't be the task of those devoted to the *Dhamma*.'

'Does this cause the *Dhamma* to decline? What do you think will happen to Thai Buddhism if the monks become propagandists and welfare workers?'

'It's hard to say. *Dhamma* is in decline. We need more spiritual teachers like Ajahn Chah.'

'Are there others?'

'A few. Nobody quite like him.'

The Ajahn's expression is weary as he plods beside me. Suddenly he looks like a very old man. Perhaps the night vigil was a strain on him. I remember his ulcer. From the way he has been speaking to me I know he is painfully aware he is not the kind of example his teacher was. Yet there is such an obligation for him to be one. He sees a great need. Alongside renunciation he must endure the burden of frustration and possibly a sense of failure. Certainly no one can accuse him of complacency.

'There are some orders these days which are determined to go back to the old ways. Some monks still prefer to *tudong* in a forest rather than live in a comfortable *wat*. Just a few good examples and the tradition will continue.' His eyes hold to the ground as he walks. He avoids puddles.

'Is going back to the old ways enough of a response? Maybe the monks who are willing to be socially active are the ones who will preserve Buddhism. A lot of young Thais don't seem to find their faith relevant to the world they're going to live in. Between the American and the Vietnamese forms of materialism, I'll bet people need to know the relevance of *Dhamma* more than ever, just to keep a little sanity and serenity in their lives.'

'Make the message relevant?' says the Ajahn without looking up. 'Like the Salvation Army did at the turn of the century, taking old drinking songs and a brass band and turning them into Christian hymns? The *sangha* should spice up *Dhamma* with a little *samsara*, do you think?'

We reach the tiger gates of the *wat*. The Ajahn does not use Ruk's short cut. He carries on over the sharp gravel road. I keep up with him, unwilling to let go of the question.

'The Salvation Army revived the message of Christian charity by dedicating themselves to the poor' I say. 'They were revolutionaries because they knew it wasn't church structures that contained the message. It was the un-nameable Spirit. But that's what Buddhism has done in every culture it entered. It took local myths and values, remoulding the symbolic meanings of their images. It used whatever was familiar to common people to teach them *Dhamma* – which has no form itself. When times changed for the Sally Anne, they became trapped in their own set of rules. Now they seem like one of the most old-fashioned denominations of the church.'

'That's the way it always is' says the teacher absently as we arrive at the *sala* door. He steps into the footbath and lets Nimalo wash his feet. He looks very tired. The walk has exhausted him, but he continues, 'People don't realize that conditions change. What was once a message becomes a dead ritual. People become so attached to words and ideas.'

Meow, waiting with a towel, dries the senior monk's feet. I give the extra bowl to Nimalo, who carries it into the *sala*. The Ajahn takes one step into the hall and gazes at the Buddha images, still glowing like silver fire after their recent burnishing. He turns around and comes back out to me. I'm still splashing my toes in the footbath. He stares down at them with his pale blue eyes.

'That's why I'm glad I'm a part of a tradition that is time-less, and a *Dhamma* that is unchanging.' He turns again and disappears into the temple.

'Forever and ever. Amen' I whisper under my breath. I step out of the footbath and hold one dripping foot up to Meow, who still stands with the towel in his hands. He flashes me his Cheshire cat grin and runs inside after the head monk.

> Impermanent are all conditioned things.
> Unsatisfactory are all conditioned things.
> Not-self are all conditioned things.
> This is the Dhamma taught by the Buddha.

The morning Herbie left for China, I smuggled an orange out of the *sala* and gave it to him for good luck. Then he was gone. Percy has decided to remain a while longer. He still uses the spindly broom and is asking me questions about the ordination ritual for a *pahkow*. Nimalo has moved to a *kuti* deeper in the jungle so he will not be disturbed. Mr Chicago has not returned from Bangkok. Dukita's scholar-ship to the States may be delayed for a year because she did not bother to apply to a college until summertime. Tan Casipo is helping her sort out the forms. Ruk and Sun Tin have filled the wood bins to the roof of the robe-dyeing shed. The *wat* is fully stocked for the rains retreat, and they have no more work to do. Yenaviro worries that his bowl sticks are again too small. He may have to start a third set. Fre-quently the Ajahn's seat is empty during morning chanting. The teacher takes medicine and grows pale. Tan Bodhipalo lets us sit through morning meditation until dawn in silence. No one ever notices little Tan Wee. Occasionally I hear recorded music. It comes from the jungle near the *kuti* of the Cheshire cat. Mum has announced that before she leaves she will hire a van to take a group of us on a picnic to the Laos border. Four of the monks want to go. The time of *pansa* is coming. Heat and humidity permeate the jungle air. Monsoons fall daily, flooding the compound. Mosquitoes breed. They swarm over us at coffee time. It has become unbearable. Slowly the season rolls by.

The king cobra greets me as I walk down his path one morning. He looks at me lazily, not bothering to arch his black hood. I squat less than two metres away, watching him smell me with his tongue. I am glad to be in his presence again. He has more compassion than us all. He could rise and kill, but he chooses to let me work out my *kamma* for myself. I wish I had his peace. Slowly the long muscular body surges across the trail, gliding like a flowing stream. I wait until the tail is swallowed up in jungle, then raise my hands high up to my forehead in a respectful *wai*.

There is only one thing left to be done. Ruk agrees to be my companion and on the appointed day we begin the three-hour walk to visit Wat Pah Pong, where I will bow three times before Ajahn Chah, the monk whose books and reputation led me to Pah Nanachat. Ruk comes not only as my guide, because I don't know the way, nor just because his company along the twelve-kilometre walk will be a joy. He is the one disciple of the master who seems to reflect some of the holiness I would expect to find in the great teacher. Ruk's words and stories about Ajahn Chah are full of gentle devotion. I fear my own aversion could rear up suddenly like a viper if I go alone. I don't want that. I am not visiting to pass judgment, only to pay my respects, as a pupil to a master. I wonder if the Ajahn has a teaching left for me.

Ruk leads me through Bung Wai village and across a set of railway lines. We walk down along a maze of country trails. The sky is clear, except for a few dark clouds boiling on the horizon. The breeze is fair. It keeps us from wilting under the hot afternoon sun. Ruk is true to his name. His conversation fills us both with laughter. He tells me stories about the villages we pass, about the strange and colourful crops in the fields, about Thai monks he has known and about the history of our destination, Wat Pah Pong.

'Ajahn Chah was born in a village near where the *wat* is now. His family still lives there. For fifteen years he wandered through the countryside. Most of his time he spent in the deep jungle, meditating. One day he came back to this area and went to stay in the old cremation grounds to practise.'

'Old cremation grounds seem like a popular spot for monks' I add.

'They are really popular. Most villagers are afraid of the ghosts, so they are good for solitude.'

'Every monastery should enlist the aid of *pee bahs*.'

'Word soon got around that the famous forest monk had returned. The villagers asked him if they could build a monastery for him and the small group of disciples who followed him. Ajahn Chah didn't object, so they built Pah Pong around him. By the time he had his stroke, he had forty branch monasteries all over Thailand.'

'They say there's over sixty now.'

Before we can begin a discussion on the merit of monastery building, we reach a three-metre high concrete wall at the end of our trail.

'It looks like a prison' I say to Ruk as we pass through a large iron door. Ruk tells me it's the back entrance to the grounds of Pah Pong. Inside, a two-metre high cement wall runs along the right-hand side of a dirt road. It continues straight ahead for a kilometre, out of sight. On the left, a barbed-wire fence protects dense forest. It feels eerie.

'I doubt if Ajahn Chah would have designed it this way himself' says Ruk as we begin to walk alongside the inner wall.

After half a kilometre we come to a wooden ladder leaning against the wall. I follow Ruk up it and down another one on the other side. A dog-proof entrance to the main grounds. The trees are thinner here. As we approach an open grassy area ahead, I notice dozens of wooden *kuties* raised on stilts.

Unlike the ones at Pah Nanachat, there is no attempt to isolate the huts from one another. It looks like a monastic suburb. A few Thais in ochre robes watch us as we pass. Ruk leads me to the *sala*. From the outside, the temple looks like a curling rink with a corrugated tin roof. Inside, it can easily accommodate five hundred worshippers. The floor is covered with old patches of linoleum of different colours and patterns. Incense burns before the giant brass Buddhas on the altar. Human skeletons encased in glass stand in each front corner. A double suicide?

A monk arrives who recognizes Ruk. They speak together in Thai for a few minutes. Ruk carries with him a pile of visa renewal forms sent by our Ajahn to the senior monk at Pah Pong. They will be sent to Bangkok for processing. Pah Pong handles all the paperwork for Pah Nanachat's *farang* monks. The Thai tells Ruk that the elder is at Ajahn Chah's bungalow. The master himself will receive visitors only between five and six pm, when he is taken out in his wheelchair.

It is too early to go, so we stroll through the vast grounds of the *wat*. We pass a new bell tower six storeys tall, built in an ancient baroque style. Carved deities, demons and gargoyles stare down at us. Near a glade, large rock totems jut up from the carefully trimmed grass. Ruins from the cremation site. Further on is a small green hill which slopes gently upward to the new *bhote*. Ruk tells me the hill is man-made, a huge underground water tank, kept full as a reserve for the dry season. The *bhote* is modern, completed less than two years ago. Its smooth white lines soar upwards gracefully like an abstract sculpture. We climb the white stone steps. It awes me that such a building could be created in Thailand. The ceiling is composed of white arches. The walls are semi-open, made up of large relief mosaics depicting scenes from the life of Ajahn Chah. In one, a king cobra peacefully crosses his path; in another, two tigers observe him with respect as he sits in deep contemplation; in a third, villagers build a forest *kuti* for him while he blesses them; in the fourth, the master sits alone in *samadhi*. The front of the *bhote* has about an eight-metre high statue in grey metal of a standing Buddha, both arms raised at right angles from the elbows. It's an unusual posture for a Buddha. Beneath the idol and slightly in front of it on the floor is a life-sized statue of a monk. The iron figure sits crosslegged in Thai meditation posture, right leg resting on top of the left. The toes of the right foot arch casually upwards. He is a relaxed-looking old man, perhaps a little tired. His lips turn down slightly at the corners, yet the expression is not dour. Somehow it seems like a smile. The artist gave the piece a rough texture, creating a harmonious contrast with the sleek modern lines of the *bhote*. We kneel and bow three times to the Buddha and three times to the statue of Ajahn Chah.

Leaving the *bhote*, we walk back past the *sala* and down a long road to the front gate of the *wat*. Pah Pong's boundaries are wide, more than two kilometres from end to end. The place seems strangely empty, ghost-like. Ruk tells me there were over sixty Thai and *farang* monks in Pah Pong when he came four years ago. Now there are fewer than ten, although more will return for *pansa*. The walk to the gate takes us through another tall forest. Painted signs written in Thai are nailed to trees next to the road. Ruk explains that they are sayings from the *Dhamma*. One-liner *dasanas* for visitors.

'Some monks think even the trees should have a teaching for us here' says Ruk. It is difficult to tell if he speaks with irony.

> Wooden signs are tacked to trees
> For those who cannot read.

We pass through the inner gate. In front of us is a building under construction. The foundation is complete. Wooden beams have been erected over it. To one side is a hill of bamboo which will be used as scaffolding. Beyond, there is an outer gate with an iron door next to it. Through the gate I see a small and rickety shack. I know it's a noodle shop. I have been here before, the night I searched so long in the dark and rain for the place which was now my home.

'What are they building?' I asked Ruk. 'When I last saw it, it was just a big hole.'

231

'It's a museum.'

'A museum? I thought you said the monastery was built when the master got here. It's not so old. A museum – Ruk, you mean a mausoleum. It's for Ajahn Chah, isn't it? The main attraction will be his ashes. Or will they just goldplate him and set him on display? The teacher isn't even dead and already they are setting up the market to make money from his relics.' Anger flares inside. I don't want it to strike out at my gentle friend. 'Tell me, am I wrong to think such negative things? What do you think? Are they just keeping his body breathing for the sake of the merit industry?' I feel as cynical as Jim.

'His disciples love him very much' says the monk in a soft voice. 'You can't expect them to let him die. Some days I think he has very clear eyes. See for yourself.'

We walk along the outside of the wall to a corner. Around it to the right, about four hundred metres away, is a bungalow. Three or four clusters of monks sit at various places on the green lawn surrounding it. Several cars and a few vans are parked in a nearby lot. Moving slowly around the perimeter of the building is a small figure in an orange-ochre robe, slumped in a wheelchair. A second figure pushes the chair around a cement strip which encircles the house. A third, also in a monk's robe, carries a long-handled fan which he waves over the one in the chair.

We leave our sandals near the front gate of the bungalow, pass through and follow the walkway to the rear of the building. An attendant novice motions us to sit on the grass. We wait for the wheelchair to come around to us. The threesome rounds the corner at a slow speed. I follow Ruk's example and kneel as the slumped figure in the chair approaches. We press our palms together in a respectful *wai*. The novice pushing the chair halts in front of us. We bow three times, touching our foreheads to the grass.

Ajahn Chah's eyes are closed, his head fallen to the side. It leans against the back of the wheelchair. The lower jaw is slack. The mouth hangs open at an unnatural angle, forming a triangle from which a pale tongue protrudes. White spittle covers the corners of the lips. The attendant keeps a cloth ready which he uses to wipe away the drool from the master's chin. The old hands are folded one on top of the other. They are mottled and pale for a Thai. The right one twitches occasionally like a dying fish. This is the only movement other than the gentle heaving of the great and collapsing chest buried beneath the robes. I hear him groan, a faint rumble within the sunken frame.

Having given us our audience, the Ajahn is swung around again to face the path. The novice slowly nudges him forward. I watch the young Thai's wide lips smile blissfully. He gazes tenderly at his helpless charge, the famous teacher. How much merit will he earn for his *karuna* towards the great monk? The novice is one of those Thais whose sex and age are undeterminable. He could be anywhere from sixteen to fifty. His features are soft and effeminate, a characteristic common among monks, accentuated by their shaven heads. He has pudgy cheeks and a fat neck which bulges at the back. As he steers past us I notice his thick ankles and his flat feet which make no sound as he walks. He reminds me of a young mother fawning over her new-born baby in a pram. The novice with the fan is skinny and tall. He wears glasses and an earnest expression. His lips are pressed together in concentration on his humble task. Actually, the late afternoon air is a little cool, now that clouds have come up to blot out the sun. He has to fan very slowly or else the Ajahn will catch cold.

The attendant who seated us returns with a plastic sitting mat. He speaks a few words with Ruk in Thai, then brings a plastic tray holding two glasses and a bottle of drinking water. Ruk thanks him while I pour for the two of us. My throat and body are dry. It has been a long walk. We have to return to Pah Nanachat tonight. I drink, surprised by the chill. The water has been refrigerated. The Ajahn comes around to us again. His left eye is partially open. The right opens as well as he approaches. I think they are blue, but they can't be. He is a Thai. I have just spent too long in a *wat* full of nordic *farang*. His gaze seems to fix on me for a moment. Then it flickers to Ruk. I watch intently for some sign of recognition by the master of the monk he named

'Laughter.' There is none. The eyes begin to wander aimlessly. The twitching right hand has fallen still. He does not
even moan. This is a body, I think, a living corpse. The
personality – whether ego or inner spirit, whatever it is that
gives life – is gone.

It was only illusion to begin with.

Is this freedom from suffering? Certainly there is the chill
of emptiness in those wandering eyes. He is detached. A
stroke is as effective as *samadhi*-suicide for that. Does the
Ajahn also serve as our example? Is he preserved for our
edification? Perhaps now he has become the embodiment
of the monks' ideal. Jim would criticize his complacency.
Wheeled around all day, fed through a tube, dressed and
bathed by devotees, he doesn't contribute anything concrete
to society. . . . They will not let him die.

A new group of Thai *bhikkhus* comes and joins us on the
grass. Ruk tells me they are on *tudong* from the far south.
They have come all this way to meet the holy monk. They
wait patiently for him to make his next pass. The novice
with the fat neck halts the chair to face the newcomers. After
they bow, he begins to turn again to his round but a feeble
groan comes from the body in the chair. The novice's eyes
widen with joy like a mother's when her baby burbles. He
moves the chair back in front of the visitors, letting his charge
enjoy their company a minute more. The master's right arm
begins to twitch violently. It flops from his lap, dangling
loosely beside the chair. The attendant carefully replaces it,
tucking the errant limb securely under an orange lap blanket.
The Ajahn's focus seems poorer than on the previous round.
The eyes wander independently of each other. The visiting
monks seem pleased with the interview. They bow again.
As the wheelchair swings back to face the path, they stand
and return to their van.

Fourth time around, Ruk and I also kneel for our parting
bows. These are the most sincere vows I will ever make
wearing my *pahkow* robes. I learned much because of this
man. His books showed me living wisdom in the Theravada
tradition. His skill as a teacher resulted not only in Pah
Nanachat, but in fifty-nine other centres dedicated to the

Dhamma. His special ability to work with Westerners attracted enough of them for me to be able to experience life in a Thai monastery without having to learn a new and difficult language. He opened this all to me. He is my teacher and I owe much reverence to him. Even if nothing but a shell and symbol remains. With my final bow I pray that this is so, for his sake.

At the front of the bungalow, Ruk finds the senior monk. He asks me to wait on the lawn while they go through details of the visa forms. I stand by the cement pathway and watch the black clouds gathering in the direction of Bung Wai. A monsoon rain is coming our way with the night. Already it is past six. We will walk home in darkness. I feel the blades of grass with my bare feet. A bird flies by, swoops down the hill of the bungalow and over the trees of Pah Pong's jungle. A jagged streak of lightning cuts the black horizon.

Behind me, the wheelchair approaches along the path as the Ajahn rolls through his last few rounds. The novice frowns and motions that I should quickly kneel and *wai* before the teacher passes. Ajahn Chah's eyes are open again. They seem to fix on me as he comes close. I read a look from them which cuts to my spine, pulls the muscles in my neck and stomach tight. My skin is suddenly cold. I hold that look, unable to determine whether or not what I see is really there. He passes, leaving me frozen like stone.

I have seen this look once before, in the eyes of an old woman in the examining room of a busy hospital. Her body was failing. Emphysema. Fluid choked her lungs and lack of oxygen was slowly suffocating her mind. Too slowly. She was gradually going insane. The doctor had prodded her naked body and shone a light at her. He wrote on a clipboard and disappeared. She could not speak. Her hand clutched at my shirt like a drowning woman. Her eyes came clear for a moment, pleading me to help. Not like this, not months longer. My eyes darted around the room. But they found nothing sharp. My grandmother's horror possessed me too. In that instant we both realized how long it can take to die.

A crack of thunder releases me. I jerk myself around on

the grass to face the black storm, wrenching the muscles in my back. A heavy rain will catch us this night. Good.

Ruk and I are tired as we begin the walk home. My body feels leeched of strength. There is ice in my spine. It stiffens my pace. The plastic sandals have worn blisters in the toes of both my feet. Where the path is sandy I walk barefoot. At dusk a viper surprises Ruk and makes me jump. We clutch at each other, as if to keep us from falling on top of the little snake. After that we use the flashlight. With it Ruk soon discovers a ten-centimetre long black scorpion. It remains as still as a rock while we kneel to examine it. The dark squiggle of a centipede wriggles in front of me, then zigzags behind Ruk. Again and again lightning shatters the sky. Heavy drops soon fall out of the night.

'All we need now is a tiger' I say to my companion.

'I think the plaster ones at the front gates will do' he says with a laugh.

'Death seems available tonight. For some of us.'

Ruk doesn't respond. He doesn't connect death with the creatures he loves best, those with claws, teeth, fangs or stings.

'How many more monasteries do you think they will build before the Ajahn dies?' I continue, feeling my own venom flash.

'Few. He predicted before his stroke he would die in 1985.'

'Six more months. That's too bad for you, Ruk.'

'Why?' He sounds astonished.

'I thought you wanted to set up a branch monastery in Germany.'

'Monastery? Not for me. Five years in a *wat* will be enough. When my fifth *pansa* is through, I only want to *tudong*.'

'In Germany?'

'That's right. I like the homeless life, just to wander from village to village. I would like to do that back home, in the Black Forest.'

'A Buddhist monk in the Black Forest? People would think you are pretty strange.'

'Sure they would. Who would know enough even to feed

me? I can't even ask for food. But I know I wouldn't starve. If I have to, I will work for my bread. Cold doesn't bother me, so most of the time I can sleep outdoors. I'll do whatever comes to my hand.'

'You mean you'll wander the market places, a potential for spontaneous goodness wherever you go?'

Ruk chuckles quietly at my words.

'Do you know what my ideal of a monk is?' I ask.

'No.'

'Laughter in the villages.'

I feel the beginning of warmth running down my spine, relaxing the muscles. A rush of joy floods through me. There is an example to carry on the master's teachings! A hundred new questions leap to mind. Is Ruk enlightened? What has he grasped of Ajahn Chah's wisdom? How is it that he sees clarity in the teacher's eyes, when I see only living death?

I want to ask, but the words won't come. I know what he'll say: that the only answers to take with me are the ones I have found for myself. Ruk never tried to convince me of anything. Asking if he's enlightened would make him laugh. And what would he care whether or not he fits *my* ideal of what a monk should be? Next thing you know, I'll be building his mausoleum and gilding his corpse.

I let the questions rise and fall, then sweep them, unasked, into the jungle. Without the questions, the craving for answers soon disappears. The euphoria fades – but the warmth in my back remains. It's an answer of sorts. I fall into place behind Ruk and his flashlight. Together we take up the steady walking rhythm of morning *bindabhat*. I realize that tomorrow I'll be leaving Pah Nanachat. Time to go.

And suddenly, there's laughter in the rain. After so much searching for a teaching – in the texts, the practice, the Ajahn's eyes – it makes me laugh to feel, just for the moment, what the Buddha never taught.

Glossary

Ajahn	(Thai) teacher, guru.
alms	donation of food or money for the sake of gaining merit.
alms round	the monks' daily begging round for food.
anapanna	(Pali) breathing meditation.
arahant	(Pali) 'non-returner.' A monk who has attained enlightenment.
asuras	(Sanskrit) the demi-gods.
bhat	Thai currency (1 bhat = about 7 cents U.S. in 1985).
bhikkhu	(Pali) literally, a devotee (male), a monk.
bhote	(Thai) ordination hall for monks and novices.
bindabhat	(Pali) the monks' daily begging round for food.
bodhisattva	(Pali, Sanskrit) a being who has followed the path to enlightenment and is near to nibbana.
Buddha, the	the Awakened One. The Historica Gautama Siddhartha, founder of Buddhism. (bodhi = awakening).
Buddhamas	Ajahn Chah's name for the Thai celebration of the birth, death and enlightenment of Gautama Buddha.
bunte	(Pali) term of respect for an elder monk.
chakras	(Sanskrit) centres of energy in the body.
dasana	(Pali) a sermon about dhamma or the Dhamma.
deva	(Pali) a god.
deva-realm	world of the gods, a paradise, except that the gods eventually die and are reincarnated in lower realms.
dhamma	(Pali) truth.
Dhamma, the	(Pali) teachings of the Buddha, the Pali suttas, the doctrine of Buddhism.
dhamma talk	a talk on truth, a sermon.
farang	(Thai) foreign, not Thai, foreigners. Use is both singular and plural. Mildly derogatory.
jhana	(Pali, Sanskrit) There are four jhanas, each a distinct level of meditation.

kamma	(Pali) all deeds which determine the present and future lives of a being. Kammic formations are both volitions and memories which cause one to act.
karuna	(Pali) compassion towards all beings, one of the four great Buddhist virtues.
koppy	(Pali) to make allowable. This word, when spoken to a monk, permits him to cut a plant.
kuti	(Thai) small one room hut where a forest monk lives.
Mahayana	the 'greater vehicle' form of Buddhism practised in northern Asia (Japan, China, Tibet, Korea).
merit	positive benefit added to one's kamma as a result of performing good deeds resulting in better rebirth in future lives.
metta	(Pali) friendliness towards all beings, one of the four cardinal virtues of Buddhism.
nibbana	(Pali) the state of enlightenment, freedom from desire, often misrepresented as a place like heaven. Literally means 'despirited', like a candle which has been blown out. (Sanskrit, nirvana).
pah	(Thai) forest, as in Pah Nanachat, pee (p)ah.
pahkow	(Thai) one who takes the eight precepts and lives in a monastery. In Thailand, usually women.
paise	Indian penny.
pansa	(Pali) the rains retreat, lasting the three months of monsoon season as determined by the lunar calendar. Monks must not spend a night away from their monastery at this time of year.
pee bah	(Thai) forest ghost.
precepts	rules taken by a devotee to develop moral purity. Laypeople take five; pahkows, eight; novices, ten; monks, two hundred and twenty seven.
rupee	Indian currency (1 rupee = about 8 cents U.S. in 1985).
sabong	(Thai) sarong, a skirt-like cloth worn by members of a monastery in Thailand.
sala	(Thai) main temple of a monastery.
samadhi	(Pali) absorption meditation, 'one-pointedness.'
samsara	(Sanskrit, Pali) illusion, 'the world.'
sangha	(Pali) the community of Buddhist monks.
sankaras	(Pali, Sanskrit) kammic formations, the concept combines memories and willing.
sati	(Pali) mindfulnes, concentration.
Shiva	(Sanskrit) the destroyer, one of the three chief divinities of the Hindu pantheon.
sila	(Pali) moral purity.
swaddie krup	(Thai) polite greeting (spoken by a male).
Tan	(Thai) respectful title for a monk, similar to 'reverend,' or 'sir.'

tantric	ritualistic and magical teachings or schools, found in both Hinduism and Buddhism.
Theravada	The old school of Buddhism, now practised in Thailand, Burma, Sri Lanka and on the Indian subcontinent, called the 'lesser vehicle' (Hinayana) by Mahayana Buddhists.
tudong	(Thai) a monk's pilgrimage from place to place.
tuk-tuk	(Thai) three-wheeled motor taxi.
Vinaya	(Pali) rulebook and summary of Theravada doctrines.
vipassana	(Pali) insight meditation.
wai	(Thai) Buddhist gesture of respect, palms pressed together, hands held up to the face.
Wai Phra	(Thai) weekly holy day in Thailand, held on new, full and half moon nights, four times a month.
wat	Thai Buddhist temple or monastery.

The Community at Wat Pah Nanachat May–June 1985

Senior Monks:

The Ajahn head monk of Wat Pah Nanachat (ex-jazz guitar player from Australia)

Tan Bodhipalo the dour cave monk (ex-gospel singer from England)

Tan Sumeno Mr Chicago (ex-real estate millionaire)

Junior Monks:

Ruk the industrious German monk whose Thai nickname means 'laughter'.

Sun Tin the ex-Thai farmer with the crooked grin.

Tan Casipo the helpful junior monk from New Zealand in charge of taking care of newcomers.

Tan Wee the tiny Thai monk.

Yenaviro the timid Chinese ex-accountant from Malaysia.

Novices:

Edward the Brit who disappeared (possibly a pee-bah?)

Mark the 'wat doctor' from New Zealand.

Meow Thai teenager and Cheshire cat.

Nimalo the 'professional novice' from Australia.

Richard the talkative Texan.

Pahkows:

Michael veteran pahkow from the U.S.A.

241

Tim
Jim   the twins, as far as the community was concerned.

Laymen
(though perhaps a dozen laymen came and went, only those central
to the story are listed here):

Herbie   the teenager from Canada.
Percy   the Brit with the limp and the not-so-stiff upper lip.
Julian   the earnest seeker from Australia.
Dukita   the young Thai woman who lived in the woman's
                section
Mum   mother of Mark the novice

Other monks outside the community:

Ajahn Chah   the revered forest monk, founder of many monaster-
                 ies including Pah Nanachat.
Ajahn Sumedo the farang monk who first headed Pah Nanachat,
                 living at a Wat in England at the time of this story.
Tan Sumana   a Bangladeshi Theravada monk and friend of the
Tissa   author, studying in Bangkok.